NATIONAL GEOGRAPHIC
TRAVELER
Madrid

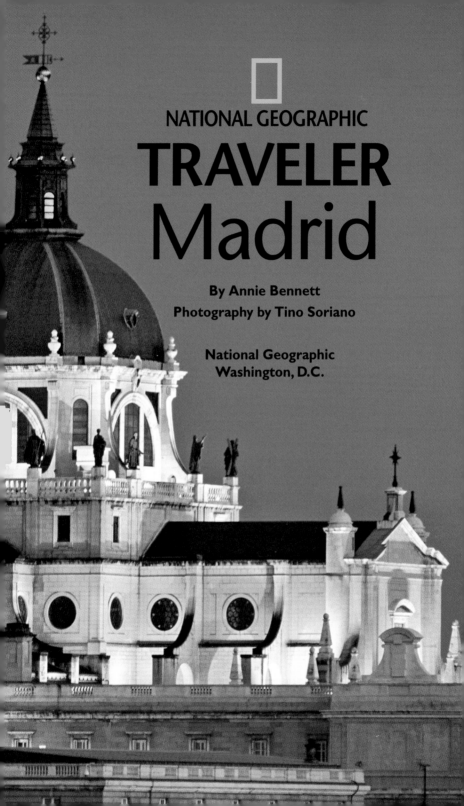

NATIONAL GEOGRAPHIC

TRAVELER
Madrid

By Annie Bennett
Photography by Tino Soriano

National Geographic
Washington, D.C.

Contents

Page 1: Puerta del Sol, symbol of Madrid
Pages 2–3: Nuestra Señora de la Almudena, Madrid's grandiose cathedral
Page 4: In front of La Fontanilla tavern, on Calle Cuchilleros

How to use this guide

See back flap for keys to text and map symbols.

The *National Geographic Traveler* brings you the best of Madrid, in text, pictures, and maps. Divided into three main sections, the guide begins with an overview of Madrid today, its history and culture.

Following are nine area chapters with featured sites selected by the author for their particular interest. Each chapter opens with its own contents list for easy reference. A map introduces the parameters covered in the chapter, highlighting the featured sites and locating other places of interest. Walks (and, in the Excursions chapter, a drive),

plotted on their own maps, suggest routes for discovering the most about an area. Features and sidebars offer intriguing detail on the area.

The final section, Travelwise, lists essential information for the traveler—pre-trip planning, special events, getting around, practical advice, and emergency contacts—plus provides a selection of hotels and restaurants arranged by area, shops, activities and entertainment.

To the best of our knowledge, information is accurate as of press time. However, it's always advisable to call ahead when possible.

Color coding

158

Each area of the city is color coded for easy reference. Find the area you want on the map on the front flap, and look for the color flash at the top of the pages of the relevant chapter. Information in **Travelwise** is also color coded to each region.

Visitor information

Museo Nacional del Prado
www.museoprado.es
Map p. 125
Paseo del Prado
91 330 2800
Closed Mon.
$$. Free Sun.
Metro: Banco de España, Atocha

Practical information for most sites is given in the side column (see key to symbols on back flap). The map reference gives the page number of the map and grid reference. Other details are address, telephone number, days closed, entrance charge in a range from $ (under $5) to $$$$$ (over $25), and metro stop. Other sites have information in italics and parentheses in the text.

TRAVELWISE

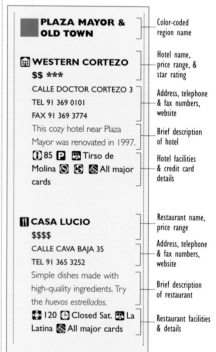

PLAZA MAYOR & OLD TOWN — Color-coded region name

WESTERN CORTEZO
$$ ★★★ — Hotel name, price range, & star rating

CALLE DOCTOR CORTEZO 3
TEL 91 369 0101
FAX 91 369 3774 — Address, telephone & fax numbers, website

This cozy hotel near Plaza Mayor was renovated in 1997. — Brief description of hotel

85 Tirso de Molina All major cards — Hotel facilities & credit card details

CASA LUCIO
$$$$ — Restaurant name, price range

CALLE CAVA BAJA 35
TEL 91 365 3252 — Address, telephone & fax numbers, website

Simple dishes made with high-quality ingredients. Try the *huevos estrellados*. — Brief description of restaurant

120 Closed Sat. La Latina All major cards — Restaurant facilities & details

Hotel & restaurant prices

An explanation of the price bands used in entries is given in the Hotels & Restaurants section (beginning on p. 241).

AREA MAPS

Important featured site

Neighborhood

Street closed to vehicular traffic

Point of interest

Metro station

- A locator map accompanies each area map and shows the location of that area in the city.

WALKING TOURS

Street closed to vehicular traffic

Walk route

Featured site on walk route

Start point

Direction of route

Building outline

Gray numbered bullets link sites on map to descriptions in the text.

- An information box gives the starting and ending points, time and length of walk, and places not to be missed along the route.

EXCURSION MAP

Road number

Important featured site

Drive start point

Point of interest

Important featured town

Grid letter

Road number

- Towns and cities described in the Excursions chapter (pp. 211-232) are highlighted in gray on the map. Other suggested places to visit are also highlighted and are shown with a red diamond.

NATIONAL GEOGRAPHIC
TRAVELER
Madrid

About the authors & photographer

Annie Bennett writes about Spanish travel, food and culture for UK national newspapers including *The Daily Telegraph, The Sunday Telegraph,* and *The Times,* and has won the Spain Travel Writer of the Year award for her articles. She has written the Blue Guides to Madrid and Barcelona, and *Art Shop Eat Barcelona.*

After studying Spanish and German in London, she lived in Madrid for ten years, working as a journalist and translator for Spanish magazines specializing in art, architecture, and design. She has translated books on the Prado museum and Spanish food and wine. Annie divides her time between her home on the Gower coast in South Wales and bases in Madrid and Barcelona.

Born and raised in Barcelona, Spain, photographer **Tino Soriano** divides his work between photojournalism and travel photography. He has received a first prize from the World Press Photo Foundation as well as awards from UNESCO, Fujifilm, and Fotopres.

In addition to Sicily, since 1988 Tino has photographed in Spain (Catalonia, Andalucía, Galicia), France, Italy, Portugal, Scotland, and South Africa on assignments for National Geographic. His work has also appeared in *Geo, Merian, Der Spiegel, Paris Match, La Vanguardia,* and *El Pais* as well as many other major magazines around the world. He also photographed the *National Geographic Traveler: Sicily* and the *National Geographic Traveler: Portugal.*

Tino likes to write, and he has published *El Futuro Existe* (a story about children with cancer). He also regularly lectures and teaches workshops at the University of Barcelona.

Damien Simonis, a travel guide writer since 1992 and the author of more than 20 guidebooks, wrote the History and Culture chapter. He lives in Barcelona, Spain.

Xander Fraser, who wrote the Travelwise section, is a writer and editor based in Andalucía, Spain.

History & culture

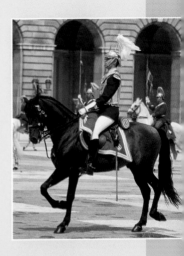

**Changing of the Royal
Guard at the Palacio Real**

Madrid today

SITTING AT THE GEOGRAPHICAL HEART OF IBERIA, ON A HIGH CENTRAL plain far from the sea, Madrid has been Spain's capital only since 1561, when Felipe II decided to settle the country's court in one place. Madrid may be short on history compared with the other great capitals of Europe, but these days it more than makes up for it with a forward-looking dynamism and zesty energy few can match. Possibly the busiest nightlife capital on the continent, it is also a magnet for art lovers.

You'll sense right away Madrid's modern verve, with its wide, bustling boulevards and fashionable shopping quarters. Modern high-rises mingle seamlessly with grand turn-of-the-19th-century edifices. Around the tight web of old town lanes unfolds a dynamic metropolis. Next to timeless taverns glitter the bright lights of the latest gourmet restaurants. Immaculately maintained old-time hotels vie for guests with 21st-century showpieces and boutique charmers. The whole city is suffused with a lively unstoppable quality. It would be difficult to get bored in Madrid.

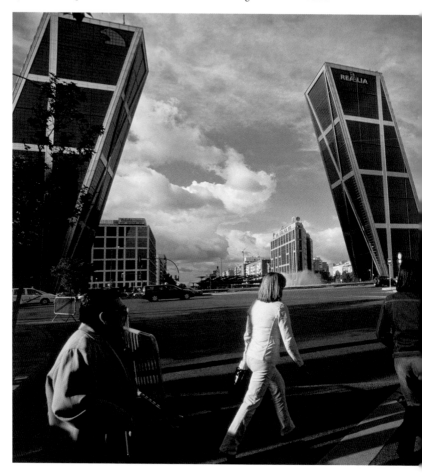

Above all, Madrid is known for its legendary nightlife. Where else are you likely to encounter traffic jams at 5 a.m. on a Sunday? In summer, café terraces, whether along the Paseo de la Castellana or across the city's main squares, fill to bursting throughout the long, hot evenings until well into the wee hours. Everything and everyone seem to blur together in an effusive atmosphere of loudly chattering bonhomie. Madrileños, known as *gatos* (cats) for their urban savvy, parade from one tapas joint to another, from flamenco den to music venue, from historic vermouth bar to all-night club.

Madrid is a powerful art magnet. In its three leading museums, along with countless smaller ones, you'll discover a wealth of masterpieces. The Prado, which has been given a major overhaul, offers a concentration of Spanish masters that is second to none. Among them are such greats as Velázquez, El Greco, José de Ribera, Zurbarán, Murillo, and Goya, just to name a few. The Prado collections encompass thousands of precious works from the Middle Ages to the 19th century. The Thyssen-Bornemisza is a more broad-ranging and eclectic international collection stretching from medieval Italian art to late-20th-century icons such as David Hockney and Francis Bacon. The Centro de Arte Reina Sofía concentrates on modern and contemporary art, with a heavy Spanish quota but with some international flights of fancy woven in as well. Among the gems there is Picasso's powerful antiwar painting "Guernica."

Art and precious artifacts as well can be seen in the stately baroque and Renaissance buildings that line the narrow lanes twisting off Plaza Mayor. The nearby Palacio Real (Royal Palace), filled with magnificent treasures, was long the residence of Spanish monarchs. Even today it remains an official home of the Bourbon dynasty, although it is rarely occupied now. A steady flow of visitors passes through its seemingly endless grand halls, guest rooms, and labyrinthine nooks and crannies.

The hectic pace in Madrid and the danger of over stimulation in its myriad museums may leave you gasping for air. Luckily, the city is blessed with plenty of green spaces and tranquil parks. Just behind the Prado stretches the Parque del Buen Retiro, a grand stretch of sculpted gardens, woods, and artificial lakes where you can paddle about in little rented boats. Also nearby is the splendid Real Jardín Botánico (Royal Botanic Garden), which is educational as well as relaxing.

THE GOOD TIMES: FOOTBALL, FESTIVALS, & BULLFIGHTING

Ask many Madrileños their religion, and you might almost expect them to reply football (soccer). The city's team, Real

A city of constant construction, Madrid is rapidly expanding northward beyond the sloping Puerta de Europa towers in Plaza Castilla—itself a busy commuter hub.

Madrid, one of the best in Europe, is the object of adoration of much of the city's population. (It is also one of the richest teams, which is how it can afford to pepper its ranks with multimillion-euro international stars.) Officially founded in 1902, the *merengues* ("meringues" because of the white stripe on their uniforms) lead the field in Spain, with 29 national championships under their belts since they won their first cup in 1932. In 1998, the world football federation, FIFA, declared Real Madrid to be the best team of all time.

Just as important as football and the fate of Real Madrid, and celebrated with just as much gusto, are Madrid's numerous traditional festivals. In the summer especially, the heat drives Madrileños into the streets for neighborhood celebrations, where eating, drinking, music, and dancing into the wee hours are the norm.

One of the greatest events is the Fiesta de la Comunidad de Madrid in May, which commemorates the Dos de Mayo uprising against the French in 1808 (see pp. 104–105). The bars in the Malasaña district, particularly around Plaza Dos de Mayo, are especially lively, and a host of cultural events is organized for the following week or two across central Madrid. Also in May, the Fiestas de San Isidro Labrador, the city's patron saint, not only mark the beginning of the month-long bull-fighting festival at Plaza de Toros Monumental de Las Ventas (see p. 46) but also inaugurate

The splendid Plaza de Toros Monumental de Las Ventas—Las Ventas for short—is *the* place to see a bullfight. Bullfighting is an integral part of cultural life in Madrid for many people, although not as popular as soccer or basketball.

another packed program of concerts and cultural events. After the Festimad outdoor rock concerts in May, the Gay Pride marches in

June, and the packed concert and theater calendar of Veranos de la Villa ("Summers in Town," with performances at venues all over the city), comes the stifling month of August and its madcap local festivities. The Fiestas of San Lorenzo, San Cayetano, and La Virgen de la Paloma, held respectively in La Latina, Plaza de Lavapiés, and Calle de Calatrava in La Latina, are the catalyst for eating, drinking, and dancing in the streets until dawn. The remainder of the year's calendar is punctuated by all sorts of events, from the ARCO contemporary art expo and Flamenco Festival in February to spectacular Easter processions.

In Madrid one could be forgiven for surmising that the Catholic faith has long ceased to have a hold over anyone. A visit to the Iglesia de Jesús de Medinaceli, in Plaza de Jesús, on the first Friday of Lent will dispel such impressions. A place of pilgrimage, it still attracts long snaking queues of the faithful. The quest is to kiss the feet of a wooden sculp-

Plaza Mayor has been a hub of activity since its construction in the early 17th century. The site of autos-da-fé (trials of faith), criminal executions, royal marriages, bullfights, and all kinds of celebrations, it continues to hold lively markets, fairs, and special events.

of the *furia española*, the legendary fury of the Spanish troops that once made Spain's enemies tremble.

A CITY IN FERMENT

Long the political capital of Spain, Madrid has more recently dethroned Barcelona as the country's prime economic and financial center. Most multinational companies based in Spain have their headquarters in Madrid. Some studies suggest that as much as three-quarters of all international investment in Spain goes into Madrid. At 24,000 euros ($28,000), Madrileños enjoy the highest average wages in the country.

With a population of nearly 3.2 million, the city seethes with seemingly limitless energy, building new metro lines at breakneck speed. Construction carries on at such a cracking pace that critics warn of a lack of considered planning. The city seems to be ringed by thick flocks of cranes as up to 12 residential suburbs destined to house nearly a million people are created from scratch. The expansion is set to continue until at least the 2020s, although potential building land within the city limits is rapidly being used up.

The new housing may well be needed. Long a country of emigrants, Spain has become a beacon for vast waves of hopeful immigrants, legal and otherwise. Curiously, official predictions of the city's population growth are fairly modest (3.3 million by 2016), but between 2000 and 2005 more than 350,000 legal immigrants settled in Madrid alone. The number of additional clandestine migrants can only be guessed at. As late as the mid-1990s, visitors from more multicultural cities would often remark that everyone "looks the same" in Madrid. The growing presence of Moroccan, African, Asian, and South American communities has changed all that forever.

Paradoxes abound. While state-of-the-art

ture of Christ inside the church. After hearing Mass, pilgrims address three wishes to Jesus, who, tradition claims, will grant one.

The other place you'll find fervent crowds of Madrileños is at the bullfighting ring. Reviled by many foreigners and not a few Spaniards, the bullfight is nonetheless a dramatic expression of a certain theatrical Spanishness. Its pomp and ceremony, *sol y sombra* (sun and shade), the deep sense of drama, tragedy, and fatalism, are all evocative apartment blocks are being raised at the extreme edges of the city and many fine old apartment buildings in central Madrid have been loving restored, plenty of others remain as reminders of darker times. In some of the traditionally poorer quarters of central Madrid, such as colorful Lavapiés, long-term elderly residents with limited resources live alongside equally hard-pressed newcomers in poky, century-old slum apartments without gas, hot running water, or private baths.

While some architects and urban planners criticize the speed and greed of the city's growth, few carp at the city's transportation policy. Since the mid-1990s, the metro system has been expanded and modernized to such an extent that by 2012 it will consist of 143 miles (230 km) of what the town council claims will be the most modern metro in the world. While that is probably a trifle exaggerated, there is no doubting the system is slick. The Barajas airport, too, has entered the 21st

Tibaldi's ceiling frescoes crown the beautiful Royal Library of the monastery at El Escorial. The ornate decoration in the room reflects the importance of the building in the 16th century. The library houses 45,000 books from the 15th and 16th centuries.

century with an inspiring new terminal building by Sir Richard Rogers.

The building frenzy has touched the heart of the city as well. All three major galleries of the so-called Art Triangle have undergone major transformations. Senior Spanish architect Rafael Moneo is behind the expansion of the Museo del Prado, by far the most complex and controversial project of the three. Aside from running way over budget and way past deadline, it involved the destruction of what

remained of the one-time cloister of the Iglesia de San Jerónimo Real. Jean Nouvel's extension of the Centro de Arte Reina Sofía, opened in 2005, startles observers with its russet red roofed patio. Meanwhile, at the Museo Thyssen-Bornemisza, two adjacent buildings were acquired and transformed in 2004 to house the eclectic new collection of Carmen Thyssen-Bornemisza.

POLITICS IN MADRID

Given all that Madrid can boast about its modernized metro system, it seems extraordinary that no one gave any thought to extending a metro line to the futuristic new international air terminal at Barajas. The system reaches the old terminals, but neither the Ayuntamiento (town council) nor the regional government of the Comunidad de Madrid (the region of which Madrid is capital) wants to bear the financial burden of its extension into the new building.

Perhaps there is more to this than meets the eye. Esperanza Aguirre, president of the Comunidad de Madrid region since late 2003

Key events in Madrid's history are portrayed by papier-mâché figures in front of the Palacio Real during a May festival.

escape the conclusion that, with the Madrileños caught in the middle, the two have used the metro argument to continue their own tit-for-tat relationship.

Local politics is overshadowed by the antics of Spain's national politicians. Long used to assassinations and terrorism from the Basque country's ETA terror group, Madrid received a brutal introduction to Arab terrorism when, on the morning of March 11, 2004, bombs were detonated on four commuter trains, killing 190 people and injuring more than 1,800. Carried out three days before national elections, it was the biggest such attack in Spanish history. The outgoing prime minister, José María Aznar (PP), had, against the will of the majority of Spaniards (judging by demonstrations and polls), supported U.S. President Bush's invasion of Iraq. As a result, Spain sent army units in as part of the coalition occupation force in 2003. The PP's challengers, the left-wing Partido Socialista Obrero Español (PSOE), under José Luis Rodríguez Zapatero, had vowed to pull Spanish troops out of Iraq if elected. The PP's attempts to attribute the bombings to ETA terrorists unleashed the fury of many citizens, whose antiwar demonstrations turned into anti-PP marches. Zapatero won the poll on March 14, 2004, and immediately withdrew the Spanish contingent from Iraq. U.S.-Spain relations have yet to recover fully. Zapatero has been ambitious in several fields, one of the most controversial being the decision to legalize gay marriages in 2005.

As seriously as Madrileños take their politics, in the opinion of most city-dwellers, life is too short to get too worked up about the nation's politicians. The average gato has a healthy disregard for the country's political class, an irrepressible desire to enjoy today without worrying overly about tomorrow, and an innate conviviality. That live-for-the-present joie de vivre keeps the restaurants, bars, and clubs filled to bursting. So sidle up to a bar, squeeze in, shout your order for a couple of tapas and a *caña* (small glass of cold beer), and allow yourself to be swept up in the rush of a truly 24-hour city. ■

and an intimate of the most right-wing forces in the conservative Partido Popular (PP), has never been on good terms with the more moderate (and vastly more popular) mayor, Alberto Ruiz-Gallardón, despite belonging to the same party. Aguirre insists that the national government (Socialist since 2004) should pay for the extension, while the national transportation ministry (with the tacit support of Ruiz-Gallardón) says the job is the responsibility of the regional government. It is hard to

Food & drink

MADRID'S DINERS ARE A FORTUNATE LOT. SMACK IN THE HEART OF A SUN-scorched region and lacking an enormous variety of local food products, Madrid does not at first glance look like a promising place for a gourmet parade. Don't worry. Madrid has for centuries acted as a magnet for internal migrants from all over Spain, and they have brought their cuisines with them.

Madrileños are discerning customers when it comes to choosing meats.

Nowhere else in Spain can you so easily sample the whole range of Spain's cuisines, from simple Castilian soups and game dishes to the refined surf-and-turf meals of Catalunya. Disciples of Catalan super-chef Ferran Adrià and his Basque equivalent Juan Mari Arzak have long since created niches for themselves in the city. They bring to Madrid's foodies the most inventive of what has been dubbed *nueva cocina española* (Spanish new cuisine).

Madrid's own culinary tradition is meager and largely assimilated into that of Castile. A standard Castilian first course is *sopa a la castellana,* a thin broth with an egg. Meat was long a luxury for most and so

callos (tripe) became a favorite. Perhaps the best known of the city's dishes is *cocido madrileño,* a kind of hot pot into which just about anything at hand is thrown in.

Castilian dishes revolve around meat. A favorite is *cochinillo,* spit-roasted suckling pig, a speciality in Segovia and some taverns in Chinchón. Game dishes and partridge are also common. Farther west, Extremadura is known above all for its top-class *jamón de bellota,* cured ham from free-range pigs fed on acorns.

From the northwest coast of Galicia comes an amazing variety of seafood. Long among the country's poorer regions, Galicia exported two items: seafood and its inhabi-

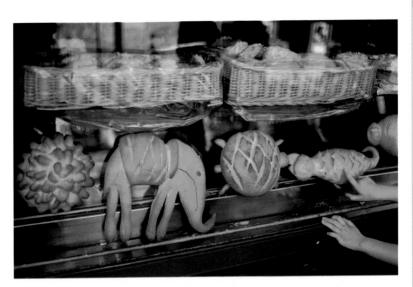

It is still traditional to buy bread daily at bakeries where the loaves are made in the back.

tants, many of whom wound up in Madrid and opened restaurants. *Pulpo a la gallega* is boiled octopus chopped into bite-size, melt-in-the-mouth pieces and prepared with potatoes in a tangy paprika sauce. A delicacy, because of their rarity, are the twisted, gnarled *percebes* (goose barnacles). Indeed, Madrileños have a special weakness for *pescados* (fish) and *mariscos* (shellfish). Despite being an inland city, it is one of the greatest consumers of seafood in Europe.

The mountain territories of Asturias, Aragón, and Catalunya have brought steaming stews to the winter table—dishes such as Asturian *fabada* (pork and beans) or Catalan (from Catalunya) *escudella* (a more general meat, sausage, and vegetable stew). Catalan cuisine is considered, along with the Basque, the best in the country. It uses seafood and meat, a rich palette of fresh products, and sauces. If anything, Basque cuisine is more refined still. From Catalunya and the coastal region of Valencia comes a series of mouth-watering rice and noodle dishes, from the world-renowned paella (a rice, saffron, and seafood stew) to the less well-known Catalan *fideuà*, basically a noodle version (without saffron) of paella.

Tapas, small saucers with bite-size snacks, originate in the southern region of Andalucía. In most traditional Madrid bars you will be offered a simple tapa of at least a few olives with your glass of wine or caña. More elaborate tapas will generally cost you a few euros apiece. Bigger servings are called *raciones*. Popular tapas include *boquerones* (white anchovies, best served in *vinagre*, vinegar) or *pincho moruno* (skewered pork). The Basque versions, elegant canapés on slices of baguette, are known as *pintxos* and best sampled with the Basque white wine, Txacoli, or alcoholic cider from Asturias.

Among the best wine-producing regions are Rioja (especially reds) in the north, the Penedès area outside Barcelona (whites and *cava*, which is champagne-style bubbly), Galician Ribeiro (whites), and Ribera del Duero (reds), the vineyards spread out along the Duero River. Some drinkable wines are produced near Madrid, but you are most likely to come across wines from Valdepeñas in southern Castilla-La Mancha. Valdepeñas was long the national supplier of cheap table plonk, but its vintners have made huge strides in producing higher quality tipples recently. From Andalucía comes *jerez* (sherry), a fortified wine ranging from bone dry to sickly sweet. ■

History of Madrid

IMAGINE THE SURPRISE (AND GLEE) OF THE RULING FAMILIES OF MADRID when, in 1561, King Felipe II of Spain, master of an empire stretching from the Andes to the Netherlands, one of the most powerful men on Earth, chose this insignificant, grubby plains town to establish the Spanish monarchy's first permanent capital. Madrid's chroniclers soon began a little rewriting of history to buff up the town's image.

FROM ROMAN VILLAS TO MUSLIM FRONTIER FORT

Even when Madrid was founded, glorifying the present was difficult, as the provincial backwater was no Rome, London, or Paris. Giving a sheen to the past was easier, even if the scholarship was dubious. The fact that the Muslims established Madrid was quietly ignored. Then a suitably noble story was concocted about Madrid having started life as the Roman town of Mantua.

Evidence for the existence of such a settlement is noticeable by its complete absence, but the old adage about not letting the facts get in the way of a good story prevailed. Excavations have revealed that the Manzanares River, nowadays little more than a dribble as it passes around the west and south of central Madrid, attracted a sparse and probably nomadic rural population as long ago as Neolithic times.

Under the Romans (who first invaded Spain during the Punic Wars in 218 B.C.), farming families lived in villas scattered about the countryside. Nothing, however, sustains the fond idea that the Romans built a town here.

In the fifth century A.D. the Roman Empire wobbled and the Visigoths invaded from France, but things down on the Roman farms around the Manzanares barely changed. The Visigoths were few in number and the Hispano-Roman population they came to rule remained largely in control of their own administrative and financial affairs, serving the Visigoths much as they had done Rome.

It was a rather different story when a zealous Muslim expeditionary force under the command of the governor of Tangier, Tariq Ibn Zayid, landed on the south coast of Spain near what is today the town of Algeciras in 711. In less than a century since the death of the prophet Muhammad in Arabia in 632, Muslim Arab legions had launched a blitzkrieg without parallel. They moved across the Middle East and North Africa, occupying and converting the peoples of territories stretching from Iraq (and later Iran) in the east to the Atlantic coast in Morocco.

In Spain, the walkover continued. Tariq and his motivated men, mostly Berbers under the command of a handful of Arabs, found the Visigoth kingdom divided and weak. They swept across the peninsula and into Frankish territory (modern France) as far as Poitiers, where Christian forces finally repulsed them in 732.

By the ninth century, the Muslims had been pushed back to a natural defensive line that followed the course of the Duero River and Ebro River from the Atlantic coast of Portugal across to the Mediterranean just south of Barcelona.

A detail from El Escorial's Hall of Battles (above). Before Madrid became the capital in 1561, the city of Toledo (right) was home to the Spanish court.

Carlos V, Holy Roman Emperor, is portrayed in an instructive mode in a 15th-century manuscript illumination. His empire stretched from Austria to America.

Although in its early centuries Al-Andalus, as Muslim Spain was known, was largely united and ruled from Córdoba, infighting was not uncommon, especially close to the front lines. Such internecine squabbling encouraged incursions by Christian forces from the north. To better ward off such attacks, the Muslims established a series of forts, of which Magerit (or Mayrit) was one, across the unstable frontier territory known as the Middle March, whose capital was Toledo.

The fort (*al-qasr* in Arabic, from which derives the Spanish word for palace or fortress, *alcázar*) was founded in 854 by Muhammad I, Emir of Córdoba (*R*.852–886), on the site of the present Palacio Real. It occupied a strategic rise that dominated key routes south to Toledo over the Sierra de Guadarrama. The fortress was the forerunner of the Alcázar that for centuries would host the kings of Spain when they stayed in Madrid.

The Caliphate of Córdoba collapsed into a series of bickering kingdoms, the *taifas*, in

1031. Magerit fell into the orbit of the Toledo *tarifa*, but the latter's rulers clearly felt exposed and abandoned the city (and Magerit) to Castile's King Alfonso VI (*R*.1065–1109) about 1085.

FROM PROVINCIAL BACKWATER TO IMPERIAL CAPITAL

Throughout the centuries of the Reconquista (the "Reconquest" by Christian armies of Spain from the Muslims), the conquering kings of Castile, León, Navarra, and Aragón had a policy of repopulating newly won territories, and so Christian newcomers quickly arrived in the fort town of Magerit.

A handful of these new families (the Vargas and Luzón clans in particular) soon had a stranglehold on municipal power. Madrid, as the town came to be mispronounced, had now lost all strategic significance and early on was largely neglected by its roaming Christian monarchs, who preferred to set up their mobile court in more important cities.

The newly Christianized town lived a moment of anxiety when a raiding Muslim army drew up before the fortress walls in 1109 and unsuccessfully besieged the town, in what has been known ever since as the Campo del Moro (Field of the Moor).

Madrid, like other medieval Christian towns in Spain, developed a feudal system of government, known in this instance as the Comunidad de Villa y Tierra. In simple terms, the peasants of the *Tierra* (Land) slaved away to supply the *Villa* (Town).

Increasingly towns were governed according to charters granted by the king. Madrid finally received its charter, or *fuero*, in 1202. Until then it had been considered a subsidiary of Toledo. The fuero put the town under the more direct control of the king, allowing the latter to intervene (theoretically at least) to curb abuses of power by local barons.

The 14th century brought catastrophe to Madrid and the rest of the country in the form of the plague. The most infamous wave came in 1348, during the epidemic of Black Death that swept across Europe. Chronicles also recount that, in the following century, the city was brought low by

Ferdinand and Isabella see Christopher Columbus off from the dock at Palos de la Frontera in 1492, in an illustration by Victor A. Searles.

terrible years of drought in the 1430s.

The unification of Christian Spain under the Reyes Católicos (Catholic Monarchs), Ferdinand and Isabella, beginning in 1474, brought stability to Madrid. The rulers completed the Reconquista with the defeat of Granada in 1492. That same year, Christopher Columbus set off on a voyage that would change the course of history. The lands he discovered in the Caribbean and South America would in the following decades be opened up by Spanish freebooters whose caravels were soon plying the Atlantic back to Spain laden with gold, silver, and all manner of exotic foods (from potatoes to tomatoes to cocoa).

By 1550, when the heir of the Catholic Monarchs, King Carlos I (R.1516–1556), came for a stay in the Alcázar of Madrid, it is estimated the city had a population of

12,000 to 15,000. The warrior king had also inherited the Habsburg throne in Austria in 1519. Thereafter he became better known as Carlos V, Holy Roman Emperor (and indeed he barely spoke Spanish), ruling over an empire that stretched from Austria to the American colonies. Spain was at the height of its power, although Carlos's interminable wars with France, rebel Dutch provinces, and Turkey were exhausting the Spanish treasury, despite the flow of precious metals from South America.

Carlos's son Felipe II (R.1556–1598) soon decided that it was inappropriate for the king of Spain to have an itinerant court. The question was, which city would he choose to make his permanent capital? Valladolid, Toledo, Segovia—all were cities with cachet.

Why Felipe finally selected Madrid, a

middle-ranking town, in 1561 has been the subject of much speculation. Some reasons seem clear. Toledo was at first glance the most obvious candidate, but, as the seat of the Catholic Church in Spain, it represented a rival power base. Noble families had vested interests in many other cities. Madrid, insignificant as it was, presented no such potential threats, and Felipe probably still recalled the 1520 revolt of many nobles and cities against his father.

Much as it surprised nearly everyone (and somewhat frightened the town's masters, who could foresee short-term supply problems when the court and its entourage descended upon the ill-prepared town), the choice clearly made sense to Felipe II and his successors. Only his son, Felipe III (R.1598–1621), would tire of Madrid sufficiently to move the court to Valladolid in 1601, a move that lasted a mere five years.

Felipe II inherited from Carlos the Spanish half of the imperial possessions, including the rebellious Dutch provinces, the American colonies, and considerable territories in Italy. In 1581 Felipe II became king of Portugal, too. At the same time, although it was not evident to many, Spain was slowly dropping from its apogee. The failure of the Spanish Armada to invade England in 1588, the secession of the Protestant Dutch provinces and constant warring there, and revolts in Granada and other largely Muslim territories in the south, all sapped the country's strength.

CAPITAL OF THE AUSTRIAS

Bad as the news often was from far afield, in Madrid the impending decline in Spanish power could not yet be felt. Felipe II built his imposing monastery-palace complex at San Lorenzo de El Escorial, just outside the city. The court attracted nobles, courtesans, artists, and writers from all corners of the country. The *Siglo de Oro* (Golden Century) of Spanish painting and letters blossomed. American precious metals continued to pour into the royal coffers.

Felipe II, who built the massive monastery-palace of El Escorial just outside Madrid in the second half of the 16th century, intended to combine all functions of Church and state.

Although Felipe II was too distracted by his wars and progress on San Lorenzo de El Escorial to lavish much attention on the expansion and embellishment of his capital, Madrid seethed with activity. Even today the core of the city is known as Los Austrias, synonymous with the grandeur of Spain under the descendants of the Habsburg emperor Carlos V. In reality, most of the city did not look the imperial part, retaining rather the air of a small town. By the time Felipe II died in 1598, the population had rocketed to about 60,000. By the 1650s it had risen to 150,000.

If Felipe II had been something of an austere control freak, conscientiously attempting to maintain a watchful eye on all the affairs of his enormous state, his successors clearly were not cut from the same cloth. Felipe III and Felipe IV both preferred to hand over the daily grind of rule to advisers such as Count-Duke Olivares.

While Olivares attempted to introduce measures to shore up a weakening internal economy (the Castilian countryside in particular had been allowed to decline), the city experienced a building boom. The Palacio del Buen Retiro was completed in 1630 and became the preferred royal residence (all that remains of it today are the Museo del Ejército building and Casón del Buen Retiro). Churches and convents were raised and noble mansions built.

The growth of the city went virtually uncontrolled. By the mid-17th century it extended from Campo del Moro in the west to the Paseo de los Recoletos in the east, and from the present-day Ronda de Toledo in the south to Calle de Sagasta in the north. The only planned space was Plaza Mayor, home to the city's main markets. Its size and good order made it ideal for bull-fighting, public executions, and autos-da-fé. Madrid's first auto-da-fé, the public execution of supposed heretics, occurred there in 1632 in the presence of the king and queen.

Since Madrid's designation as capital in 1561, people had flocked to the city from all over the country in search of opportunities. Tradesmen, desperate country people prepared to do anything for a crust, and hopeful artists and writers were joined by a

In Alonso Coello's 16th-century portrait, Felipe II is dressed without regal decoration.

stream of *hidalgos* (*hijos de algo:* "sons of something"), a peculiarly Spanish category of generally impoverished also-rans in this tightly hierarchical society. The hidalgos, scions of well-educated families but with little or no noble blood, considered themselves a cut well above the plebs. As such, they preferred not to work at any manual trade but to try their luck at landing some modest sinecure in the burgeoning court administration. Some made it, but many did not and joined the growing ranks of Madrid's poor.

The arrival of the court in 1561 meant the eclipse of municipal power. The Consejo de Madrid, the town council, although given to spending copious sums on grand parades and festivals, was rapidly subordinated to the absolute power of the royal house. Only in the 17th century did the Consejo work up the courage to request funding for the creation of a city hall. Royal approval came in 1621, but the Casa de la Villa (today the Ayuntamiento) was not completed until the end of the century.

THE SPANISH SUCCESSION & SLIDE INTO DECAY

The death of Carlos II without an heir in 1700 unleashed the War of the Spanish Succession (1702–1714). France supported Felipe V (1700–1746), the Bourbon-family grandson of France's Louis XIV and María Teresa (a daughter of Felipe IV). His lineage was hard to dispute, but in 1702 hostilities broke out between, on the one hand, France and Spain and, on the other, an alliance uniting Austria, England, Holland, Portugal, some German states, and the House of Savoy behind Archduke Charles, an Austrian pretender to the throne.

Felipe V won, but at a cost. Spain was exhausted and lost considerable territory (the island of Menorca, for instance, became a British territory). Felipe V's hard-won victory served primarily to accelerate the country's decline as a power on the European stage. An absolutist, Felipe V accelerated the process of centralizing power in the hands of the king and his bureaucracy in Madrid, abolishing the autonomous charters and local government of Catalunya, Aragón, Valencia, and the Balearic Islands.

In Madrid, the medieval Alcázar burned to the ground in 1734. This rather suited Felipe V, who found the gloomy old residence depressing. In its place he ordered the construction of a new Palacio Real (Royal Palace). It was completed 30 years later, in

The original Palacio Real, built in 1537, burned to the ground in 1734. Felipe V immediately began work on a new palace—this one only of stone. It took 36 years to complete.

time for one of Spain's most savvy monarchs, Carlos III (R.1759–1788), to enjoy it. But Madrid needed more than a nice new palace. Known, with good reason, as the *pocilga de Europa* (the pigsty of Europe), Madrid was crying out for serious urban improvement.

Known as the *rey-alcalde* (king-mayor) because of the exceptional interest he took in the improvement of his city, Carlos had streets widened and paved, sewerage and street lighting improved, and crime reduced. A central post office was established at the Puerta del Sol (the building is still there today). Carlos ordered the creation of the Real Jardín Botánico and encouraged beautification projects such as

the laying out of the tree-lined Paseo del Prado. It was at this time that the neoclassic Palacio de Villanueva, today home to the Museo del Prado, was built to house a science academy. The king even introduced a lottery in 1763.

On the wider national front, Carlos III began a program of road construction in a country that until then had been notable for its difficult travel. Trade between Spanish ports and the Latin American colonies was liberalized, and small-scale industry, such as textiles in Catalunya, began to take off.

NAPOLÉON & THE WAR OF INDEPENDENCE

Although Spain had significant problems, the long and sensible rule of Carlos III had at least given the country some sense of stability. Things were to go badly awry in the 20 years after his death.

Only one year into the reign of Carlos IV, all Europe was rocked by the violence of the French Revolution. Not only was monarchical rule suddenly called into question, it was simply swept aside. The revolutionary government soon showed itself to be an aggressive force, and conflict in Europe seemed inevitable.

Under Carlos IV, Spain at first sided with what would become Revolutionary France's most implacable enemy, Great Britain. Carlos's spokesman and minister, Manuel Godoy, then decided to switch sides. Spain paid a terrible price for this changed alliance when the bulk of its navy was sunk in the Battle of Trafalgar in 1805, in which Admiral Horatio Nelson routed the Franco-Spanish armada off the south coast of Spain.

Three years later, Napoléon persuaded Godoy to allow French troops to pass through Spain to launch an assault on Portugal, allied with Great Britain. The first French troops arrived in early 1808 and by

March they were in Madrid. As it became clear the French presence was turning into an occupation, Madrid rose in popular revolt on May 2 (see pp. 204–205). Carlos IV and Godoy had already fled. The city folk had little chance and were routed by the end of the day. Francisco Goya immor-

His Imperial Highness Prince Joseph Bonaparte, in an 1855 portrait

talized the events of that day, and the executions of rebels on the morrow, in paintings that hang in the Museo del Prado.

By July, Joseph Bonaparte (1768–1844), Napoléon's brother, was installed as king in Madrid. Across the country resistance fighters began to harry French troops, but it was not until the Duke of Wellington (1769–1852) marched into Spain with a combined British-Portuguese force that the Peninsular War (known as the Guerra de la Independencia, or the War of Independence, in Spain) got under way in earnest. The French were ousted in 1814.

Joseph Bonaparte's stay in Madrid was not all bad. The hardships of war hit the city hard and in 1812 30,000 Madrileños died of hunger. In a bid to improve living conditions in the city, numerous churches

and convents were demolished, and the area that is now the Plaza de Oriente was cleared of its warren of streets and ramshackle housing. Cemeteries were moved to the outskirts. Resented at the time, these moves were later accepted by most Spanish observers as necessary improvements.

THE AGE OF COUPS

With the French gone, Fernando VII (R.1814–1833) returned to Madrid as king. He soon showed that he was an absolutist of the old school and shut down publication of the many political and satirical pamphlets that briefly flourished in the capital after 1814. He would in no way countenance the idea of a parliamentary system of government. Rigidly rooted in the past though he was, he did open up parts of the Parque del Buen Retiro, hitherto the private domain of the royal family and intimates, to the general public. He was also behind the formation of a public art gallery in the Palacio de Villanueva. In October 1816, the first stagecoach line from Madrid to Barcelona via Valencia opened.

Overall, however, these were disastrous times for Spain. After the calamities of the Napoleonic wars, many of Spain's restless American colonies gained their independence, particularly after Spanish forces were defeated in Peru in 1824.

Fernando left his three-year-old daughter Isabel II behind as heir, and thus began the long regency of her mother, María Cristina. Fernando's brother, Carlos, refused to accept the accession of a woman to the throne and sparked off the Carlist Wars, which would sputter on through much of the 19th century, mostly in the north of the country in Navarra and the Basque country.

To fight the Carlists, María Cristina and then Isabel II turned to liberal figures in the army and politics for support. From the 1840s until Isabel was obliged to abdicate and flee the country in 1868, *pronunciamientos* (military coups), riots, and counter-coups followed one another with monotonous regularity.

Madrid had barely developed since Joseph Bonaparte set in motion his plans for urban change, plans that had been stopped in their tracks with the return to the throne of the Bourbons in 1814. In 1837, however, the government ordered the *desamortización* (disentailment) of Church property. The Church would lose 1,600 properties in Madrid in the following four decades, which in turn fueled a speculative boom. It also favored the rise of an entrepreneurial class in a city still dominated by a nobility that disdained work of any kind.

The city's first railway line, between Madrid and Aranjuez, opened in 1851 and was followed seven years later by the Canal de Isabel II, which still supplies the city with water from the Sierra de Guadarrama. Other public works included the opening of the Teatro Real (Royal Theater), the Biblioteca Nacional (National Library), and Congreso de los Diputados (lower house of parliament).

Much-needed plans to extend the city finally spluttered into motion in the 1860s, when work on an *ensanche* (extension) began around Calle de Serrano.

The flight of Isabel II to France led to still more instability. In the course of seven years, Madrid was run by an interim government, an Italian king, a series of republican governments, and, finally, after yet another coup, Isabel's son, Alfonso XII (*R.*1875–1885). He was succeeded by Alfonso XIII (*R.*1886–1931).

A NEW CENTURY & THE REPUBLIC

It would be an exaggeration to claim the early decades were ones of peaceful progress in Madrid, but progress was nonetheless felt. After the final colonial catastrophe of 1898—when Spain lost Cuba, Puerto Rico, and the Philippines, its last significant possessions, to an infinitely more powerful United States—it was almost as though the country could now concentrate on matters closer to home.

In 1891, the country's national bank, the Banco de España, opened its headquarters in Madrid. Seven years later, the first city tramlines were electrified. In 1910, work on the Gran Vía started and, in 1919, the first underground metro line was running. In October 1934, the grand Las Ventas bullring opened. Internal immigration doubled the population to one million by 1930. In the 1920s especially, Madrid was the center of the country's intellectual life, attracting the likes of poet Federico García Lorca and painter Salvador Dalí.

Madrid was a hive of activity, but the almost frenetic pace of development could not disguise the deepening political crisis in

Maria Cristina de Borbón acted as regent until her daughter was old enough to take the throne as Queen Isabel II.

Spain, fueled by serious problems at home and abroad. Remaining neutral in World War I had at first brought prosperity to Spain as it freely traded with all sides in the conflict. Boom was shortly followed by bust, however, and a pointless colonial war in northern Morocco in the 1920s proved disastrous.

In 1923, General Miguel Primo de Rivera installed himself as dictator, but he was removed by the king in 1930. The following year, a coalition of republicans and socialists won municipal elections around the country and proclaimed a republic. The king fled, but the left-wing government soon developed divisions and in 1933 was replaced by a right-wing government. In 1934, the obscure Gen. Francisco Franco Bahamonde ruthlessly put down a miners' revolt in the northern region of Asturias. Two years later, the left-wing Frente Popular (Popular Front) defeated the right-wing Frente Nacional (National Front) at national elections in February.

By this time, Madrid and other major cities were racked by spreading political violence in the streets, in what seemed an almost inevitable descent into war.

CIVIL WAR

Seeing the danger, the Frente Popular government removed suspect generals (including General Franco, sent to the Canary Islands) from the capital.

It was to no avail. In July 1936, Franco gave the go-ahead for military insurrection in Spain's North African enclaves. Garrisons on the mainland soon followed suit. What followed was three years of carnage and hardship that tore the country apart.

Madrid itself was under siege by November, about the time volunteer soldiers of the International Brigades began to arrive in the capital. Franco's forces pulled up in the Casa de Campo, and over the following years his Nationalist troops would penetrate into the university and Argüelles districts of the city, but no farther. Artillery duels between the Nationalists and government forces placed in key spots (such as Las Vistillas) became part of everyday life for Madrid's populace. The Gran Vía came to be known as Howitzer Alley, as Nationalist shells frequently fell here, but people continued to go about their business as best they could, catching the metro, going to the cinema, and just getting by.

The government fled early on to Valencia and later to Barcelona. Madrid itself did not surrender to Franco until March 28, 1939, long after much of the rest of the country (including Barcelona) had fallen. Three days later, the war was over.

FROM FRANCO TO DEMOCRACY

For years after 1939, Madrileños breathed the air of repression and reprisals. Of course, not all of them were unhappy at the outcome of the war. The middle classes generally welcomed Franco's victory, and many of those who had suffered under the republicans now turned informer. Summary trials and executions went on well into the 1940s, but figures are hard to come by. By one account, in 1939 200 to 250 executions were being carried out daily. Many of the 200,000 death sentences said to have been passed by 1944 were commuted to terms in prisons and labor camps. One trade union leader estimated that two million Spaniards went to prison or to labor camps in the three years after the war. Many were set to work on the Valle de los Caídos, a Fascist monument to the war dead outside Madrid.

After the initial euphoria experienced by some citizens, the city settled into the difficult period of the 1940s and 1950s, the Años de Hambre (Years of Hunger). Although Spain remained neutral in World War II, the regime was shunned by all the main powers after 1945. Only in 1953, when the United States decided that Spanish military bases would be handy in the Cold War, did Washington come to Madrid with aid from the Marshall Plan. Two years later, Spain had a seat at the United Nations.

Throughout the 1950s, starving peasants streamed into Madrid from the country's poorest regions—from Andalucía in the south, Extremadura in the southwest, and Galicia in the northwest. By 1960 it is estimated that 600,000 had arrived, creating massive *chabolas,* shanty towns without running water or electricity, on the city's edge.

Marshall aid and foreign investment began to breathe life into Madrid. America's Chrysler automobile manufacturer was the capital's top employer in the 1960s. A construction boom took off, and many of the towers and office blocks along the Paseo de la Castellana started going up.

Gen. Francisco Franco, who ruled Spain as a dictatorship from 1939 to 1975, gives the Nationalist salute.

Growing prosperity did not dampen political opposition to Franco's regime. Protests at the universities became more open, and clandestine trade unions began to organize themselves as well. In 1973, the Basque separatist terrorist group Euskadi Ta Askatasuna (ETA; Basque Homeland and Freedom) assassinated Adm. Carrero Blanco, Franco's prime minister and designated successor, in the streets of Madrid. The following year Franco fell ill, and he died on November 20, 1975. No one quite knew what would happen next.

Franco had groomed the Bourbon prince, Juan Carlos, to take over in his image as head of state after his death, but the newly crowned King Juan Carlos I had

other plans. As the Partido Socialista Obrero Español (PSOE; Spanish Socialist Workers' Party), Partido Comunista de España (PCE; Spanish Communist Party), and trade unions emerged from hiding, the king asked the moderate Francoist Adolfo Suárez to form a government and pass a series of reforms leading to the creation of a parliamentary democracy. By 1978 a new, federal-style constitution, with the king as head of state, was in place.

Bad memories came momentarily flooding back when, in February 1981, a Guardia Civil (Civil Guard) lieutenant colonel, Antonio Tejero Molina, led an armed detachment to occupy the Cortes (parliament). The coup attempt fizzled after 18 hours when the king ordered the army to stay in the barracks.

A year later Felipe González's PSOE won the national elections. He remained in power until 1996, when the right-wing Partido Popular (PP) under José María Aznar picked up the baton. The González years were ones of rapid growth in Spain, but many problems remained unresolved. Under the charismatic native of Seville, Spain joined the NATO defense alliance and the European Economic Community (now the European Union). The country quickly became the EU's biggest net beneficiary of cohesion funds, which were aimed at bringing the country into line with the EU's core members. Much of Spain's net-

work of freeways and other infrastructure has been built with European money. Combined with the profits from being one of the biggest tourist destinations in the world, these programs have helped turn the country around. But unemployment remained in double digits throughout González's time, and increasingly embarrassing corruption scandals blackened the name of the PSOE.

Under Aznar, a conservative economic policy helped ease unemployment and improve productivity, but by the time his party was taken out of power in 2004 (see p. 19), alarm bells were sounding. Much of the country's wealth is generated by construction and tourism, while investment in research and development is low and inflation higher than in most EU countries. Spanish wages continue to run below the EU average.

At a municipal level, the charismatic Marxist Enrique Tierno Galván was elected mayor of Madrid in 1979 in the city's first free elections following Franco's death. He governed a city in ferment until his death in 1986. These were the years of the *movida,* that sudden burst of nocturnal madness that shook Madrid out of its long gray Francoist slumber. The city partied.

Things slowed a little under Galván's Socialist successor, Juan Barranco, who was ousted after a censure motion in 1989. After a short period of centrist rule, the conservative José María Álvarez del Manzano took over in 1991. By then the downside of the previous excesses was making itself felt, with an explosion in the number of heroin addicts in the capital and a consequent rise in street crime. The arrival of AIDS in the 1980s, spread in part by needle-sharing addicts, added a further note of danger.

In May 2003 the PP's Alberto Ruiz-Gallardón, until then president of the Comunidad de Madrid regional government, was elected mayor. Six months later, his party colleague Esperanza Aguirre became the first-ever female president of a Spanish region when she took over in Madrid. ■

Leaders of Spain's 17 autonomous communities meet in Madrid in 2005 to discuss their affairs.

The arts

SPAIN AND ITS CAPITAL PRESENT SEVERAL CONUNDRUMS. THEIR MOST glorious moments in painting came at times of decline and confusion. Architecturally, Madrid began developing late, was long neglected, and expanded in fits and starts. A pleasing old center remains alongside an explosion of late 19th- and early 20th-century building. The city also has a busy music scene, ranging from flamenco performed in sultry bars to grand spectacles in the reborn opera house.

ARCHITECTURE

No more than a small provincial town until suddenly catapulted to the status of capital in the latter half of the 16th century, Madrid preserves virtually nothing of architectural interest from its early years. A pleasing concentration of historic buildings in Madrid's center does bear witness to the following two centuries. The grand boulevards and haughty edifices that most distinguish the city center are largely a product of the 19th and early 20th centuries, when Madrid got a blast of belle époque and, later, art deco beauty treatment.

From Muslim fort to the Renaissance

Of the original Muslim frontline fort that encircled Madrid, only a modest stretch of defensive wall below the Catedral de Nuestra Señora de la Almudena remains today. The bell towers of two modest churches in the Old Town, the Iglesia de San Pedro El Viejo and Iglesia de San Nicolás de los Servitas, are reminders of the Mudejar style of building. The Mudejares were Muslims who remained behind in territory conquered by the Christians. Common across much of central and southern Spain, where Catholic forces gradually ejected the Muslims, Mudejar architecture is marked by the use of brick and stylized decoration.

About the only reminders of the Gothic period in Madrid are the delightful Capilla del Obispo, a chapel in the central Iglesia de San Andrés, and the late-Gothic Casa de los Lujanes on Plaza de la Villa.

One of Spain's great Renaissance architects was Juan de Herrera (1530–1597). His robust, austere take on the era's style is exemplified by his work on San Lorenzo de El Escorial, Felipe II's mighty palace-monastery-pantheon outside Madrid.

Madrid baroque & the 18th century

Herrera's influence on construction in Madrid itself was more indirect. Juan Gómez de Mora (1586–1648) and his uncle Francisco de Mora (1560–1610) worked in a hybrid style clearly reminiscent of Herrera and known as *barroco madrileño*. The former produced the Ayuntamiento, city prisons (one is now the Ministry of Foreign Affairs on Plaza de la Santa Cruz, another the Casa de la Villa), and the Convento de la Encarnación. The latter worked on the Palacio de Úceda (now the Capitanía General on Calle Mayor). The colorful Real Casa de la Panadería on Plaza Mayor also dates from this period.

More clearly baroque, although hardly florid, are the Basílica de San Isidro, built in the 1660s, and the entrance to the Museo Municipal.

Ventura Rodríguez (1717–1785), who designed the Palacio de Liria and laid out the Campo del Moro gardens, competed for attention with the Italian Francesco Sabatini (1722–1797), who also worked on the Palacio Real and raised the Puerta de Alcalá. The other dominating figure of the 18th century was Juan de Villanueva (1739–1811), who designed the building we know today as the Museo del Prado.

The belle époque

The second half of the 19th century brought a building boom to Madrid. Boulevards like the Paseo de la Castellana and the residential district of Salamanca took form. The pace picked up at the end of the century. Spearheaded by Antonio Palacios (1874–1945), a bevy of

The 15th-century San Nicolás, with a 12th-century Mudejar tower, is one of Madrid's few remaining examples of Mudejar architecture.

The Palacio de Comunicaciones, which dominates Plaza de Cibeles, is the most extravagant of the many buildings designed by Antonio Palacios in the early 20th century.

architects joined forces to coat the capital in the glow of grandeur it still exudes today. This was the age of looking back to look forward. Palacios's gargantuan Palacio de Comunicaciones was (and remains) an extreme example of neo-Gothic.

By the early 20th century, designers felt freer than ever to indulge their whims, creating such art deco gems as the Edificio Grassy (1917) and Edificio Metrópolis (1911). The Gran Vía is laced with many such fanciful caprices.

Modern times

The Franco years did little to make Madrid a cheerier place. The Edificio de España in its eponymous square is an Iberian Fascist amalgam of New York skyscraper and Soviet dourness. Most modern development during and since Franco's day has taken place along the Paseo de la Castellana. With the exception of the inward-leaning Torres Kio on Plaza de Castilla, completed in 1998, little in the way of eye-catching construction has yet taken hold in Madrid.

In the early 21st century, the city is passing through an unprecedented spurt of urban expansion. A drive around the city's ring roads reveals whole medium-rise suburbs popping up out of nowhere, the horizon lined with cranes. Landmark buildings are in the offing. Richard Rogers's new terminal at Barajas airport is an original, undulating design. Henry Cobb is planning an exciting glass tower, the Torre Espacio, for the northern end of the Paseo de la Castellana. And Spaniard Rafael Moneo, who designed the clever restoration of the old Atocha train station building and its conversion into a tropical garden (1992), is the mind behind the remodeling and modern extension of the Museo del Prado.

PAINTING & SCULPTURE

The Old Masters of Spain, led by Velázquez, shed their radiant light in the gloom of Spain's accelerating political and economic decline in the 17th century. The capital and the court were as one, and it was largely from the latter that artistic patronage came. A couple of centuries later, the titan of early 19th-century Spanish art, Francisco Goya, would also benefit from its largesse. Civil war and the Franco years forced several Madrid artists into exile. Times have

The Bernabéu soccer stadium, home to the famed club Real Madrid, is one of the signature structures of modern Madrid.

changed, and Madrid not only is the country's greatest single repository of paintings but also hosts what has become one of Europe's top annual contemporary art fests, ARCO (see feature pp. 190–191).

Old Masters of the golden age

Felipe II's decision to make his permanent capital in Madrid in 1561 had perhaps only one serious artistic consequence. Cretan-born Domenikos Theotokopoulos (1541–1614), better known to us today as El Greco, settled in the city of Toledo, which was thought to be a prime candidate for the country's capital. From this, the seat of the Church in Spain, he tried and failed to awaken interest in the king for his ethereal figures. As it became clear that the choice of Madrid was irreversible, Toledo lost importance and El Greco's personal fortunes also slid.

The star of what came to be known as the apogee of fine arts in Spain was Diego Rodríguez de Silva y Velázquez (1599–1660), a man with extraordinary talent, a taste for glory, and a way with the powerful. Born a year after Felipe II's death, he moved from Seville to Madrid as court painter under Felipe's successors. He was born at the right

time, for Felipe had shown a penchant for Italian painters that might otherwise have left Velázquez languishing in Seville as El Greco did in Toledo.

We are fortunate that this was not so. Velázquez may have been vain (during all his life at court in Madrid, one of his biggest preoccupations was to receive a knighthood), but he was also good, and some of his grandest works now hang proudly in the Museo del Prado. Easily the best known is the enormous canvas "The Maids of Honor" ("Las Meninas," circa 1656). The painting repays close observation, for it is not merely a portrait of King Felipe IV's little daughter, the Infanta Margarita, and friends. To the left is the painter himself, painting a portrait of … whom? The clue is in the mirror at the back of the room, in which we see the king and his queen. Velázquez has captured several ideas and moments at once, including the cheeky detail of including on his vest the much desired Cross of the Order of Santiago—a decoration that the painter openly coveted but was not awarded until toward the end of his life.

In the Prado hang various of his masterpieces. Among the most powerful are his

The intriguing "Las Meninas," or "The Maids of Honor," painted by Diego Velázquez in 1656, is one of the most renowned artworks in the world.

"Christ Crucified," in which he captures the pain of Christ's death, and "The Surrender of Breda," depicting the yielding of the Dutch town of Breda to Spanish forces after a ten-month siege in 1625.

A contemporary and friend of Velázquez, the painter Francisco de Zurbarán

(1598–1664) cut his teeth in Seville, but he too came to Madrid (circa 1634–1635) to carry out commissions for the court and convents in the capital. He returned to Seville with the title of Royal Artist. He is known above all for his chiaroscuro portraits of saints and monks, in which light and shadow play a key role. Some can be seen in the Prado and the Real Academia de Bellas Artes de San Fernando. He returned to Madrid toward the end of his life, where he died in relative poverty.

Although neither had much contact with Madrid, two further masters of the period, many of whose works also hang in the Prado, require mention. José (Jusep) de Ribera (1591–1652) and Bartolomé Esteban Murillo (1618–1682) are signal artists. Ribera lived in the Spanish-controlled city of Naples (the Italians know him as Lo Spagnoletto, "the little Spaniard") and was a disciple of the Caravaggio school of chiaroscuro painting.

Murillo, like Velázquez born in Seville, carried out the bulk of his work in his native city, although he did visit Madrid to acquaint himself with the royal collections. His was a breezy, colorful style. Religious scenes dominate his paintings, as was typical in the period, but Murillo is also known for portraits of young children, often poor, in the streets.

The Madrid school

Lesser-known artists, collectively known as the Madrid school, were also busy at work in the capital. The Ricci brothers, Fray Juan (1600–1681) and Francisco (1614–1685), were active in a variety of convents and churches around Castile.

More important, and the last artist of stature to emerge in the baroque context of the Madrid school, was Claudio Coello (1642–1693). Born in the capital of Portuguese parents, he studied with Francisco Ricci. Some of his works are on display in the Prado, but the most important, the enormous "The Sacred Form" hangs in El Escorial. The panoramic portrait shows King Carlos II and his court worshipping the Eucharist, thus symbolizing the role of the monarch as guarantor of Catholic order in Spain.

Goya

Towering above the remainder of Spain's 19th-century artists, Francisco José de Goya y Lucientes (1746–1828) came to Madrid from a small town in Aragón to work in the royal tapestry factory as a designer. By 1799 he had become court painter to King Carlos III, seven years after becoming deaf.

Goya was wild at heart. In the course of his

long career his style changed continually, crashing through artistic conventions with divine indifference. He carried out religious and court portraits, but increasingly did so with a ruthless realism. Said to have had a long affair with the Duchess of Alba, it is thought that his paintings "The Clothed Maja" and "The Nude Maja" are portraits of the duchess. The scandal attached to the latter was such that it was long hidden from view.

Goya's series of etchings "The Caprices" reflects his dark views on life at the end of the 18th century.

What is most extraordinary about his works is their sheer variety, both in method and subject matter. Profoundly affected by the events of his time (above all, the War of Independence), he executed several series of engravings, for instance, "The Disasters of War." In these images the cruelty of war is portrayed without quarter. In another series, "Bullfighting," it appears the artist was repelled by the violence and cruelty of the activity.

Goya's best-known paintings refer to the Madrid uprising against occupation by Napoléon's troops. "The Second of May" and "The Third of May" depict scenes, respectively,

Juan Gris was a master of the cubist still life, as shown by "The Mandolin" (1921).

of the uprising and the execution of rebels the day after.

Surely the most bizarre of his works were his *pinturas negras*—"black paintings"—murals he painted in his house west of the Manzanares River after the War of Independence. These nightmarish images include one of Saturn devouring his own children.

Goya was far ahead of his time, providing inspiration for future generations of European painters, especially the French Impressionists.

The 20th century

Goya was a hard act to follow. Closing the 19th century in Madrid were Valencia-born Joaquín Sorolla (1863–1923), best known for his sunny beach scenes, which can be viewed in the gallery housed in his former home in Madrid. Local boy José Gutiérrez Solana (1886–1945), some of whose works can be seen in the Centro de Arte Reina Sofía, depicts in dark tones and avant-garde fashion scenes and people of his city, largely influenced by the tragic events of the Civil War.

At about the same time, Madrid's Juan

Gris (1887–1927) came to the fore as one of the most important of the cubist painters, along with his friend Pablo Picasso.

The so-called Vallecas (a Madrid suburb) school produced the likes of Benjamín Palencia (1894–1980) and Toledo-born sculptor Alberto Sánchez (1895–1962). The latter was one of the leading modern sculptors of Spain. He worked in stone, plaster, wood, and metal, and his themes, with lean human figures, are shared in the canvases of Palencia. Sánchez preferred exile in the Soviet Union to life in Franco's Spain, and much of his opus was destroyed. Works by both artists are on display in the Centro de Arte Reina Sofía. Another exile was Eduardo Arroyo (1937–), whose paintings lean to pop art lightness laden with social critique.

LITERATURE

The center of contemporary Spanish publishing is now in Barcelona, but Madrid has long acted as a magnet for great Spanish writers. For centuries they were attracted by the royal court and its patronage. Later, they came simply because the capital was the place to be for people of letters.

Generations of writers in Madrid and beyond have tended to look back in awe to the Siglo de Oro (Golden Century) of Spanish writing, when Spain had already edged away from the zenith of its power but the all-powerful court, finally established in one place, attracted writing talent from around the country to Madrid.

For many, the European novel sprang from the mind of a turbulent man born just outside Madrid in Alcalá de Henares. Miguel de Cervantes Saavedra (1547–1616) had nothing if not an interesting life. Soldier of fortune, prisoner in the hands of the Moors, public functionary, accused at one time of murder, Cervantes finally settled in Madrid where, to make a little money, he started writing a short story. "El Ingenioso Hidalgo Don Quijote de la Mancha" ("Don Quixote"), the tale of the wanderings of a ruined knight and his faithful sidekick, Sancho Panza, wound up being a rather longer story than Cervantes had intended—the forerunner of the modern novel.

The same era saw the birth of one of Spain's great poets, Luis de Góngora (1561–1627). Drama also had its stars, particularly the playwright Lope de Vega (1562–1635), whose house can still be visited in Madrid's old city center. Of the estimated 800 plays he wrote, some 300 have survived to this day. The ladies' man Don Juan was a character in the play *El Burlador de Sevilla (The Seducer of Seville)* by Lope de Vega's colleague, Tirso de Molina. At the tail end of the Golden Century also emerged another eternal great of the Spanish stage, Pedro Calderón de la Barca (1600–1681).

Born some two centuries later in the Canary Islands and often referred to as Spain's Balzac, Benito Pérez Galdós (1843–1920) lived most of his adult life in the capital. There he published one of the greatest novels of early 20th-century European literature, *Fortunata y Jacinta,* a fascinating exploration of life in 19th-century bourgeois Madrid.

Galdós lived in Madrid at a time of political and literary ferment. He watched as younger writers, led by the likes of the philosopher-essayist José Ortega y Gasset, founded the Generation of '98 movement in the wake of defeat at the hands of the United States and loss of most of its remaining colonies in 1898.

The trials of the Franco years in the capital have fascinated writers down the decades. Nobel Prize winner Camilo José Cela (1916–2002) explored the wounds of the city in the wake of the Civil War in his 1950s *La*

A museum devoted to Dulcinea, Don Quixote's great love, re-creates her fictional home in the town of El Toboso in La Mancha.

Colmena (The Beehive). While not overtly critical of the regime, it painted a bleak picture of the lives of Madrileños in the 1940s.

Like Cela, Francisco Umbral (1935–) is a winner of the prestigious national literary prize, the Premio Cervantes. A prolific writer and journalist, Umbral has penned several novels set in Madrid, most importantly the

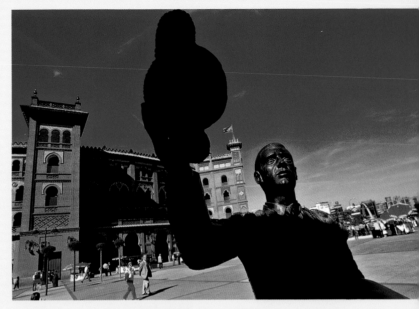

A matador statue beckons visitors to Plaza de Toros Monumental de Las Ventas.

Bullfighting

A buzz fills the arena on a brilliant mid-May afternoon. Since lunchtime, spectators have been converging on the world's greatest *corrida* (bullfight) stadium. They come from all over Madrid and across Spain to witness the finest exponents of this ancient blood sport. It is a spectacle of life and death, a dance of bravery and blood. It is not for the squeamish.

Madrid's Plaza de Toros Monumental de Las Ventas (capacity 25,000; see pp. 192–193) is a mighty setting. Built in 1931, it exudes a mix of classical grandeur and Moorish mystique. To triumph here is the ultimate dream of the *torero* (bullfighter).

Toreros seek fame and fortune through physical prowess and bravura. They all aspire to become a *matador* (killer) and reach the top by fighting at Las Ventas.

The *lidia*, as bullfighting is also known, dates from ancient Roman times and, although associated mostly with Spain, is also practiced in Portugal, southern France, and Latin America.

The one-month season of daily fights that begins at Las Ventas with the Fiestas de San Isidro Labrador (Madrid's patron saint) in mid-May is the acme of the season, but the corrida is a part of town festivals up and down the country. In bigger cities, fights can be a regular weekend fixture.

The spectacle typically begins around 6 p.m. As a rule, three matadors with their *cuadrillas* (teams of toreros) present themselves to fight six bulls from different breeders (each matador and team takes on two bulls). *Toros bravos* (fighting bulls) are bred for this day. Each encounter takes about 20 minutes. The fight is cruel and the bull is bound to lose—but no one should doubt the dangers involved. Matadors frequently wind up in the hospital with horrific wounds, although few have been killed.

A complex ritual accompanies the fight. The bull is released from a dark corral into the ring, angry and confused after being penned up. Toreros dash about with heavy rose and yellow percale capes, testing the bull's willingness to fight before the matador appears.

The matador then takes on the bull in single combat with a smaller red cape. The "art" of his fight lies in the daring and finesse of his *faenas* (moves). Particularly good maneuvers move the crowd to scream *Olé!* in encouragement.

The matador is followed by *picadores,* mounted on horseback, who fight off the bull while it charges at the horses. Next come the *banderilleros,* who rush headlong at the bull to lodge short, harpoonlike instruments (*banderillas*) in its withers. All this serves to wear down and goad the bull for the return of the matador, whose bravado is now fully tested. When he judges the bull can give no more, he steadies himself before his victim with his sword to execute the *estocada* (kill).

If the matador performs well, he is awarded one or even two of the bull's ears, and sometimes its tail. The matador's dream is to exit Las Ventas by its Moorish Puerta de Madrid—an honor reserved only for the most daring, artistic victories in the grandest bullring in the world. ■

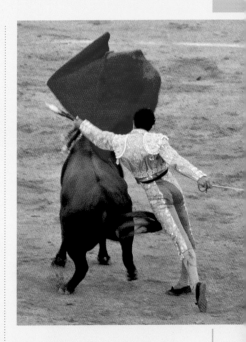

The picador on horseback (below) aims to tire and weaken the bull before the matador (above) moves in for the kill.

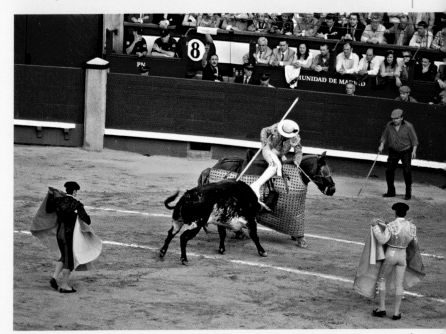

Trilogía de Madrid, a journey through the life and times of Madrid into the Franco years.

Almudena Grandes (1960–) is one of the most successful Madrid-born authors of the moment. Her novels range across a variety of settings but generally turn on complex human relationships. The protagonists are frequently Madrileños, and in her latest novel, *Castillos de Cartón* (2004), she uses a suicide as the start-

passion. For many, flamenco (be it the music, song, or dance of that name) is the quintessence of Spain. In fact, it derives from the country's *gitano* (Gypsy) community, and its original home lies in Andalucía. But Madrid, as a city of immigrants, has long been a second home for that southern heat.

The origins of flamenco remain obscure. It is thought to have its roots in the 15th

Flamenco, a Spanish Gypsy song or dance, originated in southern Spain in the 14th century and evolved into one of the icons of Spanish culture.

ing point for a look at the interlocked lives of three young people in art school.

Many other contemporary writers, whether local or not, frequently set their novels in Madrid. Juan Eduardo Zúñiga (1929–) examines the city's resistance to Franco during the Civil War in his acclaimed novel *Capital de la Gloria,* while Andalucía's Antonio Muñoz Molina (1956–) chose Madrid as the scene for such novels as *El Dueño del Secreto (The Master of the Secret).*

FLAMENCO

It rumbles from the depths of the Spanish soul, crying out with universal sorrow and

century, when Gypsies arrived in southern Spain from India via Egypt and eastern Europe. The Muslims were still in control of Granada and parts (but by no means all) of Andalucía at this time, and the immigrants soon picked up elements of Arab and Berber music.

Flamenco song evolved over the centuries into different styles, ranging from the anguished *siguiriyas* and *soleás* common in Seville to the more toe-tapping *bulerías* of Jerez de la Frontera, as well as *boleros, fandangos, alegrías, farrucas,* and more.

At the base of it all is *cante hondo* (deep song), the throaty, anguished singing that often talks of grief, loss, and injustice.

Flamenco guitar (performed by a *tocaor*), initially probably no more than accompaniment to the singing, evolved into its own virtuoso musical genre, as did the powerful dancing of the *bailaores*.

What was long a largely ignored folk music began to attract wider attention in the 19th century. In Madrid, Gypsies lived around Calle de Toledo, and Andalucían audience. Such claims are probably twaddle, but the traditionalists view dimly the tendency among the younger generation (Gypsy or otherwise) to mix genres (producing fusion, flamenco rock, and even flamenco hip-hop). Yet it is this very openness to fresh influences that has brought flamenco artists a whole new worldwide audience.

Of the more traditionally inclined per-

The story of Carmen, the tragic beauty from Seville, is told in dramatic style by the dancers of the Ballet de Madrid.

taverns on that road frequently hosted flamenco performers. The genre subsequently had its ups and downs in Madrid, but from the 1950s, the spread of *tablaos* (flamenco bars) kept it alive in the capital. A few, like the Corral de la Morería and Café de Chinitas, are active today.

Flamenco today

Since the 1980s, flamenco has undergone a revolution, and opinions on its current merits are sharply divided. The proudest of the purists, Gypsies one and all, affirm that non-Gypsies can't really acquire *duende*, that indefinable quality that allows the flamenco singer or musician to work his or her magic on the formers, the Carmona family (also known as Los Habichuela) are probably the best known, especially Juan (1933–) and Pepe (1944–), along with the Montoya family.

Universally acclaimed as the greatest of the younger generation of singers was El Camarón de la Isla (1950–1992), a friend of Paco de Lucía (1947–) and probably the best-known exponent of flamenco guitar beyond Spain. From much the same generation are the *cantaores* Enrique Morente (1942–) and Carmen Linares (1951–). A younger guitarist who has duende in spades is Vicente Amigo (1967–).

Of the contemporary bailaores, those with the greatest international profile are the fiery, highly theatrical Joaquín Cortés (1969–) and the more classical Antonio Canales (1961–). Also to be watched are Belén López (1987–), Belén Maya (1966–), Eva la Yerbabuena (1973–), and Antonio El Pipa (1971–).

The new wave

Nuevo Flamenco may attract opprobrium from the purists, but since the 1980s the groups that dare to innovate have won over a young and otherwise mostly uninterested audience for flamenco in Spain. Two groups that fall squarely into this camp of flamenco rock (also called Gypsy rock) are Ketama and Pata Negra. To the youngest generation, however, even these groups are beginning to look a little stale. This explains the growing success of singers such as Raquel Riquelme, a non-Gypsy *(paya)* whose music has been described as "paya punk."

Other musicians have gone in the direction of fusion. Radio Tarifa is a group that experiments with a mix of flamenco, medieval European, and North African sounds. Juan Peña Lebrijano (1941–), or El Lebrijano, plays more traditional flamenco, accompanied by the mellifluous music of traditional Moroccan orchestras.

Aside from the tablaos, which tend to be touristy, there is a smattering of more genuine flamenco bars in the Lavapiés and La Latina areas of central Madrid. Frequent concerts are held on principal stages like the Centro Cultural de la Villa. (For more information, visit www.deflamenco.com, with text in Spanish and English.)

MUSIC

In 1997, the Teatro Real, Madrid's grand opera house on Plaza de Oriente, opened … again. A site with a long history of mishaps and hiccups, it had been shut for restoration for nine years. Now Madrileños have a premier location with the latest technological innovations for seeing top-quality opera.

Madrileños might like hearing opera and classical music, but Madrid has produced little

The Spanish National Orchestra gives regular concerts at the Auditorio Nacional, Madrid's main venue for classical music.

world-class talent, with the mighty exception of the gentle tenor Plácido Domingo (1934–). Born in Madrid, he grew up in Mexico with his family of *zarzuela* performers.

Zarzuela, a uniquely Madrid creation, is a cross between musical, light opera, and spoken theater. It emerged in the 17th century as home entertainment for King Felipe IV, taking its name from the palace (official home to the royal family today) in which it was regularly performed. After all but dying out in the 18th century, zarzuela returned to Madrid as popular entertainment in the 19th century. Playwright Calderón de la Barca wrote many of the original scripts, in those days usually of a mythological nature.

Nowadays, any human drama can be the stuff of zarzuela. While it may come across as a music-hall genre belonging to another age, zarzuela is still popular with many Madrileños and can be seen regularly at the Teatro de la Zarzuela.

Madrid has been a serious party town since the days of the movida, but for most night owls neither opera nor zarzuela cuts the mustard. The intense nocturnal scene spawns countless rock, pop, hip-hop, and other groups.

One of the icons of Madrid soft pop remains Antonio Vega (1957–), who went solo after his 1980s group, Nacha Pop, went belly up. Local rock legends include Rosendo Mercado and band Seguridad Social. The latter has produced more than a dozen albums since it emerged in the early 1980s and, while unknown beyond Spain, has a faithful home following. Strangely, another major local group is Dover, which belts out its indie rock in English.

A new young talent to keep an eye on is Belén Arjona, Madrid born and compared by some with Canada's rock-and-roll wild child, Avril Lavigne.

CINEMA

Franco had died only seven years earlier and the movida was still in full swing. The passing of the Generalísimo had lifted the lid on the city's creative spirit. Enrique Tierno Galván, Marxist philosopher and Socialist mayor who once told Madrileños to "get stoned and watch out," was still at the municipal helm in 1982

Filmmaker Pedro Almodóvar celebrates winning an Academy Award in 2003 for best original screenplay for *Talk to Her*.

when a landmark film, *La Colmena (The Beehive)*, premiered on the city's screens.

Based on the masterpiece novel by Camilo José Cela (who makes a cameo appearance), Mario Camus's film is set in 1940s Madrid. It depicts the trials and tribulations of characters struggling in the gray days of Franco's post-Civil War capital, following them around its listless cafés, police stations, and dark apartments. Such a picture would have been unthinkable only a few years earlier, and in some ways symbolizes the birth of modern Spanish cinema.

More than 20 years later, Spanish filmmaking is more prolific than ever and sparkling with inventiveness and originality. Much of the industry is based in Madrid, and the city itself appears in numerous films. The bulk of them remain largely unknown beyond Spain's shores, but there are some exceptions.

At the same time as *La Colmena* came out,

Almodóvar's *All About My Mother*, which deals with the complex relationships between women, won the Oscar for Best Foreign Film in 1999.

a joyously outrageous young phone company employee from the south of Castilla-La Mancha, Pedro Almodóvar, was also trying his hand at moviemaking. He had arrived in Madrid in the late 1960s, and, in the wake of the dictator's death, Almodóvar and his cohorts spearheaded the movida in wickedly stylish fashion. Partying aside, he whipped off a series of uneven films, all based on zanily complex stories in deeply manic Madrid.

His first seriously successful picture did not come until 1988, with *Mujeres al Borde de un Ataque de Nervios (Women on the Edge of a Nervous Breakdown)*. A typically Almodóvarian web of hysterical relationships sweeps across Madrid. In passing, some of his favorite actors come to the fore, including Carmen Maura, Antonio Banderas, and Rossy de Palma.

An astonishing concentration of screen talent, especially actresses, comes from or at least lives in Madrid. Local icon of stage and screen Victoria Abril has down the years been another of Almodóvar's favorites, starring in

the likes of *¡Átame! (Tie Me Up! Tie Me Down!;* 1990). Others include Ana Belén, Maribel Verdú, and Penélope Cruz, the latter making her name in Hollywood after appearing in such films as Fernando Trueba's Oscar-winning *Belle Époque* (1992). Trueba co-wrote that film with Madrid-based Rafael Azcona, one of the country's most important screenwriters.

By the time Almodóvar's Oscar-winning *Todo Sobre Mi Madre (All About My Mother;* 1999) reached international screens, he and several of his Madrid colleagues had made the leap to international fame. Banderas and Cruz, in particular, have established themselves in U.S. films.

Javier Bardem, nephew of the great Madrid director Juan Antonio Bardem, is also beginning to make waves abroad. His stunning performance in *Mar Adentro (The Sea Inside;* 2004), the controversial true story of a quadriplegic who wants to die, has unlocked international doors, leading to his involvement in four non-Spanish pictures in the following years. ∎

Plaza Mayor is the hub of historic Madrid, a symbol of the importance of the city in the 17th century. Around the old square, the layout of narrow lanes has not changed since medieval times.

Plaza Mayor & Old Town

Traditional embroidered shawls

Plaza Mayor & Old Town

THE OLD TOWN IS KNOWN AS "MADRID DE LOS AUSTRIAS," MEANING "Habsburg Madrid," but this title is in fact misleading, as this area has been inhabited since the Moors established the first settlement in the ninth century. The reign of the Habsburg monarchs lasted from 1516 to 1700, during which time Madrid became the capital of Spain and the hub of an empire following the discovery of the Americas.

Murals brighten Plaza de la Puerta Cerrada, once the site of a gate in the city walls.

Although this was a buoyant period in Spain's history, the architecture of the era reflects the relatively austere tastes of the Habsburg monarchs, characterized by elegant redbrick buildings with slate roofs, turrets, and pinnacles. Exploring this area gives visitors an insight into how Madrid developed from its origins as a Moorish stronghold to become a powerful player on the world stage.

Plaza de la Villa, the administrative center of the growing town, was the most important square in Madrid for 500 years following the Christian reconquest in the 11th century. The City Hall is still situated there, in a magnificent Habsburg building, but is set to move to the former main post office building in Plaza de Cibeles in the next few years.

The construction of Plaza Mayor in the 17th century was the most important urban development of the Habsburg period. The area provided a public space for all sorts of ceremonies and entertainment. Today it is an imposing setting for enjoying a cup of coffee at one of its many cafés, but it is no longer the heart of the city.

South of these two squares is an evocative area of tiny squares and winding streets, where, although little remains from medieval times, you can still trace the course of the old city walls. Plaza de la Paja is now a pleasant spot for an evening drink under the trees; 900 years ago it was a bustling market square. Over the course of the next four centuries, some of the most important events in Madrid's history took place there. Muslims and Christians alike have deep roots in the neighborhood, and the area boasts some of the city's most interesting older churches.

Some of the apartment blocks date from the 17th century, although most have now been sumptuously restored and constitute some of the most coveted real estate in the city. The two-story buildings are the oldest, with red pan-tiled roofs and tiny attic windows. All around this area there are traditional taverns, pavement cafés, and quite a few designer bars, making it one of the most enjoyable parts of Madrid to while away a few hours whether by day or by night. ■

People soak up the sun year-round at the outdoor cafés of historic Plaza Mayor.

Plaza Mayor

Plaza Mayor
- Map p. 53
- Metro: Sol

Visitor information
www.esmadrid.com
- Madrid Tourist Center, Plaza Mayor 27
- 91 588 1636

BUILT NEARLY 400 YEARS AGO, PLAZA MAYOR IS STILL A spectacular space. Enclosed by redbrick buildings, with the slate roofs, spires, and dormer windows typical of the architecture of the Habsburg dynasty, this elegant square is now full of pavement cafés, with traditional shops and tapas bars under the porticoed arcades. At night, it is used for concerts, performances, and fireworks displays, and on Sunday mornings it holds a stamp and coin market.

For several centuries before the square was built, the area served as a marketplace outside the city walls. In view of the rapid expansion that took place in the decades after Madrid was made capital in 1561, it was decided to develop the space into a public square that could be used for official events.

Designed by Juan Gómez de Mora (1586–1648), the great architect of the Habsburg period, construction began in 1617 and was completed just two years later. The buildings forming the square provided accommodation for about 3,000 people—a population density that was highly unusual in those days and became the source of a great many local jokes about people living on top of one another.

As well as official ceremonies, the square was used for bullfights, jousting, and theatrical performances by the top playwrights of the time, attended by up to 50,000 spectators. Crowds also gathered to witness more sinister events, such as executions and the grim trials of faith, known as autos-da-fé, which were held there by the Spanish Inquisition.

Walking into the square, you are inevitably drawn to the extraordinary frescoes adorning the building on the north side. This is the **Casa de la Panadería,** which existed on this site before the square was

The principal building on the opposite side of the square is the **Casa de la Carnicería,** where butchers used to pack, store, and sell their meat.

The appearance of the square today dates back to the end of the 18th century, when a fire caused severe damage. The architect of the Prado museum, Juan de Villanueva, remodeled the space by making the buildings more uniform and adding the entrance arches. These changes made the square a much more enclosed

built and for centuries was the headquarters of the bakers' guild. The frescoes, featuring the signs of the zodiac and allegories of temperature and time, were created in 1992 by Carlos Franco. The royal family had apartments in the building and used to watch events from the balcony overlooking the square. Only the doorway remains of the original structure. It is now occupied by the Madrid City Council, and the main **tourist center** is on the ground floor.

space than it had previously been, which some Madrileños blame for its decline in popularity. The equestrian statue of Felipe III by Giovanni de Bologna and Pietro Tacca was created in 1616, but not installed here until the mid-19th century.

Nowadays, the square is more popular with tourists than locals, and the bars and restaurants have tailored their menus to cater to the largely foreign clientele. Check the prices before ordering and count your change carefully. ■

A stamp and coin market takes place beneath Plaza Mayor's arches on Sunday mornings.

Plaza de la Villa & around

Plaza de la Villa
- 🗺 Map p. 53
- 🚇 Metro: Sol

Casa de la Villa
- ✉ Plaza de la Villa 5
- ☎ 91 588 1000
- 🕐 Free guided tours on Mon. at 5 p.m.

PLAZA DE LA VILLA, WHICH TODAY EXUDES A QUIET dignity, was the most important square in Madrid until Plaza Mayor was built. The buildings framing it on three sides were built between the 15th and 17th centuries. In medieval times, the city council used to meet in the San Salvador church, which was situated at the top of the square until it was demolished in the 19th century.

The oldest building now is the **Torre y Casa de los Lujanes,** on the left as you look down from Calle Mayor; it dates from the end of the 15th century. The facade features bands of flint and mortar alternating with brick, a typical style of the time for aristocratic residences. While the arch on the right was built by Mudejar craftsmen, the main portal on the left dates only from the 1920s, when it was rebuilt in Castilian Gothic style by Luis Bellido. The various coats of arms are original, however, and belong to the prestigious Lujanes family.

The statue in the middle of the square is of Admiral Ivaro de Bazán, who triumphed at the Battle of Lepanto, fought between Christians and Ottomans off the coast of Greece in 1571. Author Miguel de Cervantes took part in the fighting and was wounded, losing the use of his left arm.

Taking up the other side of the square is the **Casa de la Villa,** or City Hall, one of the signature buildings of Habsburg Madrid. Designed by Juan Gómez de Mora in the 1640s, the building was not completed until 1693 due to a shortage of funds. This was because mayors in Madrid did not have royal support, making it much more difficult to finance construction. In the late 18th century, Juan de Villanueva added the colonnaded loggia, which gives onto Calle Mayor.

Inside Casa de la Villa you will find 18th-century tapestries from the Royal Tapestry Factory and a late 16th-century silver monstrance that is carried through the neighboring streets for the Corpus Christi processions. In the Assembly Room, where the councilors meet, there are 18th-century red leather banquettes and ceiling frescoes by Antonio Palomino (1655–1726).

The **Casa de Cisneros** *(Plaza de la Villa 4, tel 91 588 2906/7),* which takes up the bottom of the square, was built in 1537 as the residence of Benito Jiménez de Cisneros, the nephew of Cardinal Cisneros. It currently forms part of the City Hall, to which it is linked via a gallery. The mayor's office is in the tower overlooking the square. It is in the Plateresque style, which is the term used to describe the use of filigree decoration, similar to the work of silversmiths, popular with Spanish Renaissance architects in the 16th century. This facade, which was remodeled by Luis Bellido in the early 20th century, is now the main entrance, but originally this was the rear of the building. Walk around the building in order to see the elaborately carved doorway on Calle Sacramento.

Next to the Casa de Cisneros is the elegant **Basílica Pontificia de San Miguel** *(Calle San Justo 4, tel 91 548 4011),* a truly baroque church with a concave facade that was designed by the Italian

**Opposite:
Slate pinnacles crown the austere Casa de la Villa, or City Hall, the civic center of Madrid since the 17th century.**

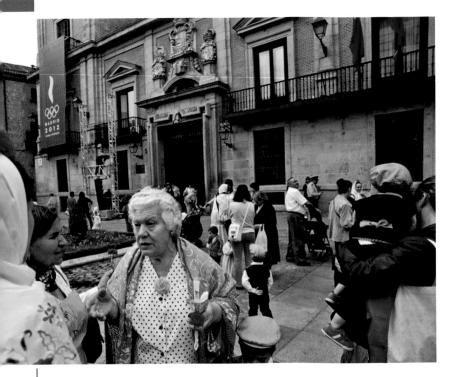

Plaza de la Villa, where Madrid has been governed since its inception. The Plateresque Casa de Cisneros, dating from 1537, anchors the square's south end.

architect Giacomo Bonavia in 1739–1745. It was built for Prince Don Luis—the youngest son of Felipe V and Isabella Farnese—who was Archbishop of Toledo at the time, even though he was still a child. The church was originally dedicated to the child saints Justo and Pastor, who were martyred in Alcalá de Henares, east of Madrid, in the time of the Roman emperor Diocletian. Carvings of these saints appear in a circular relief over the doorway. It is now run by the Opus Dei organization, and there is a highly realistic statue of the group's founder, José María Escrivá de Balaguer, in the second chapel on the left.

Next to the church is the **Palacio Arzobispal** (Archbishop's Palace), built at the same time. Turn left up Calle de la Pasa and walk through Plaza

Conde de Barajas to Plaza Conde de Miranda. On the left is the **Convento de las Carboneras** (*tel 91 548 3701, closed Sun.*), which was founded in the 17th century and belongs to the Spanish Hieronymite order. If you ring the bell marked *monjas* (nuns), you can buy cakes through a *turno*, a rotating drum that allows the cloistered nuns to deal with the outside world without being seen. The church features an elaborate altarpiece by Antón de Morales as well as a painting of "The Last Supper" by Vicente Carducho.

Leaving the square along the narrow Calle del Codo—the name means "elbow," reflecting the shape—by the convent brings you back to Plaza de la Villa. If you turn left out of the square along Calle Mayor and turn immediately right up Calle San

Nicolás, you come to the **Iglesia de San Nicolás de los Servitas** *(Plaza de San Nicolás, tel 91 559 4064)*. Begun in the 12th century, this is the oldest church in Madrid, although it has been altered and restored over the years. It is thought that a mosque once stood on this site. Built by Arab craftsmen, the bell tower with its horseshoe arches resembles a minaret. The presbytery features 15th-century Gothic vaulting, framed by the pointed horseshoe arch of the nave. Juan de Herrera, the architect of El Escorial (see pp. 228–231), was buried inside.

Returning to Calle Mayor, you will see a bronze angel across the way that commemorates the bomb, hidden in a bouquet of flowers, that was thrown on May 31, 1906, at the wedding procession of Alfonso XIII and Victoria Eugénie of Battenberg. The new Queen of Spain was the granddaughter of Britain's Queen Victoria and the grandmother of the current King Juan Carlos. The two monarchs were not injured, but 23 other people died, and the bride's gown was stained red with blood.

Behind the monument is the **Iglesia Arzobispal Castrense** *(Calle del Sacramento 11, tel 91 547 3624)*, started in the 17th century and completed in the mid-1740s by Bartolomé Hurtado for the powerful Duke of Úceda, whose palace is next door. Originally it was part of a convent that was demolished in 1970. The frescoes on the ceiling vaults were painted in 1744 by the González Velázquez brothers, who worked on several Madrid churches of the time. It is now the church of the Spanish armed forces in the capital. ■

Having a conversation on a public phone is serious business in the cacophonous city center.

A couple snatch a kiss outside the Taberna de San Isidro in Plaza de la Puerta Cerrada.

A walk around Habsburg Madrid

This walk takes you through the lanes of the oldest part of the city, known as Madrid de los Austrias, or Habsburg Madrid. Only a few buildings survive from the period, but the medieval atmosphere still permeates the streets, particularly at dusk.

Leave **Plaza Mayor** ❶ (see pp. 54–55) through the arch in the northwest corner, along the passageway called Calle Ciudad Rodrigo. The Bar Valle del Tiétar, on the left at No. 5 with a typical red wooden frontage, was a notorious criminal den in the 19th century. The **Mercado de San Miguel** ❷ *(Plaza de San Miguel, tel 91 548 1214, closed Sat. p.m & Sun., metro: Sol, La Latina)*, constructed in 1916, is the last ironwork-built market in Madrid. Sadly, in recent years many stalls have closed as Madrileños increasingly favor supermarkets over traditional markets.

Turn immediately left down Calle Cava San Miguel, which was originally a ditch outside the city wall. The 17th-century houses get taller as you progress down the hill, forming the wall of Plaza Mayor. Now it is lined with tapas bars, known as *mesones,* each one specializing in a particular dish.

The street becomes **Calle Cuchilleros,** named after the knife- and swordmakers who used to be based along it. **Casa Botín** at No. 17 is the oldest and best known restaurant in Madrid (see p. 242). You reach **Plaza de Puerta Cerrada** ❸, where one of the city gates used to stand. Murals were painted onto the buildings in the 1980s.

Turn right down the steeply sloping **Calle Segovia,** which was a stream in medieval times, flowing down to the Manzanares River. Paleolithic, Roman, and Visigothic remains have been found around here. The imposing concrete bridge up ahead is known as the **Viaducto** and was built in the 1930s. The leaning Mudejar tower of the church of **San Pedro el Viejo** ❹ (see pp. 62–63) rises up on the left.

On the right is the sloping **Plaza de la Cruz Verde,** which got its name from a green wooden cross that once stood there.

These crosses had a sinister significance, as they marked the spots where the Inquisition held trials of faith and carried out executions. These days, café tables sit peacefully under the trees.

Opposite the square, turn right along Calle Alamillo, which leads to the tiny, triangular **Plaza de Alamillo** ⑤. This plaza, where the Arab law courts were situated, was the hub of the Moorish quarter after the Christian conquest.

Turn up Calle Alfonso VI, which leads to **Plaza de la Paja,** with the church of **San Andrés** at the top (see p. 63). Walking just beyond San Andrés you emerge into a large open space with pavement cafés. This part is called **Plaza de los Carros** ⑥, but each side has a different name. This was the site of another city gate, the **Puerta de Moros,** where wine merchants used to arrive from the vineyards of La Mancha. Turn off the square into **Calle Cava Baja** ⑦, which,

like Calle Cava San Miguel, was originally a ditch around the city wall. The many bars and restaurants lining the street today are vestiges of the medieval inns that provided accommodation for the wine merchants.

Cava Baja leads back to Puerta Cerrada. Cross the road and cut up Calle Latoneros to Calle Toledo, then walk back up through the arch to Plaza Mayor. ∎

🔼 See area map p. 53
▶ Plaza Mayor
↔ I mile (1.6 km)
🕑 30 to 40 minutes
▶ Plaza Mayor

NOT TO BE MISSED
• Plaza Mayor
• Calle Cuchilleros
• Plaza de la Paja

The Capilla de San Isidro was originally even more ornately decorated, but it was severely damaged in the Civil War.

Plaza de la Paja
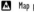 Map p. 53
🚇 Metro: La Latina

Plaza de la Paja & around

PLAZA DE LA PAJA IS A LAID-BACK URBAN SPACE NOW, BUT in the Middle Ages it was the busiest spot in town. It was the most important marketplace in Muslim Madrid, and, for centuries afterward under Christian rule, it was flanked by grand residences where the most important families lived. Farmers who worked in the nearby fields were obliged to donate a tenth of their crop to the church of San Andrés, which became a powerful economic institution.

At the beginning of the 12th century, a young man named Isidro worked as a laborer for Iván de Vargas, a nobleman who lived in the square and owned land on the other side of the river. Deeply religious, Isidro did all he could to help the sick, children, animals, and people down on their luck. More than 400 miracles were attributed to him, and he is now the patron saint of Madrid.

When Ferdinand and Isabella, the future Catholic Monarchs, came to Madrid to claim their right to the throne at the end of the 15th century, they stayed at a palace in the square, where No. 14 is now. At the bottom of the square you can take a break in the **Jardín del Príncipe de Anglona.** This small garden was laid out in 1920 adjoining the Palacio de Anglona, a grand residence that is now apartments. Just off the square beyond the palace is the **Iglesia de San Pedro el Viejo** (*Calle Nuncio 14, tel 91 365 1284*), which was built in the mid-14th century on the site of a mosque and has a leaning tower with loophole windows built by Arab craftsmen. The church was largely rebuilt in the 17th century, but it still has 15th-century Gothic vaulting and a Renaissance door from 1525.

The **Iglesia de San Andrés** *(tel 91 365 4871)*, at the top of Plaza de la Paja, was one of the first to be built following the Christian Reconquest, in the heart of what was then the Moorish quarter. The church was mostly destroyed by fire in the Civil War. The facade facing Plaza de la Paja belongs to a separate private chapel called the **Capilla del Obispo,** one of the finest late-Gothic structures in Madrid. This was built in 1520 by the Vargas family to provide a grand setting for the tomb of San Isidro. Now being rehabilitated, the chapel may become part of the Museo de San Isidro (see below) by the end of 2007.

The octagonal dome rising up behind it belongs to the recently restored **Capilla de San Isidro,** built alongside San Andrés in the

San Isidro

Isidro became Madrid's patron saint after performing a series of miracles, including getting angels to plow a field for him, making jets of water spring from the ground on a hot day, and reviving his baby son after he fell down a well. ■

17th century using stone from an old Arab wall. The remains of San Andrés are now incorporated into the rear section of this structure. The Capilla de San Isidro was also built to house the tomb of San Isidro, but in the late 18th century the tomb was transferred to the nearby Iglesia de San Isidro el Real (see p. 67).

On the other side of the church, on Plaza de San Andrés, is the interesting **Museo de San Isidro,** on a site where the saint is believed to have lived, and, indeed, died. Exhibits chart Isidro's life and also deal with the development of Madrid from prehistory to the 17th century. ■

Museo de San Isidro

www.munimadrid.es/museo sanisidro

✉ Plaza de San Andrés 2

☎ 91 366 7415

🕐 Closed Sat. p.m., Sun. p.m., & Mon.

🚇 Metro: La Latina, Tirso de Molina

The Iglesia de San Andrés stands in the heart of medieval Madrid.

Traditional taverns

The fashion for bars and cafeterias meant that Madrid lost dozens of its traditional taverns in the second half of the 20th century. In recent years, however, the Madrileños have realized that the taverns are an important part of their heritage and those that have survived are firmly back in vogue.

Taverns are closely connected to the history of Madrid, as they started to appear soon after the Christian Reconquest in 1085. Muleteers brought wine from the Valdepeñas vineyards in La Mancha to the city gate at Puerta de Moros in the heart of the old town. By the 14th century, there were about 40 bars, a figure that had risen sixfold by the 17th century, in the reign of fun-loving Felipe IV.

Classic taverns have wooden frontages painted a deep red or brown, a tradition dating back to the 19th century. Signs are either hand-painted or acid-engraved on glass. In the 1920s, the facades began to be decorated more ornately with hand-painted tiles. Inside, the taverns typically have a marble or carved wooden bar with a long shallow trough at one end made of tin or zinc. A tap is left running all the time to

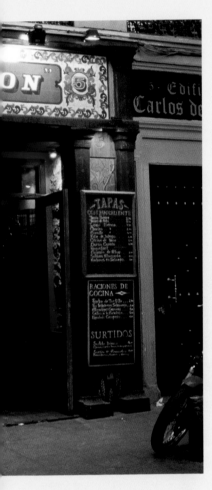

Believed to the oldest surviving tavern in the city, **Casa Alberto** *(Calle Huertas 18, tel 91 429 9356, closed Sun. p.m. & Mon.)* opened in 1827. A couple of centuries earlier, Cervantes lived in a house on this site, where he wrote the second part of *Don Quixote*. These days, a range of traditional tapas is displayed on the onyx counter, with more substantial meals served in the tavern's restaurant.

Characterful taverns such as Venta el Buscón (left) and Bodega de Ángel Sierra (above) are making a revival in Madrid.

Casa Labra *(Calle Tetuán 12, tel 91 531 0081)* has a typical brown wooden frontage with an acid-engraved glass sign, a skill that sadly is dying out. Founded in 1860, it was a favorite haunt of Ernest Hemingway's, as well as of the bullfighters Antonio Ordóñez and Luis Miguel Dominguín. In 1879, the Spanish Socialist Workers' Party was founded in a back room by Pablo Iglesias. Everything but the counter is original, and people flock here from the surrounding shopping streets for exquisite cod in batter, croquettes, and excellent draft beer.

With its mosaic tiles from 1908, **Taberna de la Dolores** *(Plaza de Jesús 4, tel 91 429 2243)* is easy to spot. There were tiles inside too until the 1960s, when the owner thought them old-fashioned and tore them out. The draft beer is renowned as the best in Madrid, as it is still pulled by the traditional method of leaving it to settle, then putting a head on it before serving. ■

keep everything cool and clean, and flasks of wine sit chilling in the pool of water in the trough.

Totally authentic, **La Taberna de Antonio Sánchez** *(Calle Mesón de Paredes 13, tel 91 539 7826, closed Sun. p.m.)* was founded in 1830 and has always been run by ex-bullfighters, as borne out by the paintings and photographs adorning the paneled walls—not to mention the enormous bull's head. Customers sit at marble tables to drink draft vermouth and eat tasty canapés. There are restaurant tables at the back, where they specialize in braised bull's tail and blood sausage, as well as *torrijas,* a delicious dessert made from bread soaked in milk, sugar, and cinnamon.

Plaza de San Francisco

🗺 Map p. 53

☎ 91 365 3800

🕐 Closed Sat. p.m., Sun., & Mon.

💲 $

Ⓜ Metro: La Latina, Puerta de Toledo

Basílica de San Francisco el Grande

SAN FRANCISCO WAS MADRID'S UNOFFICIAL CATHEDRAL until the Almudena was completed in 1994, and many Madrileños still consider it to be the most important church in the city. After decades in the doldrums, it is gradually being restored to its former grandeur. An early work by Goya is just one of its artistic treasures.

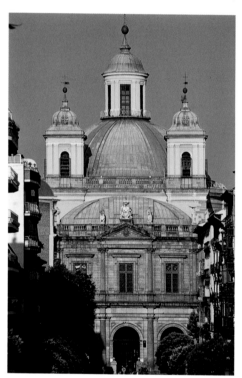

The huge dome of the Basílica de San Francisco el Grande rises above the Old Town's narrow streets.

According to legend, St. Francis of Assisi founded a monastery on this site in 1217, making it one of the earliest such buildings in Madrid. In 1760, Carlos III decided a grander structure was required and had the original buildings demolished.

The inexperienced architect Brother Francisco Cabezas drew up ambitious plans for the new cathedral, which included a dome 183 feet (56 m) high with a diameter of 108 feet (33 m), making it one of the biggest in the world. The design posed many problems, which the leading architects of the time—Francesco Sabatini, Ventura Rodríguez, and Diego de Villanueva—all helped to overcome, amid much acrimony. The monks had to leave following the disentailment of the monasteries in 1836. The structure later served as an army barracks and a national pantheon.

The cathedral's main altar was restored in 2005 and features paintings depicting the life of St. Francis by Manuel Domínguez and Alejandro Ferrant. The Goya painting, dating from 1782–1783, is in the first chapel on the left as you enter the church; it shows St. Bernardino of Siena preaching a sermon to King Alfonso V of Aragón and his court. Goya painted himself into the picture on the right, wearing a yellow jacket. The artist was only 37 years old at the time and had not yet been appointed court painter. The church also contains paintings by Francisco de Zurbarán, Alonso Cano, and Francisco Pacheco, who was Velázquez's father-in-law.

On the right of the main entrance is the **Capilla del Cristo de los Dolores de la Venerable Orden Tercera.** Built in the 17th century, the chapel features a baldachin containing a sculpture of Christ. ∎

Iglesia de San Isidro el Real

ONE OF THE MOST IMPORTANT CHURCHES IN MADRID, San Isidro acted as the city's cathedral for a century, until Nuestra Señora de la Almudena (see pp. 78–79) finally opened in 1993. Built in 1622–1664, it was originally the church of the Colegio Imperial de la Compañía de Jesús, a prestigious Jesuit school funded by Empress María of Habsburg. The royal patronage attracted some famous names to the school, including such golden age writers as Lope de Vega, Calderón de la Barca, and Francisco de Quevedo.

Iglesia de San Isidro el Real

- 🅰 Map p. 53
- ✉ Calle de Toledo 37–39
- ☎ 91 369 2037
- Ⓜ Metro: La Latina

The baroque structure with twin towers and a slate dome was designed by Pedro Sánchez and Francisco Bautista, who was inspired by Il Gesù in Rome. After the Jesuits were expelled from Spain in 1767 by Carlos III, Ventura Rodríguez revamped the interior in neoclassic style. The remains of San Isidro and his wife, Santa María de la Cabeza, were transferred here from the nearby Capilla de San Isidro in 1789 (see p. 63).

In the reign of Fernando VII, the church returned to the Jesuits, but tragedy struck in 1834 when rumors spread through the city that the priests were responsible for poisoning the water in fountains around Madrid. An angry mob burst into the church, killed 14 priests, and seriously wounded five others. The building was badly damaged in 1938 during the Civil War and had to be largely rebuilt. There is still a school alongside, the Instituto San Isidro, which retains its original baroque granite courtyard.

The main altar, built in the 18th century by Ventura Rodríguez, contains the tombs of the saint and his wife. On the left of the main altar, an oval chapel holds figures of the two saints. The three chapels on the right as you enter have figures of the Virgen de los Reyes, the Virgen de la Esperanza Macarena, and Jesús del Gran Poder, images that are revered by the Andalusian community in Madrid. ■

Festival-goers at San Isidro venerate Madrid's patron saint.

Palacio de Abrantes, now the Italian Institute of Culture, dates back to the 17th century.

More places to visit in Plaza Mayor & Old Town

IGLESIA DE SANTA CRUZ

The neo-Gothic church with a distinctive neo-Mudejar tower was designed in 1878 by the Marquis of Cubas (1826–1899), although it was not completed until 1902. It contains a rich collection of religious paintings, sculptures, and monstrances from local convents that were demolished in the 19th century. ⚠ Map p. 53 ✉ Calle de Atocha 6 ☎ 91 369 1239 🚇 Metro: Sol, Tirso de Molina

PALACIO DE ABRANTES

Now the Italian Institute of Culture and formerly the Italian Embassy (1888–1939), the palace was built in 1652 and restored from 1842 onward when it was bought by the Duke of Abrantes. During the Civil War, the building was occupied by the Italian battalions of the International Brigades. Fragments of the 12th-century church of Santa María and the 9th-century Arab wall are visible alongside it. ⚠ Map p. 53 ✉ Calle Mayor 86 ☎ 91 547 5205 🚇 Metro: Ópera

PALACIO DE SANTA CRUZ

With its redbrick facade and slate turrets, this palace is a fine example of Habsburg baroque architecture. Designed by Cristóbal de Aguilera, it is now the Ministry of Foreign Affairs, but was built as a prison between 1629 and 1643 and later housed law courts and the Overseas Ministry. The stone portal features the coat of arms of Felipe IV, sculpted by Antonio Herrera Barnuevo. George Borrow (1803–1881), the British writer, linguist, and salesman for the Bible Society, spent three weeks in the prison in 1838, accused of promoting heretic beliefs, but he was treated as an honored guest rather than a prisoner. Other famous inmates included the colorful bandit Luis Candelas and the playwright Lope de Vega. ⚠ Map p. 53 ✉ Plaza Provincia 1 ☎ 91 379 9550 🚇 Metro: Sol, Tirso de Molina

PALACIO DE UCEDA

Built in the early 17th century for the Duke of Úceda, the favorite of Felipe III, the palace set a design precedent for some of the most important civil buildings of the period, including the Casa de la Villa (see p. 56). It no longer looks so imposing, as its two towers were destroyed by fire in the 18th century. The palace now houses the Council of State and is also the army's military headquarters. ⚠ Map p. 53 ✉ Calle Mayor 79 ☎ 91 516 6262 🚇 Metro: Ópera ■

The grandeur of the Palacio Real (Royal Palace) is complemented by the elegance of the surrounding area, where opulent buildings bear witness to the French and Italian influences prevalent in Madrid in the 18th and 19th centuries.

Palacio Real & around

A young Madrileño in traditional dress

The Changing of the Royal Guard outside the palace occurs the first Wednesday of most months.

Palacio Real & around

THE PALACIO REAL (ROYAL PALACE) stands on the edge of a promontory in the west of the city. This excellent vantage point, with views across the plains to the Guadarrama mountains, was the reason the Moors chose this site for their citadel in the ninth century. The palace began its existence as part of a string of fortresses that spanned the countryside to protect the important city of Toledo to the south. After the Christian Reconquest at the end of the 11th century, the new rulers occupied the fortress, known as the Alcázar, and established their first churches nearby, often converting existing mosques.

After Felipe II made Madrid his capital in 1561, religious orders flocked to the city and convents sprang up all over town. One of the most important, the Descalzas Reales, was founded by his sister, and its amazing treasures are now open to the public. Fifty years later, Felipe III's wife set up a less extravagant but equally fascinating convent, the Encarnación, close to the Palacio Real.

In the 17th century the royal family was still living in the ramshackle structure left over from the Muslims. A devastating fire in the 18th century gave monarch Felipe V the chance to build a much more fitting residence, which was not completed until 1764, when his son, Carlos III, was on the throne. Future Bourbon monarchs added to the palace's decoration and extensive collections to create the lavish residence seen today.

Madrileños are still getting used to the Almudena cathedral next to the palace. It was completed in the 1990s after more than a century of delays and setbacks. Local resistance to the new

church was softened to some extent by the widespread delight arising from the royal wedding in 2004 between Prince Felipe, heir to the Spanish crown, and Letizia Ortiz, a former television journalist. The couple had their first public kiss on the balcony of the Palacio Real overlooking Plaza de Oriente, a huge landscaped space created in the 19th century.

The construction of the opera house on the opposite side of the square strengthened the stylish character of the area, where the handsome apartment buildings are now some of the most coveted addresses in the city. Sit at a café and soak up the elegant atmosphere in this area, a world away from the medieval streets of the nearby Plaza Mayor. ■

Palacio Real

Palacio Real & gardens

THE PRESENT SPANISH ROYAL FAMILY PROJECTS A
relatively modest, low-key image, but their forebears in the 18th and
19th centuries loved nothing more than blatantly flaunting their
importance and wealth. Their residence, the Palacio Real (Royal
Palace), is a dizzying ensemble of ornately decorated rooms filled
with countless artistic treasures. It was the main royal residence until
1931, when Alfonso XIII, the grandfather of King Juan Carlos, abdi-
cated and went into exile. Nowadays, the royal family lives in the less
ostentatious Palacio de la Zarzuela west of Madrid, and the Palacio
Real is used for state ceremonies.

The palace stands on the site of a
ninth-century Moorish fortress,
which became a royal residence
after Felipe II moved the court to
Madrid in 1561. After much of
the building was destroyed by fire
in 1734, the Bourbon Felipe V
ordered the construction of a new
palace. The design was influenced
by the tastes he had acquired
while growing up at Versailles in
France, as well as by the opinions
of his forceful Italian wife,
Isabella Farnese.

The original architect was the
Italian Filippo Juvarra, who
planned a palace twice the size of
Versailles. However, he died
before his ideas got any further
than the drawing board, and his
plans were then modified by
Giovanni Battista Sacchetti, with

contributions by Ventura Rodríguez and Francesco Sabatini. To reduce the risk of further fires, the palace was built using limestone from Colmenar and granite from the Guadarrama mountains northwest of Madrid.

VISITING THE PALACE

To enter the palace, you walk across the vast parade ground, where the Changing of the Royal Guard takes place at noon on the first Wednesday of each month, except in July, August, and September. The visit starts in a hall where a statue of Carlos III as a Roman general stands at the foot of a grand staircase made from Toledo marble. The surprisingly shallow steps were designed so that ladies could go upstairs in their restrictive clothing or be carried in sedan chairs.

The ceiling above the staircase is covered with frescoes by Corrado Giaquinto (1703–1765) and leads up to the **Hall of Halberdiers,** which was used by the royal guards and is decorated with tapestries. The ceiling was painted by Giovanni Battista Tiepolo (1696–1770). Bronze sculptures symbolizing the planets and Roman busts in the **Hall of Columns** were saved from the 1734 fire. The dictator General Franco lay in state there after his death in 1975.

The ceiling of the lavishly decorated **Throne Room,** also painted by Tiepolo, is an allegorical representation of the power of the Spanish monarchy. The decor dates from the original monarchs. The room also contains mirrors, Venetian chandeliers, and several ornate clocks. The two thrones, made in 1977 for King Juan Carlos and Queen Sofia, feature their portraits in miniature. Spanish monarchs are not crowned, only proclaimed, so the king and queen do not wear crowns when sitting on their thrones.

The **King's Rooms** were occupied by Carlos III when he moved into the palace in 1764. The antechamber contains four portraits by Goya of Carlos IV and Queen María Luisa of Parma, which are the highlight of all the

The soldiers of the Royal Guard stand at attention while parading in Plaza de Armas.

paintings on display in the palace. Carlos III used to get dressed, aided by his courtiers, in the rococo **Gasparini Room,** which is named after the Italian decorator responsible for the embroidered silk walls, swirling marble mosaic floor, and ornately stuccoed ceiling. The blue walls in the **Bedroom,** where the king died in 1788, are decorated with lions, castles, and fleurs-de-lis, the symbols of the Spanish monarchy.

The **Porcelain Room,** which was used for smoking, is decorated with china panels on the theme of Bacchus, god of wine. Tapestries adorn the walls of the adjoining **Yellow Room,** where the ladies would eat chocolates, sitting on marquetry chairs, while the men puffed away next door.

The **Banqueting Hall** takes opulence to new heights with Flemish silk tapestries, Chinese and French vases, and gilded stucco on the walls. It was created in 1879 in the reign of Alfonso XII from a series of smaller rooms. A row of 25 chandeliers illuminates the table, which seats 144 and is used for entertaining foreign heads of state. Diners can gaze up at the ceiling painting of Christopher Columbus announcing his discovery of the New World to Ferdinand and Isabella. The slightly larger dining chairs are used by the king and queen.

The next series of rooms is used to exhibit some of the palace's extensive collections. The first room was used as a cinema by Alfonso XIII. These days, an orchestra occasionally plays in the room to entertain guests in the Banqueting Hall. Although much of the royal silver was melted down by Joseph Bonaparte, the **Silver Room** contains some interesting exhibits, including a punch bowl brought to the palace by Alfonso XIII's English wife Victoria Eugénie. The queen wanted to introduce the custom of drinking punch, but the Spanish resisted her efforts and chose to stick with sangria.

Felipe V commissioned Antonio Stradivari (1644–1737) to make a cello, a viola, and two violins, which now form the most valuable collection of his instruments in the world and are on display in the **Stradivarius Room.** They are still played occasionally at concerts in the Hall of Columns. The **Ceramics Room** contains chinaware made by the East India Company, Meissen, and Sèvres.

PALACIO REAL

Gasparini Room

Plaza de Armas

Royal Armory

Visitor Center

After the original wood-and-stone palace burned down in 1537, a new palace was built beginning in 1734—of stone only. It has 2,800 rooms filled with lavish artworks and ornamentation, 16 of which are open to the public.

Dining Room

Porcelain Room

Chapel

Entrance

Hall of the Halberdiers

Hall of Columns

Throne Room

Carlos III Rooms

Carlos IV Rooms

Other rooms

After emerging into the gallery around the inner courtyard, you enter the **Capilla Real** (Royal Chapel), designed in neoclassic style by Ventura Rodríguez. Black marble columns surround the single nave; frescoes on the dome are by Corrado Giaquinto.

The final series of rooms

Suits of armor worn by kings and princes in the Palacio Real's Armory (above). Visitors climb the grand staircase to visit the palace's state rooms (right).

made up the apartments of Queen María Luisa of Parma. Alfonso XII remodeled part of this section to create a walnut-paneled billiard room and a smoking room in Japanese style. The final room is a rococo study with marble marquetry and embroidered silk wall panels.

Much more remains to be seen when you return to the outside courtyard. On the right is the **Armería Real** (Royal Armory), which was founded by Felipe II and displays armor worn by kings and princes over the centuries, as well as shields, helmets, and swords.

On the other side of the outside courtyard is the **Farmacia Real** (Royal Pharmacy), founded in 1594. It contains a reconstruction of a distillery and an alchemy laboratory based on the ones at El Escorial. Exhibits include ceramic jars from Talavera, copper stills, and pestles and mortars. Huge books record the treatments prescribed for members of the royal family, and leather trunks contain the pharmacy kits the family used when traveling. Next door there is a visitors' center with a café and a good bookshop on the top floor.

THE GARDENS

You cannot currently reach the gardens from this end of the palace. Leaving the complex, turn left and walk the length of the building to reach the **Jardines de Sabatini.** Although these landscaped gardens were not created until the royal stables were demolished in the 1930s, the designs were drawn up in the 18th century. From this angle, you get a good view of the chapel's dome and can appreciate the way the palace is built into the hillside.

To get to the main palace gardens, known as the **Campo del Moro,** you have to cross the Sabatini gardens, then walk down Cuesta de San Vicente and turn left along Paseo de la Virgen del Puerto to reach the entrance. The name, which means "Field of the Moor," arose from the encampment held there by besieging Arab soldiers in 1109, 24 years after Alfonso VI and his Christian army had taken over Madrid.

Until the gardens were created at the end of the 19th century, the palace stood on a steep escarpment. The sloping hillside was devised by the architect Narciso Pascual y Colomer and features avenues flanked by magnolias, chestnuts, acacias, cedars, and bamboos. The impressive lawn leading down from the palace was added in the 1960s. The 16th-century Triton fountain was originally found in the palace gardens in Aranjuez (see p. 220). ∎

Nuestra Señora de la Almudena & around

Nuestra Señora de la Almudena

🅰 Map p. 71

✉ Calle Bailén 10

☎ 91 542 2200

$ Cathedral: free.
Temporary
exhibitions: $

Ⓜ Metro: Ópera

MADRID DID NOT HAVE ITS OWN CATHEDRAL UNTIL THIS structure was consecrated by Pope John Paul II in 1993. It took more than a century to build, proceeding in several phases with long periods of inactivity. Every time construction resumed, the new architects altered the plans to suit changing architectural tastes. To describe the end result as "eclectic" is putting it mildly.

Construction began during the period of economic buoyancy that followed the restoration of the monarchy in the late 19th century. The cathedral started out as a neo-Gothic structure with a large neo-Romanesque crypt, designed by the Marquis of Cubas. Although the crypt was completed in 1911, the main cathedral was only partly built. Further development was hindered by political upheaval, financial restraints, and the Civil War (1936–1939). In the 1940s, Fernando Chueca Goitia and Carlos Sidro came up with a design that encased the crypt and what had been built of the main structure in a neoclassic shell.

The name "Almudena" is of Arabic origin and refers to the grain store situated on the edge of the Muslim enclave. According to legend, a figure of the Madonna was hidden in the wall in the eighth century by Visigothic settlers to protect it from the invading Moors. After the Reconquest, the figure miraculously reappeared, flanked by burning candles, thereby lending some weight to Madrid's tenuous Christian heritage.

The most elegant element of the cathedral is the slate dome, which sits on an octagonal drum over the Latin-cross transept. Light floods into the side naves through rose windows. As you enter, look for the figure of St. John the Baptist by 18th-century French sculptor Robert Michel. In the chapel opposite is an exceptional "Christ Tied to the Column," sculpted by Giacomo Colombo in the 17th century.

Don't miss the **crypt,** which is arguably of greater interest than the cathedral itself. You can reach it either by the main door on Cuesta de la Vega or via a stone staircase just inside the entrance to the cathedral. It features more than a hundred neo-Romanesque capitals, intricately adorned with plants, castles, and animals, illuminated by the multicolored light of the stained-glass windows. The chapels contain the tombs of important 19th-century families. Presiding over the presbytery behind the high altar is a copy of the figure of the Madonna of the Almudena. If you turn right out the main door on Cuesta de la Vega, you'll see a plaque marking the spot where the figure was discovered nearly a thousand years ago.

Crossing the Cuesta de la Vega, you can also see a small section of the ninth-century **Arab wall,** which now forms part of the open space known as the Parque del Emir Mohamed I. ∎

Arab wall

- Map p. 71
- Parque del Emir Mohamed I
  Cuesta de la Vega
- Metro: Ópera

The Almudena cathedral fits neatly alongside the Palacio Real on the edge of the old town.

Visitors cool off by the fountains in Plaza de Oriente, between the Palacio Real and Teatro Real.

Plaza de Oriente

THIS VAST, SEMICIRCULAR SPACE WAS CONCEIVED DURING the brief reign of Joseph Bonaparte (1808–1813) as king of Spain. The development was the most important of the many urban changes he instigated, but the square was not completed until the second half of the 19th century. The lead mansard roofs and stuccoed facades reflect the French influence at that time. Unlike the popular, practical Plaza Mayor, Plaza de Oriente was always intended to be a grand plaza for ceremonial events. General Franco used the square for huge gatherings of his supporters, addressing the crowd from the balcony of the Palacio Real.

Work began in 1811 and drastically altered the area, destroying several churches as well as the library of the Palacio Real. When Fernando VII returned as king in 1814, he was eager to continue the project, commissioning new plans that would include a grand opera house. The square remained a mass of rubble for 30 years, however, until the architect Narciso Pascual y Colomer (1801–1870) was put in charge of the project in 1842.

Colomer came up with the idea of installing the bronze equestrian statue of Felipe IV in the square as its centerpiece. The monument had been made in 1639 for the gardens of the Buen Retiro palace, which by the mid-19th century had become the Parque del Retiro. The figure of the king, modeled by Juan Martínez Montañés, was based on a portrait by Velázquez. Pietro Tacca designed the rearing horse with the help of the great Italian scientist Galileo Galilei, who figured out that the horse needed to be hollow at the front and solid at the back to stop it from falling over.

The stone statues around the landscaped gardens were originally intended for the parapet of the Palacio Real. They represent Roman emperors, Visigoth kings, and Christian monarchs. Carlos III vetoed the idea of placing them on the palace, claiming that they would be too heavy and might crash down. It is more probable, however, that the figures simply did not comply with his neoclassic tastes.

The square underwent large-scale restoration at the end of the 20th century. Most of the traffic was routed into tunnels, allowing the square to become pedestrian-friendly and a much more pleasant area for people to rest their feet after visiting the palace.

TEATRO REAL

The curving east side of the square is presided over by the gray bulk of the Teatro Real. Madrid's opera house has had a checkered history, to say the least. Although this structure dates only from 1850, there have been makeshift theaters on the site since the early 18th century. In medieval times, several streams flowed down from the adjacent hills to form a small lake here. Bathhouses and washtubs were later built to take advantage of this abundance of water, while the surrounding sandbanks provided a convenient stage for theatrical performances.

The lake, which is still underneath the site, caused construction problems from the outset. The project was always running out of money, too, and in 1826 a special tax was levied on cork trees in Spain to raise funds to carry out the work. Designed by Antonio López Aguado (1764–1831), the theater was completed in 1850 and was opened by Isabel II on her 20th birthday with a performance of Donizetti's *La Favorita*.

The opera house soon became the hub of cultural and social life. It had a ballroom, now a restaurant, where people would dance after the performances. In 1863, Verdi attended the premiere of *La Forza del Destino*, and in 1916–1917 Diaghilev's Ballets Russes performed there, starring Nijinsky and Pavlova.

The water problems persisted, however, causing problems over the years. During the Civil War, a gunpowder store exploded inside, producing extensive damage. The building reopened as a concert hall in the 1960s, closed again in 1988 when the Auditorio Nacional opened across town, and opened again after remodeling in 1997.

The building rises up nine stories, with a further six stories below ground. It has a spectacular interior. The stage covers an area of approximately 15,400 square feet (1,390 sq m), and there is room for an audience of 1,740. Galleries around the theater on the second floor are decorated with paintings, tapestries, chandeliers, and mirrors. The restaurant, by Catalan designer Pascua Ortega, has a midnight blue ceiling studded with stars. ■

Teatro Real
www.teatro-real.com
Map p. 71
Plaza de Oriente
91 516 0600
Closed Mon.
Guided tours: $

Chocolate & churros

One of Madrid's great traditions entails forgetting all about calories for an hour or so. Dipping churro fritters into thick hot chocolate is an experience everyone should have while visiting the city. You can have churros for breakfast, in the late afternoon, or at the end of a long night out. They are also an essential part of local festivals, when they are sold from street stands.

The fritters are made from a dense, smooth batter of flour, water, and salt. The mixture is piped through a container, emerging as long, ridged strips, which are dropped into huge vats of boiling oil. Once fried, the strips are drained, cut into short lengths, and sometimes dipped in sugar. In Madrid, the two ends of the churros are typically pressed together to form a loop, although sometimes they are served simply in strips. They must be eaten straightaway, otherwise they become chewy and indigestible.

The Spanish have been drinking hot chocolate since the conquistadors brought cocoa beans back from the Americas in the 16th century. Be prepared for a different taste and texture when you try a cup at a *chocolatería*, as the specialty cafés are called. Spanish hot chocolate is made by melting slabs of bitter dark chocolate with milk, cornstarch, and sugar. It is usually so thick that you can stand the churros up in it, and not as sweet as you might expect.

Madrileños love going out to bars for breakfast, often as a break from the office at around 11. This is a good time to try churros, as the turnover of customers means the pastries will almost certainly be freshly made. Not all bars make their own, however, as there are little shops around town, called *churrerías*, that specialize in churros and potato chips. You can buy some to eat as you go if you are short of time.

After a day's sightseeing, you may well be tempted to pop into a café for a break, and this is when you will see people having their *merienda*, the Spanish version of afternoon tea. Coffee or hot chocolate is often accompanied by a plate of churros. This is a great way to restore your energy levels, as dinner is unlikely to be before 10.

Perhaps the most typical time to consume churros, however, is between 4 and 7 in the morning. Unlikely as it may seem, this is the busiest time for chocolaterías, as starving revelers emerge from dancing the night away in the city's clubs.

The best known place in Madrid for

chocolate and churros is undoubtedly the **Chocolatería San Ginés** (*Pasadizo de San Ginés 5, tel 91 365 6546*), which has been in business since 1894. Before dawn, waiters in black bow ties and green vests attend exhausted nightclubbers seated at marble tables, and throughout the day they serve office workers, families, and shoppers.

This is one tradition that shows no sign of dying out. In fact, it has moved easily into the 21st century by keeping up with these fast-food times. **Maestro Churrero** (*Plaza Jacinto Benavente 2, tel 91 369 2406*) was founded more than a century ago as a street stand on the Paseo del Prado, but these days it is a franchise where the baseball-capped waiters have handheld devices that send your order straight to the kitchen. It may be fast, but it is certainly not junk, as the cooks use natural ingredients and everything is fresh. You can order traditional churros or versions that are coated in chocolate or filled with custard or strawberry cream. ∎

Opposite: Ladies restore their energy with hot chocolate and churros at a local festival. This page: The fritters are served with ceremony and rich hot chocolate at the Chocolatería San Ginés, where they are freshly made by skilled chefs.

Real Monasterio de la Encarnación

JUST NINE NUNS STILL LIVE IN A CLOSED ORDER IN THIS Augustinian convent, which was founded in 1611 by Margarita de Austria, the wife of Felipe III. Although right by the royal palace, the convent is situated in a quiet corner, just off Plaza de Oriente. It contains paintings and sculptures by important Spanish artists of the time, many of which were created specifically for the convent.

A deeply religious lady, Queen Margarita wanted a convent close to the Alcázar, the fortress that preceded the current palace. Sadly, she died in childbirth soon after it was built, at the age of 26.

The convent was designed by Juan Gómez de Mora and Fray Alberto de la Madre de Dios, who created a beautifully proportioned structure within brick and rubblework walls. A covered wooden bridge linked it to the Alcázar, so that the queen could move easily between the two buildings. It was originally a much bigger structure, with a huge vegetable garden at the back, much of which was built on in the 19th century. The courtyard in the front became a popular meeting place where people would get the latest royal gossip.

VISITING THE CONVENT

You have to follow a one-hour guided tour, which begins in a hallway containing one of the most interesting paintings in the convent. Created by Peter van der Meulen, it depicts the ceremony that took place in 1615 on the Bidasoa River between Spain and France. The Habsburg Princess Ana was being sent to France to marry Louis XIII, whose sister, Princess Isabel of Bourbon, crossed into Spain to marry the future Felipe IV.

The tour continues through rooms containing paintings by Vicente Carducho, José de Ribera, Corrado Giaquinto, Antonio Pereda, and Juan Carreño de Miranda. The elegant, simple cloister, which is undergoing a long restoration process, was influenced by Juan de Herrera's designs at the monastery of El Escorial (see pp. 228–231).

In the **upper antechoir** there are two superb wooden sculptures of Christ by Gregorio Hernández. The rooms still have some of the original furniture and decoration from the 17th century, including hand-painted tiles from Talavera. The **antechoir** contains tiny figures in polychrome wax of St. Anthony of Padua and St. Teresa of Jesús.

Perhaps the most intriguing exhibit in the convent is to be found in the **reliquary room,** which has a coffered ceiling and walls lined with mahogany cases containing about 700 relics. A tiny vial is said to contain the blood of Pantaleón, the doctor saint, who lived in the fourth century in Turkey. Every year, on the saint's day, July 27, the thick substance mysteriously liquefies. If it does not happen, it is a sign of impending doom.

Ventura Rodríguez designed the neoclassic Latin-cross **church** in 1767 after the original structure burned. One of the most beautiful churches in Madrid, it is decorated with marble from various parts of Spain and has ceiling frescoes by the González Velázquez brothers and Francisco Bayeu, Goya's brother-in-law. ∎

Real Monasterio de la Encarnación

www.patrimonionacional.es/encarna/encarna.htm

- Map p. 71
- Plaza de la Encarnación 1
- 91 454 8800
- Closed Fri. p.m., Sun. p.m., & Mon.
- $. Free Wed. for E.U. citizens.
- Metro: Ópera

Monasterio de las Descalzas Reales

The Monasterio de las Descalzas Reales's reliquary contains treasures from around the world, donated by royal patrons over the centuries.

EVERY DAY, THOUSANDS OF PEOPLE FLOCK TO EL CORTE Inglés department store on Calle Preciados in the heart of the city. Most of them are unaware that hidden away behind the store is a building containing artistic treasures of far greater value than anything in Spain's favorite shop. Formerly a powerhouse of the Habsburg empire, the Descalzas Reales is now one of Madrid's most fascinating museums.

Monasterio de las Descalzas Reales

www.patrimonionacional.es/descreal/descreal.htm

⚅ Map p. 71

✉ Plaza de las Descalzas Reales 1

☎ 91 454 8800

🕐 Closed Fri. p.m., Sun. p.m., & Mon.

💲 $

🚇 Metro: Ópera, Callao, Sol

The building was originally a palace, built for Emperor Carlos V's treasurer, Alonso Gutiérrez. The emperor and his wife, Isabel of Portugal, also lived there for a period, and their daughter, Juana of Austria, was born there in 1535. In 1557, Juana, who was Felipe II's sister, decided to found a convent in the palace, which was converted to its new use by Antonio Sillero and Juan Bautista de Toledo. The structure was restored in the 18th century by Diego de Villanueva.

In 1582, Felipe's other sister, the Empress María of Austria, came from Prague to live in the convent, where she had also been born. This prestigious patronage meant that the convent always had close ties with royalty and the aristocracy. Over the years it received a number of lavish donations, many of which are on display today. These include Flemish tapestries and paintings by El Greco, Zurbarán, Velázquez, Goya, Titian, and Rubens.

The convent is still home to 22 nuns belonging to the closed Franciscan order of the Poor Clares, who live in complete privacy in part of the building, while visitors follow a 50-minute guided tour around the public areas.

VISITING THE CONVENT

The **grand staircase** survives from the original palace, but the frescoes were added at the end of the 17th century by artists including Claudio Coello (1642–1693) and Francisco Ricci (1608–1685). The portrait of the family of Felipe IV, on a trompe l'oeil balcony, is attributed to Antonio Pereda (1611–1678).

In the **upper cloister,** look

Eucharist," based on cartoons by Peter Paul Rubens (1577–1640).

The **choir,** which the nuns use every day, contains the marble tombs of Empress María and her daughter Margarita. There is also an astoundingly realistic Madonna by Pedro de Mena (1628–1688), as well as a portrait of St. Teresa.

A series of rooms overlooking the nuns' vegetable garden contain paintings including a "Ship of

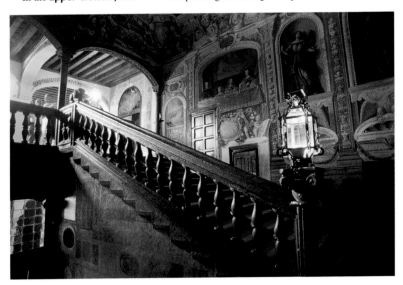

for the "Guardian Angel" by Luisa Roldán (1656–1704), the panel of the "Madonna and Child" by Bernardino Luini (circa 1480–1532), and a particularly stunning recumbent Christ by Gaspar Becerra. One of the more ornate chapels is dedicated to the Virgen de Guadalajara, with unusual portraits on mirrors.

Upstairs, what was once a dormitory is now the **tapestry room.** You'll see a portrait of the Infanta Isabel Clara Eugenia, Felipe II's daughter, who bought the tapestries for the convent. The hangings were made in Brussels and depict "The Triumph of the

Fools," attributed to Brueghel the Elder, and others by Isenbrandt and Rubens.

One of the most intriguing paintings in the convent is "The Journey of Empress María from Prague to Madrid," which depicts a procession of young orphan girls with masked faces who were accompanying the empress to the convent.

The interior **church** was altered in the mid-18th century when Diego de Villanueva introduced neoclassic decoration. It contains the tomb of Juana of Austria with a marble statue of the princess by Pompeo Leoni. ■

The monastery's staircase is decorated with royal portraits, including the family of Felipe IV, who seem to be observing the scene from a balcony.

Residents of the Ópera area attend Mass at their local church, the Iglesia de Santiago.

More places to visit around the Palacio Real

FUNDACIÓN CAJA MADRID

The cultural foundation of the Madrid savings bank has a permanent collection of contemporary art and stages temporary art and photography exhibitions in an elegant restored late 19th-century building. The foundation also sponsors shows in other venues, organizes concerts, and funds the restoration of historic buildings. ▲ Map p. 71 ✉ Plaza de San Martín 1 ☎ 91 379 2050 🚇 Metro: Ópera, Sol

IGLESIA DE SAN GINÉS

Although this baroque structure was built in 1645, there has been a church on this site since the 12th century. Playwrights Lope de Vega and Quevedo attended the church in the 17th century. It was largely rebuilt after a fire in 1824, and in 1872 the entrance was moved to Calle Arenal. The Capilla del Santísimo Cristo contains "The Expulsion of the Merchants from the Temple" by El Greco. ▲ Map p. 71 ✉ Calle Arenal 13 ☎ 91 366 4875 🚇 Metro: Ópera, Sol

IGLESIA DE SANTIAGO

This simple neoclassic church was built in 1811, replacing a Romanesque structure demolished to create space for Plaza de Oriente. Dedicated to the Order of St. James, the church contains a painting of "St. James the Moor Slayer" by Francisco Ricci and works by other 17th-century artists. ▲ Map p. 71 ✉ Plaza de Santiago 24 ☎ 91 548 0824 🚇 Metro: Ópera

PALACIO DE GAVIRIA

Built by the Marquis of Gaviria in 1851, this is one of the few grand buildings remaining from the reign of Isabel II. One of the great social venues of the 19th century, the palace saw many glamorous events in the ornate ballroom. The palace is now a nightclub, but it still retains some of its rich decoration. ▲ Map p. 71 ✉ Calle Arenal 9 ☎ 91 526 6069 🚇 Metro: Ópera, Sol

PALACIO DEL SENADO

Built in 1581 as a convent school, this Renaissance structure became the Senate—the upper house of the Spanish Parliament—when the two-chamber system was introduced in 1834. The Senate now uses a new debating chamber added to the rear of the building in 1991. ▲ Map p. 71 ✉ Plaza de la Marina Española 8 ☎ 91 538 1000 🕐 Guided tours by appt. 🚇 Metro: Plaza de España, Ópera ■

Brash, noisy, and always busy, the Puerta del Sol is the linchpin of downtown Madrid. Grand buildings on Calle Alcalá and the Gran Vía show how the city shook off its provincial past a century ago.

Downtown Madrid

Caryatids adorn the facade of one of the palatial bank buildings on Calle Alcalá.

Crowds stream along the Gran Vía at all hours of the day and night.

Downtown Madrid

THE PUERTA DEL SOL HAS BEEN AN IMPORTANT GATHERING PLACE through most of Madrid's history, forming the backdrop to many pivotal events. The heart of the commercial center, it is also the point from which all distances in Spain are measured. While the majestic avenues of Calle Alcalá and Gran Vía have a big-city feel, the narrow streets of the areas immediately to the north have a more intimate character.

With ten streets leading off the square and one of the busiest metro stations in Madrid, the Puerta del Sol is always packed with people and traffic. Unlike Plaza Mayor (see pp. 54–55), however, this is not a place for sitting at pavement cafés and watching the world go by. It seems as if everyone is rushing to somewhere else, whether to office jobs on Calle Alcalá, to the shops of Calle Preciados, or simply to catch a bus or metro train to another part of the city.

Calle Alcalá, which leaves the square to the east, has changed character over the centuries. In medieval times, this section was the beginning of the ceremonial royal route to Alcalá de Henares (see p. 222). After many of the religious buildings flanking it were demolished in the 19th century, it became the heart of café society, the place to see and be seen.

The lively atmosphere of those days was, however, gradually diluted as the banking sector moved in at the turn of the 20th century. This led to the appearance of some signature buildings, illustrative of the way Madrid was booming as a financial center. Their foreign influences show Madrid's eagerness to project itself as a modern European city. This trend was continued along the Gran Vía, which did not exist at all until the first half of the 20th century and changed the face of central Madrid.

The areas north of the Gran Vía have a much longer history, with parts dating back to the 15th century. Most of what is standing today was built in the late 19th century, and is made up of elegant brick apartment buildings with wrought-iron balconies. At ground level, these traditional neighborhoods are changing radically. Chueca has become the center of gay life in Madrid, leading to the emergence of dozens of bars, restaurants, and boutiques.

Neighboring Malasaña, always a bohemian quarter, is becoming more gentrified, but it still exudes its own particular charm. ■

The Puerta del
Sol is the central
point not only for
Madrid, but for
the whole of
Spain.

Puerta del Sol

Puerta del Sol
 Map p. 91
Metro: Sol

THE PUERTA DEL SOL TOOK ON ITS PRESENT APPEARANCE
in the mid-19th century, when society was becoming less influenced
by the church and more interested in shopping and entertainment.
Convents bordering the square were demolished and replaced by
residential and commercial buildings, which form a semi-elliptical
shape. The pedestrian areas have been extended recently, but the
sheer density of people makes it difficult to negotiate at peak times.

The name Puerta del Sol—Gate
of the Sun—originated when the
east gate of the 15th-century city
wall stood where the Hotel París
is now. Popularly known simply
as Sol, the gate was a social hub
in the 17th and 18th centuries,
when people used to meet on the
steps of the San Felipe church
(situated where McDonald's is
now). Long before the invention
of celebrity magazines, people
came here to exchange snippets
of gossip. Until a century ago,
there was a café on nearly every
corner, where writers and intellectuals would gather to discuss
the issues of the day.

The square is dominated by
the redbrick and stone **Casa de
Correos,** which was designed by
Jacques Marquet in 1768 as the
central post office. The facade is
crowned by a baroque pediment
featuring the coat of arms of
Carlos III, in whose reign it was
built. The clock tower was added
in 1866. The clock, Spain's official
timepiece, is one of Madrid's
most famous landmarks.

In the mid-19th century, the
building housed the Ministry of
the Interior; then, during the dictatorship of General Franco, from
1939 to 1975, it became the headquarters of the sinister security

police. Many people were tortured or killed in the cells below the building. It is now home to the regional government, the Comunidad de Madrid, and used for ceremonial purposes.

In front of the building, look for the semicircular paving stone known as *kilómetro cero*, kilometer zero, which is considered to be the center of Spain. Distances to every town in Spain are measured from here. On May 2, 1808, this was also one of the main scenes of the uprising against Napoléon's army (see pp. 204–205), which is commemorated on a plaque to the left of the main door.

The equestrian statue of Carlos III on the north side of the square was not installed until 1997, but it manages to look as if it has been there for centuries. Just beyond it, at the entrance to Calle del Carmen, is one of Madrid's best known symbols: a bronze statue of a bear jumping up at an arbutus tree, also known

New Year fortune

On New Year's Eve, thousands of people gather in the Puerta del Sol to take part in the tradition of eating a grape with each chime of the clock. In theory, this will bring good fortune in the coming year. Once the feat has been accomplished, bottles of sparkling cava wine are opened and shared among the crowd. ■

as wild strawberry. The bear is female and represents the fertility of the land around Madrid, while the tree represents the aristocracy, who traditionally owned everything above ground level.

The pedestrian streets north of the statue are packed with shops, dominated by the several buildings occupied by different sections of the El Corte Inglés department store. ■

A statue of Carlos III presides over the Puerta del Sol, which is dominated by the Casa de Correos.

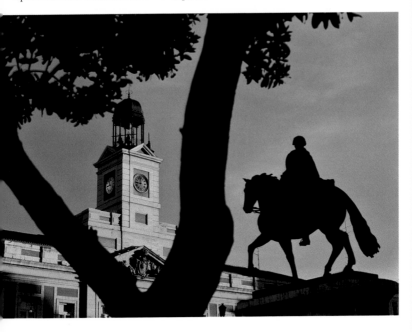

Calle Alcalá

Calle Alcalá

🗺 Map p. 91

Ⓜ Metro: Sol, Sevilla

ORIGINALLY PART OF A DROVERS' TRACK USED TO DRIVE herds from Extremadura to the north of Spain, Calle Alcalá acquired grand mansions and convents in the 17th and 18th centuries. In the early 20th century, the street became Madrid's financial center, resulting in the construction of the impressive buildings seen today. Although the business area has now shifted to Paseo de la Castellana, many banks still keep their headquarters here.

The Casino de Madrid reflects the lavish architectural style prevalent in the early 20th century.

Círculo de Bellas Artes

www.circulobellasartes.com

🗺 Map p. 91

✉ Calle Alcalá 42

☎ 91 360 5400

🕐 Exhibitions closed Sun. p.m. & Mon.

💲 $

Ⓜ Metro: Banco de España, Sevilla

The first imposing building is the vast **Ministerio de Hacienda** (Treasury Department) on the left at No. 5. Built as the Customs House in 1769, it was designed by Francesco Sabatini (1722–1797), who was inspired by Rome's Palazzo Farnese. Next door is the **Real Academia de Bellas Artes de San Fernando** (see pp. 96–97), the Fine Arts Academy.

The opulent **Casino de Madrid** at No. 15 (*tel 91 521 8700*) is a private gentlemen's club. Although not open to the public, you can see inside to the opulent hallway and staircase. You do not have to be a member to eat at the superb restaurant (see p. 246) on the top floor, which has a Michelin star.

The first major commercial building on the street, the **Banco Español de Crédito**, is the triangular structure on the right on the corner of Calle Sevilla. It was designed by Catalan architect José Grases Riera in the 1880s. Look for the stone elephant heads that support the balcony.

The **Banco Bilbao Vizcaya Argentaria,** which curves around the facing corner of Calle Sevilla, was designed by Richard Bastida at the beginning of the 20th century. Look up at the two chariots, each drawn by four horses, which seem to be galloping off the roof.

Looming up on the left is the slate dome of the **Iglesia de las Calatravas** (*Calle Alcalá 25, tel 91 521 8035*). Built in the 17th century as part of a convent, the church's facade was altered to reflect Milanese Renaissance influences in the mid-19th century—a change that detracts from the baroque style of the church itself. Inside there is a magnificent altarpiece by José Benito de Churriguera (1665–1725).

The junction of Calle Alcalá and the Gran Vía is marked by one of Madrid's signature buildings: the **Metrópolis** (*Calle Alcalá 39*). Designed by French architects Jules and Raymond Février between 1907 and 1910, the elaborate facade features Corinthian columns, sculptures, and a slate dome crowned with a bronze figure of Winged Victory. It looks spectacular lit up at night.

The large eclectic structure opposite the Metrópolis is the

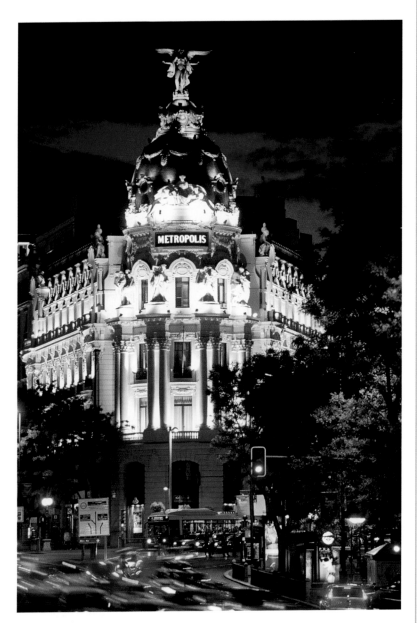

Círculo de Bellas Artes, or Fine Arts Circle. Designed by Antonio Palacios in 1919–1920, it looks like different buildings stacked on top of each other. Several exhibitions are usually running concurrently at this lively cultural center, along with films, theater, and concerts. The large café on the first floor is known as the *pecera,* or goldfish bowl, owing to its panoramic windows; it is a popular spot with writers and artists. ■

The grandiose Metrópolis building dramatically heralds the beginning of the Gran Vía.

Real Academia de Bellas Artes de San Fernando

IT IS A SHAME THAT SO FEW PEOPLE VISIT THE MUSEUM OF the Royal Fine Arts Academy, as it contains some first-class artworks. It is worth going in just to see the 13 Goya paintings, not to mention those by Velázquez, El Greco, Zurbarán, Van Dyck, and Rubens. The fine 18th-century building also contains important collections of drawings, prints, and engravings.

An artist hard at work at the Real Academia de Bellas Artes de San Fernando

Real Academia de Bellas Artes de San Fernando
rabasf.insde.es
🅰 Map p. 91
✉ Calle Alcalá 13
☎ 91 524 0864
🕐 Closed Sun.–Mon. year-round & Sat. p.m. mid-Sept.–June
💲 $
🚇 Metro: Sol, Sevilla

The building was designed in the 1720s by José Benito de Churriguera (1665–1725) as a private residence and altered in 1775 in neoclassic style to house the Fine Arts Academy. The Academy, which taught painting, sculpture, and architecture until 1967, was founded in 1752 during the reign of Fernando V and originally housed in the Palacio Real. It began collecting works by Spanish and foreign artists who were working in Madrid at the time, and later received valuable private legacies. New members also have to donate a piece of their work when admitted.

The collections now comprise more than a thousand works from the 16th to 21st centuries. Only a small fraction is currently exhibited, on the building's third floor, although there are plans to rearrange and expand the displays. Two series of Goya etchings are occasionally on display as part of the National Chalcography Collection on the second floor.

The displays begin in **Rooms 11–14** with 17th-century Spanish artists and include flower paintings by Juan de Arellano (1614–1676) and "Christ Collecting His Vestments" by Alonso Cano (1601–1667). José de Ribera (1591–1652) is well represented with several portraits of saints, including a "Penitent St. Jerome." Two portraits of Felipe IV and Mariana of Austria were previously thought to be by Velázquez, but are now attributed to artists from his studio. Francisco de Zurbarán contributed a series of five portraits of Mercedarian monks (1598–1664), along with his masterly "Vision of the

This room also contains "Susanna and the Elders" by Rubens (1577–1640) and works by Martin de Vos, Leandro Bassano, and Van Dyck.

The Goya (1746–1828) paintings are displayed in **Rooms 20 and 21** and include two small self-portraits. One, painted in 1793–1795, is a full-length portrayal of the artist at work in

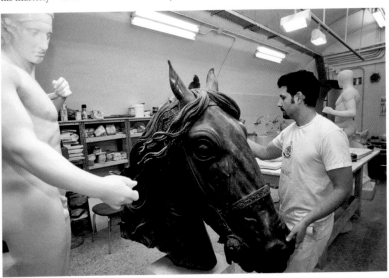

Blessed Alonso Rodríguez."

Room 17 contains several works by Bartolomé Esteban Murillo (1618–1682), including "La Magdalena," which reflects the tendency in the Counter-Reformation to depict madonnas in a gentler, more realistic way.

One of the Academy's most famous paintings is "Spring" (circa 1563) by Giuseppe Arcimboldo (1527–1593), which is in **Room 19.** This intriguing canvas shows a man in profile, made up entirely of flowers and plants. It was presented to Emperor Maximilian II by the artist in 1569 and is one of a series depicting the four seasons.

front of a canvas, dressed in a stylish suit and hat. The other, painted 20 years later, shows the artist looking much more relaxed as he approached the age of 70.

The six portraits include one of Juan de Villanueva, architect of the Prado, and a sensitive depiction of writer Leandro Fernández de Moratín. "The Burial of the Sardine" (1813–1814) shows a ritual from the Madrid carnival that still exists today, but at another level refers to the French occupation of the city. "Procession of Flagellants" and "The Madhouse" show the sinister themes with which Goya became obsessed in later life. ■

An expert re-creates a classical sculpture in a museum workshop.

Gran Vía

Gran Vía
 Map p. 91
 Metro: Banco de España, Gran Vía, Callao

THE GRAN VÍA SWEEPS THROUGH THE CENTER OF Madrid, choked with traffic at all hours of the day and night. The avenue was conceived more than a century ago to connect the new residential districts of Salamanca and Argüelles. It is still a crucial link between the east and west sides of the city.

A showcase for 20th-century architecture, with strong French and American influences, the Gran Vía was developed in three stages and took 50 years to build.

The first stretch, which was built between 1910 and 1917, runs from Calle Alcalá to the junction with Montera, Hortaleza, and Fuencarral. The ornate buildings with art nouveau decoration reflect the buoyant economic situation at the time. The Grassy jeweler's at the foot of the street on the left sets a suitably grand precedent with its colonnaded cream facade. Downstairs there is a **museum** of clocks and watches, some dating back to the 16th century *(tel 91 532 1007, closed Sun.)*.

One of Madrid's great institutions is on the right at No. 12. The **Museo Chicote** cocktail bar *(tel 91 532 6737, closed Sun.)* still has its original art deco interior from the 1930s. A haunt of Ernest Hemingway, Orson Welles, and Salvador Dalí—to name but a few—these days the bar is a chic place for a late-night drink.

On the left at No. 17, you see the curving rear facade of the **Real Oratorio del Caballero de Gracia** *(entrance on parallel Calle Caballero de Gracia at No. 5, tel 91 532 6937)*. Recently restored, the church was designed by Juan de Villanueva at the end of the 18th century and is one of the best examples of neoclassic architecture in Madrid. The narrow nave is flanked by a Corinthian colonnade; there is a stunning baroque figure of Christ from the mid-17th century by Juan Sánchez Barba.

The second stage of the street, built in the 1920s, is lined with movie theaters and shops. The massive **Telefónica** building on the right, which is 290 feet (88 m) tall, was designed between 1926

and 1929 by the American architect Louis S. Weeks and was the first skyscraper in Madrid. The Fundación Telefónica holds temporary exhibitions on the first floor, and there is a permanent telecommunications display on the second floor *(tel 91 522 6645,*

Theater posters

Movies showing along the Gran Vía are advertised by hand-painted posters rather than official promotional material. Decades ago, the artists' union cannily got the theaters to agree to long-term contracts. Madrileños now regard these posters as part of their city's artistic heritage. ■

Opposite: The cacaphonic Gran Vía cuts through central Madrid. Above: The apse of the Real Oratorio del Caballero de Gracia is visible through an arch on the Gran Vía.

closed Sat. p.m., Sun. p.m., & Mon.). This section ends at Plaza de Callao, named after the naval battle off Callao in Peru in 1866.

The third stretch of the Gran Vía, which runs to Plaza de España, was developed from the 1930s to the 1950s. It is heralded by the spectacular art deco **Cinesa Capitol** *(No. 41)*, a theater designed by Luis Martínez Feduchi and Vicente Eced in the 1930s. Opposite is the towering redbrick **Palacio de la Prensa** at No. 46, designed by Pedro Muguruza in 1926. ■

Pedro Almodóvar's Madrid

Pedro Almodóvar, Spain's most renowned moviemaker, has been depicting Madrid in his films since his career began a quarter of a century ago. He has used several well-known landmarks as backdrops, but also likes to portray the sorts of neighborhoods that do not usually feature in the itineraries of people visiting the city for just a few days. You might recognize some of Almodóvar's locations as you explore Madrid.

Volver (2006) is based in La Mancha, where Almodóvar was born, but he also filmed in Vallecas, a blue-collar neighborhood in the south of Madrid, and in Cuatro Caminos,

Spanish star Victoria Abril plays an obsessive investigative journalist in *Kika*, set in Madrid in the early 1990s.

an area that has changed character over recent years owing to the influx of foreign workers. Almodóvar concentrated on the streets in the north of the district, which has become known as "The Little Caribbean" owing to the proliferation of shops, restaurants, and businesses catering to the needs of the new community.

Almodóvar has always been eager to show new developments in the city. *Kika* (1993) featured scenes at the new terminal at Atocha station. Built for the AVE high-speed train to Seville, it had just started operating at the time. The picture itself is based in an apartment near the Paseo de la Castellana, Madrid's north-south axis, and

includes views of the Torre Picasso, Madrid's tallest building.

In *Live Flesh* (1997), he shows the Torres Kio, the leaning twin towers at the top of the Paseo de la Castellana. At that time, the area beyond the towers was rough ground with a few run-down houses, but now it is a burgeoning business district of high-rise buildings, extending the city to the north.

Labyrinth of Passions (1982), Almodóvar's second film, starts with the lead actors, Imanol Arias and Cecilia Roth, wandering through the crowded streets of the Rastro market on a Sunday morning. They have breakfast at La Bobia, a legendary café on Calle San Millán. The café, now an ice-cream parlor called Wooster, has shed its notorious reputation, but you can still sit at the pavement tables just as the characters do in the movie.

Hardly changed at all is the café of the Círculo de Bellas Artes (see p. 95), where Victoria Abril and Peter Coyote sit at a window table in *Kika*. In *High Heels* (1991), the lead characters go to a drag show at Villa Rosa, a famous flamenco bar with ornately decorated tiles on Plaza Santa Ana. Also easily recognizable is the Cine Doré, Madrid's national film theater, featured in *Talk to Her* (2002), which won an Oscar for best original script.

In *High Heels,* Marisa Paredes lives in a basement apartment in Plaza de Alamillo, on the corner of Calle Alfonso VI in the heart of Habsburg Madrid. This neighborhood also features in *The Flower of My Secret* (1995), which again stars Marisa Paredes. In that film she is seen trying to take her boots off while sitting on the edge of a fountain in the Puerta de Moros, by the church of San Andrés.

Paredes also strolls late at night with the actor Juan Echanove through Plaza Mayor, which looks even more dramatic without the usual crowds. He lives in a spectacular apartment in the Palacio de la Prensa on the Gran Vía, with panoramic views across the city.

The Oscar-nominated *Women on the Verge of a Nervous Breakdown* (1988) is based in an even grander penthouse apartment in the upscale quarter of Los Jerónimos, between the Parque del Retiro and the Prado.

Perhaps the most dramatic location, however, is the Viaducto, spanning Calle Segovia, which appears in *Matador* (1986). Assumpta Serna, her black and yellow satin cape billowing in the breeze, stands on the bridge and awaits her fate as she gazes at the mountains of the Sierra de Guadarrama in the distance. ■

The original section of the Atocha train station, designed by Alberto del Palacio at the end of the 19th century, features in *Kika*.

The dense mesh of streets in the Malasañ quarter lace north of the Gran Vía.

North of the Gran Vía

North of the Gran Vía

🅰 Map p. 91
🚇 Metro: Banco de España, Chueca, Gran Vía

Iglesia de las Salesas Reales

🅰 Map p. 91
✉ Calle General Castaños 2
☎ 91 319 4811
🚇 Metro: Colón, Alonso Martínez

THE AREAS JUST OFF THE GRAN VÍA GIVE A FASCINATING insight into how people live in downtown Madrid. While the atmosphere at street level is resolutely commercial, look up and you see rows of balconies adorned by flowerpots and shaded by green wooden blinds. These traditional neighborhoods of Chueca and Malasaña are becoming increasingly fashionable, with boutiques and bars fast replacing the grocery shops and small workshops occupied by carpenters, upholsterers, and electricians.

By far the oldest building is the **Casa de las Siete Chimeneas** (House of the Seven Chimneys), built in 1577 on Plaza del Rey in Chueca. It has been restored and is now part of the head office of the Ministry of Culture. A young woman who died there is rumored to haunt the building, appearing occasionally on the roof in a white dress. In the early 17th century, the future Charles I of England stayed in the house when he came to Madrid to meet Princess María, the sister of Felipe II, with a view to marrying her.

Calle del Barquillo leads north from Plaza del Rey and is lined with stores specializing in music equipment. Originally, this street was part of the royal route up to the majestic **Iglesia de las Salesas Reales.** Also known as Santa Bárbara, this church was built in the mid-18th century as part of a convent intended as a retreat for the Portuguese wife of Fernando VI, Bárbara de Braganza. It was designed by French architect François Carlier, whose plans were modified after his death by Francisco Moradillo.

The lavish late-baroque interior contains the tombs of

Fernando VI and Bárbara of Braganza, which were designed by Francesco Sabatini and sculpted by Francisco Gutiérrez. Statues of San Fernando and Santa Bárbara adorn the high altar, which is flanked by green marble columns. The convent was rebuilt following a fire in 1915 and now houses the Supreme Court.

The street in front of the church is also named after Bárbara de Braganza. One block west it becomes Calle Fernando VI. At the end on the left is the extraordinary building housing the **Sociedad de Autores** (*Calle Fernando VI 4, tel 91 349 9550*), the Society of Authors, an organization that deals with the copyrights of authors and artists. Designed by José Grases Riera in 1902 as a private residence, it is the best example of art nouveau in Madrid. Influenced more by the architecture of Hector Guimard than the *modernisme* of Catalunya, the building's stone plants seem to trickle down the caramel walls, which are encircled by twisted green railings. Around the corner on Calle Pelayo, you get a glimpse of the exotic garden behind the building.

MUSEO ROMÁNTICO

Take the first right off Calle Pelayo into Travesía San Mateo, which leads to Calle San Mateo. The unusual Museo Romántico (*closed at press time for renovation*) is housed in the late 18th-century mansion that was the home of the Marquis of Vega-Inclán (1858–1942). This eccentric aristocrat collected not only art but also musical instruments, fans, and chinaware. An avid promoter of Spanish tourism, he was the man behind the reconstruction of El Greco's house in Toledo

---

Caped crusaders

The Italian Marquis of Squillace caused a mutiny in 1766 when he banned long capes and wide-brimmed hats, claiming that thieves were wearing them to conceal what they had stolen. Madrileños refused to give in and rioted at several places in the city center, including Plaza del Rey in Chueca. ∎

---

and the Santa Cruz quarter in Seville. He later came up with the idea of turning disused historic buildings into hotels, which gave birth to the highly successful Parador chain.

The marquis was a leading exponent of the Romantic movement, which lasted approximately from the 1820s to the 1870s, during the reign of Isabel II. Artists and writers, influenced by Liberal politics, began to throw off the constraints of academicism to explore free expression in their work. Visiting this museum gives an insight into this fertile period of Spanish culture.

The displays begin on the first floor with exhibits charting the many achievements of the marquis. You then enter into the mind-boggling world of his collections on the main floor upstairs. A highlight is a painting by Goya of "St. Gregory the Great." There are portraits by leading 19th-century artists including Leonardo Alenza and José and Federico de Madrazo, and scenes from everyday life—a style known as *costumbrista*—by Valeriano Bécquer and Eugenio Lucas. One room is devoted to the writer Mariano José de Larra (1809–1837), who shot himself after a lover abandoned him.

Museo Romántico

http://museoromantico.mcu.es

- ▲ Map p. 91
- ✉ Calle San Mateo 13
- ☎ 91 448 1071 or 91 448 1045
- 🕐 Closed for renovation
- 💲 $. Free Sun.
- Ⓜ Metro: Tribunal, Alonso Martínez

Frescoes richly decorate the baroque church of San Antonio de los Alemanes.

MUSEO MUNICIPAL

Around the corner, the Museo Municipal has also been undergoing refurbishment, but it is at least partially open during the alterations. The building, designed in the early 18th century by Pedro de Ribera, has an elaborate baroque portal, a characteristic feature of his style. Originally a poorhouse, the building also housed workshops where the political activist Pablo Iglesias trained as a printer.

Even if you are short of time, be sure to pop into the museum to see the extraordinary wooden scale model of Madrid. Measuring 17 feet by 11.5 feet (5.2 x 3.5 m), it was made in 1830 by León Gil de Palacio, just a few years before the disentailment of religious property led to the disappearance of many churches, convents, and monasteries. It shows how very different Madrid looked before the urban development of the mid-19th century.

During refurbishment, only a limited selection of the museum's rich art collection is on display. When it is fully open again, exhibits will chart Madrid's histo-

Manuela attacked the French soldiers who tried to detain her,
using her sewing scissors as a
weapon. The soldiers shot her
dead on the spot.

This area has been a nightlife
hub since the 1960s, when artists
and musicians moved into the
traditional apartments, attracted

Museo Municipal
- 🅰 Map p. 91
- ✉ Calle Fuencarral 78
- ☎ 91 588 8672
- 🕐 Closed Sat. p.m.,
  Sun. p.m., & Mon.
- Ⓜ Metro: Tribunal,
  Bilbao

**Iglesia de San
Antonio de los
Alemanes**
- 🅰 Map p. 91
- ✉ Calle Puebla 22
- ☎ 91 522 3774
- Ⓜ Metro: Gran Vía,
  Callao

Historic soup kitchen

At the beginning of the 18th
century, a brotherhood set
up a refuge next to the church
of San Antonio de los Alemanes.
Every night the monks would
take to the streets with baskets
of bread and boiled eggs to hand
out to the many vagrants in the
area. The tradition has continued into the 21st century with a
soup kitchen that still feeds
dozens of people every day. ■

ry from Paleolithic to Roman
times, before showing how the
town grew during the Muslim
period and after the Christian
Reconquest.

MALASAÑA DISTRICT
Calle Fuencarral marks the
boundary between Chueca and
the district of Malasaña (see also
pp. 106–107). The area is named
after Manuela Malasaña, a hero-
ine of the uprising against the
French army on May 2, 1808 (see
pp. 204–205), which took place
nearby. A 17-year-old seamstress,

by low rents in what was then a
run-down district. By day it is
peaceful, but at night the atmosphere changes drastically when
the many bars and clubs open up.

One of Madrid's most surprising churches is hidden in this
neighborhood. **San Antonio de
los Alemanes** looks unassum-
ing from the outside, and most
people walk by with no idea of
the baroque riches inside. It was
built between 1624 and 1633 by
Pedro Sánchez, a leading church
architect of the time. The elliptical interior is covered with frescoes related to the life of St.
Anthony of Padua (1195–1231),
a Franciscan monk who died in
Padua, Italy. The frescoes were
painted by leading artists of the
day, including Francisco Ricci
(1608–1685) and Juan Carreño
de Miranda (1614–1685). ■

A walk around Chueca & Malasaña

This walk takes you around the rapidly changing areas north of the Gran Vía. While not rich in monuments, these traditional neighborhoods have taken on a new lease of life and now have the most avant-garde boutiques and bars in Madrid. Early evening is a good time to explore these areas, particularly on weekends when the streets are thronged with people.

From the **Gran Vía metro station,** walk up Calle Hortaleza, a busy shopping street. The mesh of streets to the right is the Chueca district, now well known as one of the liveliest gay quarters in Europe. The success of the area has led to its becoming much more mainstream, and it is now popular with a young, trendy crowd.

Turn right down Calle Augusto Figueroa, which is lined with shops selling designer shoes at discount prices. Turn left

apartment buildings around the square, most dating back about a hundred years, have been spruced up, turning this formerly scruffy space into an attractive focal point.

Walk down Calle Gravina, which after crossing Calle Barquillo becomes **Calle Almirante,** renowned for its boutiques with clothes by top Spanish designers. Turn left up Calle Conde de Xiquena, where the elaborate doorways, wide enough for carriages to enter, show the wealth of this area

Children play in the shady Plaza Dos de Mayo, the heart of the Malasaña district.

down Calle Barbieri, which leads into **Plaza de Chueca ❶,** a square that epitomizes the changes taking place in the area. The pavement cafés are a popular place to meet on summer nights, while the **Taberna de Ángel Sierra** *(Calle Gravina 11, tel 91 531 0126),* on the far side of the square, is a great traditional tavern with a zinc bar, tiled walls, and good tapas. The

at the end of the 19th century. At the end of the street is the magnificent **Iglesia de las Salesas Reales ❷** (see pp. 102–103).

Turn left along Calle Fernando VI, with the **Sociedad de Autores ❸,** the Society of Authors (see p. 103), at the end on the left. Continue straight ahead along Calle Mejía Lequerica, then turn left into Calle Barceló. On the right at No. 11 is the curving facade of Pachá *(tel 91 447 0128)*, one of Madrid's most famous nightclubs. Built in the 1930s as a cinema, the building is a good example of functionalist architecture. The **Museo Municipal** ❹ (see pp. 104–105), on the left, is well worth a look.

Crossing Calle Fuencarral takes you into Malasaña, where the gay scene disappears, replaced by a New Age atmosphere. Walk down Calle Velarde to **Plaza Dos de Mayo** ❺, which is named after the uprising that began here on May 2, 1808 (see pp. 204–205). The monument in the middle features statues of Pedro Velarde and Luis Daoíz, the heroic army captains who lost their lives in the fighting.

Leave the square by walking south down Calle San Andrés, which leads to **Plaza de Juan Pujol**. Don't miss the Farmacia Juanse (Juanse pharmacy) on the corner on the right; hand-painted tiles on the facade depict a variety of ailments. Turn left along Calle Espíritu Santo, which gets its name from the Cross of the Holy Spirit that was installed here in the 17th century to commemorate the fact that several brothels were struck by lightning.

See area map p. 91

▶ Gran Vía metro station

3 miles (5 km)

2 hours

▶ Gran Vía metro station

NOT TO BE MISSED
- Plaza de Chueca
- Calle Almirante
- Iglesia de las Salesas Reales

Turn right at the end into Corredera Alta de San Pablo, which leads to **Plaza de San Ildefonso** ❻, dominated by its 19th-century church. Turn left into Calle Colón, where there is a tiled bar at No. 13, **Bodegas La Ardosa** *(tel 91 521 4979)*. Turn right down Fuencarral, one of the trendiest places to shop in Madrid. The **Mercado de Fuencarral** *(tel 91 521 4152, closed Sun.)*, at No. 45, is a small shopping mall with an Internet center in the basement. Carry on down the street to return to the Gran Vía. ∎

More places to visit in downtown Madrid

CENTRO CULTURAL BLANQUERNA

This new center promotes the culture of the Catalunya region in northeast Spain. Although it specializes in Catalan authors, the center also provides a good range of fiction, art, and travel books in both Spanish and English. The space downstairs is used for exhibitions, talks, concerts, and other events. www.gencat.es/blanquerna Map p. 91 ✉ Calle Alcalá 44 ☎ 91 524 1890 🕐 Closed Sat. & Sun. 🚇 Metro: Banco de España

CONVENTO DE SAN PLÁCIDO

Built in the mid-17th century by Fray Lorenzo San Nicolás, this convent was soon immersed in a scandal involving the novices, their confessor, members of the aristocracy, and even the king, Felipe IV. The rich decoration in the church is at least partly the result of donations aimed at silencing the rumors and includes an amazingly realistic "Recumbent Christ" by Gregorio Fernández. A Velázquez painting, "Christ on the Cross," painted for the convent on the orders of Felipe IV, is now in the Prado museum, replaced in this collection by a copy. The convent's dome is decorated with frescoes by Francisco Ricci, and the painting of the Annunciation on the high altar is by Claudio Coello. 🅰 Map p. 91 ✉ Calle San Roque 9 ☎ 91 531 7999 🕐 Closed Sat. a.m. & Sun. 🚇 Metro: Gran Vía

The Tribunal metro stop serves the Museo Romántico and other sights in north Madrid.

IGLESIA DE SAN JOSÉ

Designed by Pedro de Ribera in 1730, the baroque church is now slotted between grand commercial buildings. It originally adjoined a Carmelite convent, which was demolished following the disentailment of religious property in 1836. The church contains 18th-century sculptures by Robert Michel and Juan Pascual de Mena. A plaque commemorates the wedding of Simón Bolívar (1783–1830), the great Venezuelan general, to Maria Teresa Rodríguez del Toro y Alaysa, the daughter of a Spanish nobleman. The ceremony took place in the church in 1802. 🅰 Map p. 91 ✉ Calle Alcalá 43 ☎ 91 522 6784 🚇 Metro: Banco de España

MUSEO COLECCIONES ICO

This interesting exhibition space is run by the cultural foundation of the state credit organization, the Instituto de Crédito Oficial. The permanent collection contains works by leading Spanish contemporary artists including José María Sicilia, Jaume Plensa, Miquel Barcel, and Pablo Picasso (the Suite Vollard). There is usually at least one temporary exhibition running, featuring Spanish and international artists. www.ico.es 🅰 Map p. 91 ✉ Calle Zorrilla 3 ☎ 91 420 0717, free cellphone 900 121 121 🕐 Closed Sun. p.m. & Mon. Free guided tours on Tues. & Thurs. at 11:30 a.m., 5:30 p.m., & 6:30 p.m. 🚇 Metro: Banco de España

TEATRO MARIA GUERRERO

Designed in 1885 by Agustín Ortiz de Villajos, the theater is named after the renowned actress who for many years owned the building and performed there regularly. Originally it was called the Teatro Princesa, after the daughter of Alfonso XII, which is why the letters T and P feature entwined in stone on the neo-Greek facade. One of the best examples of 19th-century cast-iron architecture in Madrid, the theater has a neo-Mudejar interior with intricate red and gold decoration. It is now home to the Centro Dramático Nacional, which specializes in contemporary theater, particularly the work of Spanish playwrights. www.mcu.es 🅰 Map p. 91 ✉ Calle Tamayo Y Baus ☎ 91 310 2949 🚇 Metro: Colón ∎

Packed with cafés, bars, and restaurants, Plaza de Santa Ana draws huge crowds on weekend nights. It has been an entertainment hub since Madrid's first theaters were set up in courtyards there four centuries ago.

Around Plaza de Santa Ana

A ceramic portrait of the 17th-century writer Francisco de Quevedo

Around Plaza de Santa Ana

THE TRIANGLE OF STREETS EAST OF THE PUERTA DEL SOL IS USUALLY known as the Barrio de las Letras, the Literary Quarter. Bordered by Carrera de San Jerónimo, Paseo del Prado, Calle Atocha, and Calle de la Cruz, the area got its name from the concentration of poets, playwrights, journalists, and novelists who flocked to the area after Madrid's first makeshift theaters were established at the end of the 16th century.

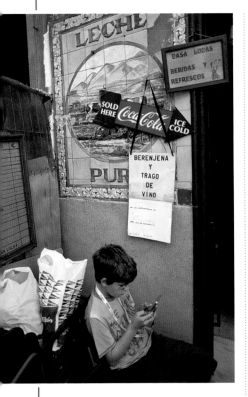

Hand-painted tiles advertise a brand of milk outside the Casa Locas tapas bar.

Known as *corrales,* the first two courtyard theaters were the Príncipe, where the Teatro Español now stands on Plaza de Santa Ana, and the Cruz, on the street of the same name. The 17th century was the golden age of Spanish theater, and plays by leading writers of the time—Lope de Vega, Calderón de la Barca, Tirso de Molina—are staged to this day both in Spain and abroad.

Madrid's population rose sharply after Felipe II made the city the capital in 1561.

Many of these people were unemployed and kept themselves amused by spending their time at the corrales, which were open from noon until 10 p.m. Most stood throughout the performances and were anything but a passive audience. Only the clergy and aristocracy sat down, either at the front or in private compartments around the sides.

There was an enormous turnover of plays, which led to dozens of workshops being set up to print them. Bookshops opened, too, along with taverns to cater to the thousands of people who flocked to the area every day. The 19th century saw the emergence of literary cafés, where the literati would meet to discuss literature, art, and current affairs (see pp. 118–119).

Though the Teatro Español remains Madrid's most prestigious theater, the Santa Ana area is now better known for its nightlife. Popular with locals and visitors of all ages, this is a good place to try a few tapas bars.

Corrales also appeared south of Santa Ana, in the area known as Lavapiés, where courtyards still exist behind the 19th-century facades. One of Madrid's most traditional neighborhoods, it features in the work of many golden age writers. In recent years, an influx of people from Africa, Latin America, and the Far East has given the area a new lease on life. On Sunday mornings, a huge flea market, the Rastro, attracts thousands of visitors in search of bargains. ■

Local residents exercise their dogs in Plaza de Santa Ana, the hub of the Literary Quarter.

Plaza de Santa Ana

PLAZA DE SANTA ANA GETS ITS NAME FROM THE CONVENT that stood here until the 19th century. This large, open space is now a popular meeting place with lots of cafés and tapas bars. The square is dominated by the Teatro Español, which has developed over the centuries from a courtyard playhouse into a grand edifice.

Plaza de Santa Ana

▲ Map p. 111

Teatro Español

✉ Calle Príncipe 25

☎ 91 360 1480

🚇 Metro: Antón Martín, Sevilla

Patrons' revenge

Back in the 17th century, if the audience did not like either the play or a particular actor, they would shout, throw rotten fruit, and bang kitchen utensils to make their feelings known. Their unequivocal reaction could get a play closed down after just one performance, with disastrous consequences for the actors and writers. Spectators sometimes became so immersed in the play that they believed it was real, and would jump onto the stage to attack the actors with knives and other weapons. ∎

Known as the Corral del Príncipe, the theater was originally founded by a charity to generate income for a hospital on Calle Toledo. The theater was highly successful, although tight controls had to be introduced to stop unruly crowds from getting in without paying.

The open, wooden playhouse was replaced in 1745 by a covered Italian-style theater, which was rebuilt by Juan de Villanueva following a fire at the beginning of the 19th century. After the square was created by the demolition of the convent, owners added a new neoclassic facade, featuring medallions with busts of famous playwrights. The interior was rebuilt after another fire in 1975, and the theater now stages classical and contemporary plays under the directorship of Mario Gas.

A likeness of poet and playwright Federico García Lorca (1898–1936) stands in front of the theater. The marble statue at the other end depicts playwright Pedro Calderón de la Barca (1600–1681), one of the best known golden age dramatists; scenes from four of his plays surround the base.

The most famous of the many bars on the square is **Cervecería Alemana** at No. 6 *(tel 91 429 7033)*, which was founded in 1904 and has changed little over the years. The bar was a favorite haunt of bullfighters; Ernest Hemingway was also a regular.

The bullfighters, including Manolete and Luis Miguel Dominguín, favored the **Hotel Reina Victoria** (see p. 248), with its gleaming cream facade and distinctive corner beacon at the top of the square. Built in 1919, it closed in 2005 and was converted into the first Hard Rock hotel in Europe.

Just off the square, to the left of the hotel, is the **Iglesia de San Sebastián.** The original structure, from the 16th century, was destroyed in the Civil War. In the 17th century, the church became the base for the charitable organizations that had set up the two courtyard playhouses. Funds from these organizations helped actors and writers cover basic expenses and medical care.

Lope de Vega was buried in the church's crypt, and although his remains were lost, he is commemorated by a monument inside. Many other writers, including Valle-Inclán, Bécquer, Larra, and Zorrilla, were married there. Through a glass screen in the church, you can see the neoclassic **Chapel of Our Lady of Bethlehem,** originally designed by Ventura Rodríguez in the 18th century and meticulously rebuilt by the Architects' Guild. Leading architects, including Juan de Villanueva, are buried there, as is Ventura Rodríguez himself. ∎

Iglesia de San Sebastián

✉ Calle Atocha 39
☎ 91 429 1361
Ⓜ Metro: Antón Martín

With its tapas bars and cafés, Plaza de Santa Ana is a popular meeting place.

Bars and restaurants with literary associations line the lanes around Plaza de Sana Ana.

A walk in the Barrio de las Letras

This walk is more about atmosphere than sights. As you stroll through the narrow streets, let your imagination take you back to the 17th century, when the area was the seedbed of cultural life in Madrid.

From the **Puerta del Sol** ①, walk along Carrera de San Jerónimo and turn right up Calle Victoria. One of Spain's most renowned authors, Benito Pérez Galdós (1843–1920), set his first novel, *La Fontana de Oro,* in a café of the same name on this corner. Although the café disappeared a century ago, the novel is commemorated by a marble plaque a little farther along outside a bar that now uses the name.

Bearing right up Calle de la Cruz, on the left at No. 23 is **Capas Seseña** *(tel 91 531 6840),* which makes and sells traditional capes. You come almost immediately to a small square. Facing you is a large mural of this street as it is now, featuring Felipe IV in the bottom right-hand corner. The Corral de la Cruz, one of Madrid's first theaters, was set up in a courtyard here in the late 16th century. Felipe IV often attended performances, and famously had an affair with La Calderona, a leading actress of the day.

Turn left down Calle de Álvarez Gato, a lane with a series of distorting mirrors on the left, the originals of which featured in Ramón del Valle-Inclán's play *Bohemian Lights* (1924). At the end on the right, hand-painted tiles of Spanish cities decorate **Villa Rosa** *(tel 91 521 3689),* a flamenco club that dates back to 1919.

Turn right into **Plaza de Santa Ana** ②, with the **Teatro Español** at the far end (see p. 112). Walk diagonally across the square and turn right into Calle Príncipe. On the first corner on the right, you reach the **Palacio de Santoña,** which was designed in 1734 and features ornate baroque doorways by Pedro de Ribera on Calle Príncipe. It is not usually open to the public, but the Madrid Tourism Center *(tel 91 588 1636)* organizes occasional tours of the lavish interior.

In 1614, Cervantes lived across the street, where the **Casa Alberto** tavern (see pp. 64–65) is now. Turn left down Calle Huertas, one of the busiest streets for nightlife in Madrid, where quotes by authors including Galdós, Góngora, and

Cervantes are set into the sidewalk in bronze letters.

The austere neoclassic building on the corner with Calle León was designed by Juan de Villanueva in 1788 and houses the **Real Academia de la Historia** (Royal Academy of History) ❸. It was originally used by monks from the monastery at El Escorial (see pp. 228–231), who used to print their prayer books here.

Turn right up Calle León—whose name derives from a lion that was kept in a cage here in the 17th century—then left down the broad Calle Atocha. At No. 87 you come to the **Sociedad Cervantina** ❹ *(tel 91 420 3437)*, which promotes the work of Cervantes. As shown by a plaque, this was the site of the printing press that published the first part of *Don Quixote* in 1605.

Turn left up Costanilla de los Desamparados and take the third left back up Calle Huertas, then walk up the hill on the right, Costanilla Trinitarias. The wall running the entire block on the left belongs

- See area map p. 111
- Puerta del Sol
- 1.4 miles (2.25 km)
- 45 minutes
- Plaza de Santa Ana

NOT TO BE MISSED
- Plaza de Santa Ana
- Teatro Español
- Casa-Museo de Lope de Vega

to the **Convento de las Trinitarias Descalzas** ❺ (see p. 117). Turning left up Calle Lope de Vega, you can appreciate the size of the convent. Cut down Calle Quevedo to Calle Cervantes, where the **Casa-Museo de Lope de Vega** ❻ is situated (see p. 116), and turn left back to Calle León. A plaque on the corner marks the place where Cervantes lived. Turn right down to Calle Prado, then left to arrive back at Plaza de Santa Ana. ■

Calle Cervantes
& around

Map p. 111

**Casa-Museo de
Lope de Vega**

✉ Calle Cervantes 11

☎ 91 429 9216

🕐 Closed p.m., Sun., &
Mon.

💲 $. Free Sat. a.m.

🚇 Metro: Antón Martín,
Sevilla

Calle Cervantes & around

MANY STREETS IN THIS AREA ARE NAMED AFTER LITERARY figures who lived (or were buried!) in the neighborhood. The street now called Calle Cervantes was home to both Cervantes and playwright Lope de Vega, but only the latter's home survives. The parallel Calle Lope de Vega is also associated with Cervantes, as he was originally buried there. Calle Quevedo, which links the two streets, was home to the poet and satirist Francisco de Quevedo (1580–1645).

Although largely rebuilt, the **Casa-Museo de Lope de Vega** is a traditional 17th-century house and is worth visiting to see how professional people lived in the area at that time. One of Spain's most renowned playwrights, Félix Lope de Vega lived here from 1610 until his death in 1635 at the age of 73. He was married twice, had three lovers, and fathered at least 14 children. In the course of his tumultuous life, he wrote about 1,500 plays, as well as poetry and novels.

The house has two main floors, set around a peaceful courtyard garden, with orange, lemon, fig, and cypress trees. In Lope de Vega's time, half was used as a vegetable garden to provide food for the family.

The furniture and decoration are authentic from the 17th century, although most did not belong to the writer. In the study, the desk is near the window, as Lope de Vega worked very long hours and needed to make optimum use of the natural light. Two paintings in this room belonged to him, one of which depicts his own children, Carlitos and Lope Félix. Lope de Vega became a priest at the age of 51, and the house contains a small chapel dedicated to San Isidro, the patron saint of Madrid (see p. 63).

A room on the top floor contains a chessboard, which was a very popular game in Lope de Vega's lifetime. There was no bathroom; inhabitants simply used pitchers and bowls and threw the waste out of the window at night.

Lope de Vega and a well-known actress named Micaela de

Luján had five children together, one of whom became Mother Superior of the nearby **Convento de las Trinitarias Descalzas** *(Calle Lope de Vega 18)*. There are now just 21 nuns living in a closed order at the convent, which is not open to the public. Inside the church entrance on the left, a hatch with a revolving drum allows the nuns to communicate with the outside world without being seen. To the left of the presbytery in the church, a stone tablet commemorates the fact that Cervantes was buried there. On the anniversary of his death, April 23, the church holds a special Mass in his memory.

Calle Prado, one block north of Calle Cervantes, is lined with antique bookshops. One of the great intellectual institutions of the 19th century, the **Ateneo de Madrid** is still going strong at No. 21. Founded in 1835 by a group of liberal thinkers, the organization was dedicated to reforming the educational system. Its activities often met opposition from the government or the Church, and it was shut down several times. Designed in 1884 by Enrique Fort, the building comprises a lecture theater, library, and club room. It is a private club, but visitors are welcome to look around; the café is open to the public. ∎

Ateneo de Madrid

✉ Calle del Prado 21
☎ 91 429 1750
Ⓜ Metro: Antón Martín, Sevilla

Intellectuals have been meeting in the imposing library of the Ateneo club for more than a century.

Traditional cafés

Sitting at marble tables in cavernous cafés has been a favorite pastime for Madrileños for nearly two centuries. Although the city lost most of its original cafés following its rapid development in the second half of the 20th century, the tradition has been revitalized with dozens of newer watering spots. In these relaxing cafés, people can sit for hours, drinking coffee, watching the world go by, engaging in intellectual debate, or simply passing along the latest gossip.

Madrid's café society began during the repressive regime of Fernando VII in the early 19th century, when intellectuals used to gather to debate ways to reform the political and cultural situation. These gatherings gave rise to the term *tertulia*, meaning an informal discussion group. Tertulias usually had a special area of interest—such as politics, literature, poetry, bullfighting, or science—with each group favoring a specific café for its meetings.

One of the most renowned early tertulias included the impressive group of politicians and writers that went on to found the Ateneo institution (see p. 117), which flourishes to this day. Led by Ramón de Mesoneros Romanos (1803–1882), a writer and city councilor who chronicled life in Madrid, this group was known as El Parnasillo and met in the Café del Príncipe, now called the **Café del Español** *(Calle Príncipe 25, tel 91 420 1755)*, alongside the Teatro Español (see p. 112).

The present café opened in the late 1990s, but the traditional decor is based on descriptions by Mesoneros Romanos and the writer Benito Pérez Galdós (1843–1920). Among its colorful members was the satirist Mariano José de Larra. In his article "El Café," written in 1932, Larra said, "I don't know if it is my natural curiosity … that makes me take a seat at corner tables four times a day to eavesdrop on other people's conversations, which later

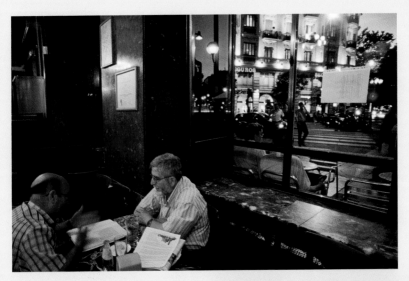

keep me entertained when I am back home … when I laugh like a lunatic at all the lunatics I have overheard."

By the end of the 19th century, cafés had proliferated all over downtown Madrid, particularly around the Puerta del Sol, Calle Alcalá, and Plaza de Santa Ana. One of the most famous was the Café del Pombo just off the Puerta del Sol. A famous tertulia group used to meet in the basement—dubbed "the Sacred Crypt"—and was led by Ramón Gómez de la Serna (1888–1963), who specialized in writing about Madrid. This group was depicted by expressionist artist José Gutiérrez Solana in his painting "La Tertulia del Café del Pombo," which hangs in the Reina Sofía museum (see pp. 154–159).

After the Civil War, many of the leading exponents of café society went into exile, and a number of cafés were turned into banks and shops. Two great institutions do, however, survive to this day: the **Café Comercial** *(Glorieta de Bilbao 7, tel 91 521 5655)* and the **Café Gijón** *(Paseo de Recoletos 21, tel 91 521 5425)*.

The Comercial opened in 1887 and has been packed with a mixture of politicians, poets, intellectuals, and office workers ever since. Originally the café featured musical performances on a stage, which sadly no longer exists. The decor has not essentially

For nearly 200 years, Madrileños have relaxed (left, at Plaza Matute), discussed (top, at Café Comercial), and worked (above, at Café Gijón) at the city's many cafés. Some are old, some are new, but all offer a prime spot to watch the world go by.

changed since 1953, when the café's marble tables were installed.

The Gijón has been going since 1888 and tertulia groups still meet there, particularly at the coveted window tables. Regulars over the years have included writers Ramón del Valle-Inclán, Federico García Lorca, and Nobel Prize-winner Camilo José Cela, whose novel *The Hive* was based on the characters who frequented the Gijón in the 1940s. ■

You never know what treasures you might discover while browsing around the Rastro flea market on a Sunday.

Lavapiés & the Rastro

THE STREETS SLOPING DOWN FROM PLAZA DE SANTA ANA form the neighborhood of Lavapiés, traditionally known as the *barrios bajos*, or low districts. Now the most racially mixed part of the city, its character is changing fast. Over the centuries, Lavapiés has provided a wealth of material for writers and artists. Lope de Vega, Cervantes, and Tirso de Molina wrote about the area in the 17th century, followed by Ramón de la Cruz and Benito Pérez Galdós. Many paintings by Francisco de Goya, who loved depicting scenes from the everyday life of the lower social classes, were inspired by events he witnessed in this area. If possible, explore Lavapiés on a Sunday morning, when the Rastro street market is in full swing.

Lavapiés & the Rastro

- Map p. 111
- Metro: Tirso de Molina, Lavapiés, La Latina

Plaza de Lavapiés was the heart of the Jewish quarter in medieval Madrid. The synagogue stood near the square on the corner of Calle de la Fé and Calle de Salitre, where the 19th-century **Iglesia de San Lorenzo** is now.

After the Catholic Monarchs expelled the Jews in 1492, this area was occupied by *conversos,* Jews who had converted to Christianity. The conversos traditionally named their first son Manuel, which led to the area also becoming known as the Barrio de los Manolos. Over the years, the term Manolo has come to mean the typical streetwise Madrid character who features in many plays and novels.

Near the square, on the corner of Calle Sombrerete and Calle Mesón de Paredes, is **La Corrala,** a 19th-century galleried building open on one side to reveal a courtyard. In summer, concerts and theatrical performances are sometimes held there, featuring local people dressed in traditional costume as Manolos and Manolas.

One block west, on Calle Embajadores, is the area's most important church, the **Iglesia de San Cayetano.** The church was rebuilt in the 1960s after most of the original structure, from the late 17th and early 18th centuries, was destroyed in the Civil War. The Greek-cross interior has Byzantine influences, with a central dome and four smaller ones.

THE RASTRO

The Rastro market takes place between Calle Embajadores and Calle Toledo, with Ribera de Curtidores as the main street. The term *rastro* has unpleasant origins, as it refers to the trail of blood left on the streets from the two abattoirs that used to exist in the area. Those are long gone, replaced by stands selling clothes, bags, books, and all manner of secondhand junk. Try to avoid carrying anything valuable, as theft is rife in the crowded streets.

Start from Plaza de Cascorro, then turn to the right into Plaza General Vara del Rey, where stands sell rustic furniture. Work your way down the hill to the stands of old records and books at the bottom, then cut through to Ribera de Curtidores and walk back up the hill. ■

Iglesia de San Cayetano

✉ Calle Embajadores 15

☎ 91 527 0790

🚇 Metro: Tirso de Molina, Lavapiés

Rastro street market

✉ Ribera de Curtidores

🕐 Sundays until 3 p.m.

🚇 Metro: La Latina

Housing story

In the 16th century, a bylaw was introduced to ease the housing shortage arising from the drastic increase in population after Madrid became capital in 1561. People in houses with more than one story were forced to provide accommodation for courtiers and the nobility. To get around this, inhabitants built houses with only one story facing the street, but rising higher at the back. ■

A prospective buyer bargains for a chess set with a market trader in Plaza del General Vara del Rey.

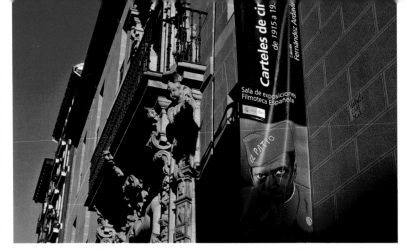

The 18th-century Palacio de la Magdalena now houses the National Film Institute.

More places to visit around Plaza de Santa Ana

LA CASA ENCENDIDA

Run by José Guirao, a former director of the Reina Sofía museum, this is an exciting new cultural center, located in a neo-Mudejar building. The varied program includes exhibitions, concerts, and performances, as well as workshops and courses. Activities often have an ecological angle, and there is also a fair-trade shop. www.lacasaencendida.com
⚠ Map p. 111 ✉ Ronda de Valencia 2
☎ 902 430 322 🚇 Metro: Embajadores, Atocha, Lavapiés

FILMOTECA ESPAÑOLA— CINE DORÉ

This pretty art nouveau cinema was built in 1923 and is now owned by the Filmoteca Española, the national film archive, which programs showings in its three theaters. In summer movies are also shown on the roof terrace. There is a good bookshop and café. www.mcu.es/cine/film/filmoteca.jsp ⚠ Map p. 111 ✉ Calle Santa Isabel 3 ☎ 91 369 2118 🕐 Closed Mon. 🚇 Metro: Antón Martín

IGLESIA DE JESÚS DE MEDINACELI

Although this structure was built only in 1920, it stands on the site of a monastery founded in the early 17th century. The church was popular with theater people, who always came to Mass on Sundays. It contains a 16th-century figure of Jesus of Nazareth that is believed to have miraculous qualities, having been rescued by Trinitarian monks from the Moors in North Africa in the 17th century. On the first Friday of every month, people stand in line to kiss the feet of the statue, in the hope it will bring them good fortune. www.archimadrid.es/jesusmedinaceli.es
⚠ Map p. 111 ✉ Plaza Jesús 2 ☎ 91 429 6893 🚇 Metro: Antón Martín

PALACIO DE LA MAGDALENA

Recently restored, the building was designed by Pedro de Ribera in 1731 and has an elaborate baroque doorway. It was built as the residence of the Marquis of Perales, who was governor of Madrid at the time of the 1808 uprising against the French (see pp. 204–205). It is now the headquarters of the National Film Institute, which organizes a program of exhibitions. www.mcu.es/cine/film/filmoteca.jsp ⚠ Map p. 111 ✉ Calle Magdalena 10 ☎ 91 467 2600 🕐 Closed Sun. & Mon. 🚇 Metro: Tirso de Molina, Antón Martín

TEATRO DE LA COMEDIA

The original 19th-century home of the National Company of Classical Theater, located behind a residential building on Calle Principe, is undergoing restoration. Until it reopens in 2007 or 2008, the company is based at the Teatro de Pavón.
⚠ Map p. 111 ✉ Calle Embajadores 9
☎ 91 528 2819 🚇 Metro: La Latina ∎

The Paseo del Prado is Madrid's museum mile, with an astounding wealth of first-rate art in the Prado, Thyssen-Bornemisza, and Reina Sofía, which are all expanding to create an even greater cultural axis.

Paseo del Prado

A life-size figure of Felipe IV decorates a shop balcony on the Paseo del Prado.

Paseo del Prado

MADRID'S THREE GREATEST ART MUSEUMS ARE ALL LOCATED ON OR NEAR the Paseo del Prado, a boulevard designed for leisure and learning during the reign of Carlos III in the 18th century. Now it is becoming known as the Paseo del Arte, or Art Walk, and in the next few years it will be developed as a grand urban promenade. The Prado, Thyssen-Bornemisza, and Reina Sofía museums contain some of the most famous artworks in the world, and for many people are the main reason for visiting Madrid.

Visitors inspect Goya's painting "The Nude Maja," rumored to depict the Duchess of Alba.

All three museums have been undergoing expansion in recent years to provide more space for their prestigious collections. The most far-reaching changes are taking place at the Prado, where work is under way on neighboring buildings that will eventually create a huge complex across the hill above the Paseo del Prado.

Visiting the Prado is a stimulating but often overwhelming experience. You could easily spend several days contemplating its treasures, but if you have only a few hours, it really pays to decide which areas interest you most and visit those first. You also need at least three hours for the Thyssen-Bornemisza, where the displays span eight centuries of art history, with masterpieces from every period. The Reina Sofía is a vast museum of contemporary art, with two or three major temporary exhibitions usually running at any given time. Again, you are likely to spend a minimum of three hours looking at the displays, and quite possibly another couple of hours in the excellent restaurant and bookshop.

The Paseo itself is also going to be altered to make it more pedestrian-friendly. A development plan devised by Portuguese architect Alvaro Siza restricts traffic to the west side of the street, with ramps and walkways improving access to the museums. Slated for completion in 2008, the plan also involves the planting of a thousand trees.

These changes will create a 21st-century version of the original concept for the Paseo del Prado. During the Enlightenment, this stretch was the most fashionable social area in the city. That situation is likely to be repeated when it is once again the preserve of pedestrians rather than cars. ■

Area of map detail

PASEO DEL PRADO

0   200 meters
0   200 yards

CALLE PRIM

Palacio
Marqués de
Salamanca

CALLE RECOLETOS

CALLE SERRANO

RECOLETOS

CALLE SALUSTIANO
OLÓZAGA

Palacio de Buenavista
(Cuartel General del
Ejército de Tierra)

CALLE BARQUILLO

PASEO RECOLETOS

Palacio de Linares
(Casa de América)

Puerta
de Alcalá

PLAZA
INDEPENDENCIA

CALLE ALCALÁ

Fuente de la
Cibeles

PLAZA
CIBELES

Banco de
España

Banco de
España

CALLE ALCALÁ

Sevilla

Sevilla

CALLE ALCALÁ

C. MARQUÉS DE CUBAS

CALLE
LOS MADRAZO

Banco de
España

Banco de
España

CALLE ZORRILLA

PLAZA
CANALEJAS

CARRERA SAN JERÓNIMO

Congreso de los
Diputados

PASEO DEL PRADO

Fuente de
Apolo

Palacio de
Comunicaciones

Museo Postal
y Telegráfico

Museo
Naval

C. RUIZ ALARCÓN

CALLE ALFONSO XI

CALLE ALCALÁ

Museo Nacional
de Artes
Decorativas

Puerta de
España

Bolsa de
Comercio

C. ANTONIO MAURA

PLAZA
LEALTAD

Monumento
a los Caídos
por España

Museo del
Ejército

PLAZA
CORTES

**Museo Thyssen-
Bornemisza**

Hotel
Ritz

CALLE FELIPE IV

C. MÉNDEZ NÚÑEZ

Puerta de
Felipe IV

Fuente de
Neptuno

Real Academia
Española

Casón del
Buen Retiro

CORTES

CALLE PRADO

CALLE SAN AGUSTÍN

Hotel
Palace

PLAZA CÁNOVAS
DEL CASTILLO
(PLAZA NEPTUNO)

CALLE JESÚS

CALLE RUIZ DE ALARCÓN

CALLE MORETO

Iglesia de
los Jerónimos

PARQUE

DEL

RETIRO

CALLE CERVANTES

CALLE LEÓN

CALLE LOPE DE VEGA

**Museo
Nacional
del Prado**

JERÓNIMOS

Puerta de
Murillo

CALLE HUERTAS

PLAZA
MURILLO

CALLE ESPALTER

CALLE MORATÍN

COSTANILLA DESAMPARADOS

Antón
Martín

C. GOBERNADOR

La Fábrica
Galería

CALLE SAN PEDRO

CALLE ALAMEDA

PASEO DEL PRADO

REAL JARDÍN BOTÁNICO

Puerta
Real

CALLE ALFONSO XII

C. TORRECILLA DEL LEAL

Antón
Martín

CALLE SANTA ISABEL

CaixaForum

Terraza
Cuadros

Terraza
Escuelas

Plano
Flor

Palacio de
Fernán Núñez

CALLE MARQUÉS DE TOCA

CALLE ATOCHA

CALLE CENICERO

Puerta del
Ángel Caído

LAVAPIÉS

Real Monasterio
de Santa Isabel

Real Conservatorio
de Música

Atocha

CALLE CLAUDIO MOYANO

CALLE SALITRE

CALLE HOSPITAL

PLAZA
EMPERADOR
CARLOS V

Ministerio
de Agricultura

CALLE DOCTOR VELASCO

CALLE ARGUMOSA

Fuente de
la Alcachofa

Atocha

PASEO DE INFANTA ISABEL

Museo Nacional
de Antropología

Atocha Renfe

Atocha
Renfe

C. DOCTOR FOURQUET

**Museo Nacional
Centro de Arte
Reina Sofía**

ATOCHA

Antigua Estación
de Atocha

AVENIDA CIUDAD DE BARCELONA

CALLE VALENCIA

EMBAJADORES

RONDA ATOCHA

PASEO SANTA MARÍA DE LA CABEZA

CALLE MÉNDEZ ÁLVARO

PASEO DELICIAS

Estación
de Atocha

To
Museo del
Ferrocarril

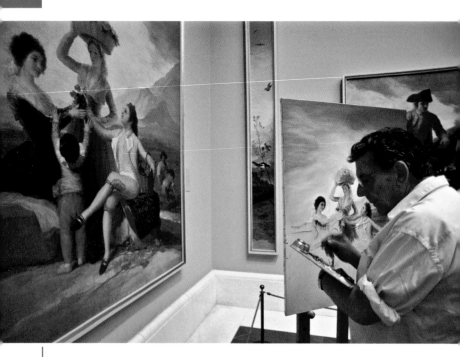

An artist
replicates "La
Vendimia," one
of Francisco de
Goya's tapestry
designs.

Museo Nacional del Prado

THE PRADO IS ONE OF THE GREATEST MUSEUMS IN THE
world, with an awe-inspiring wealth of masterpieces. Although best
known for its collections of works by Velázquez, Goya, and other
Spanish masters, it also has superlative displays of Italian and Flemish
paintings. No matter how determined you are to follow a planned
route, you will be constantly distracted by the breathtaking artworks
that assail your senses as you stroll through the galleries.

Museo Nacional
del Prado

www.museoprado.es

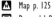 Map p. 125

✉ Paseo del Prado

☎ 91 330 2800

🕐 Closed Mon.

💲 $$. Free Sun.

🚇 Metro: Banco de
España, Atocha

The Prado has always suffered
from a severe lack of space, and it
displays only about 10 percent of
its holdings. This problem is
being at least partially addressed
by the construction of an exten-
sion at the rear of the building.
Designed by Rafael Moneo, it
opens in 2007. Neighboring
buildings are being remodeled as
well to provide more exhibition
rooms (see p. 136).

One of the most important
neoclassic buildings in Spain, the
Prado was designed in 1785 by

Juan de Villanueva (1739–1811)
as a natural history museum.
This museum was intended to be
the focal point of Carlos III's
ambitious plan for the develop-
ment of Paseo del Prado. Progress
on this grand project slowed,
however, following Carlos III's
death in 1788 and came to a
total halt during the War of
Independence (1808–1814), when
the building was used as a bar-
racks by French soldiers.

The possibility of creating a
public museum to display the

royal collections of art had first been suggested by Anton Raphael Mengs in 1775, but the idea did not come to fruition until the reign of Fernando VII. The Prado museum finally opened on November 19, 1819, with about 1,500 paintings on display.

The Prado's works were acquired by different monarchs over the centuries in accordance with their personal tastes and the political circumstances of their reigns, rather than with any intention to create a coherent collection. Carlos V and his son Felipe II were both keen on Venetian artists, particularly Titian. Felipe II was an astute art lover whose taste was influenced by his Flemish aunt. This ruler built up an extensive art collection at El Escorial (see pp. 228–231), a substantial part of which is now in the Prado, including several superb paintings by Hieronymus Bosch.

The more conservative Felipe III favored Rubens, while Felipe IV chose Diego de Velázquez (1599–1660) as court painter. Francisco de Goya (1746–1828) worked for both Carlos III and Carlos IV.

In 1872, the Prado acquired 3,000 works that had been requisitioned as a result of the disentailment of religious property. The Francisco Cambó bequest in 1941 brought an important collection of Italian and Spanish primitive art to the museum.

VISITING THE PRADO

You can enter the Prado at either the north or south end, but not by the main entrance in the middle. As mentioned above, the museum is being expanded, which may mean changes to the displays. Rooms are sometimes closed for restoration or used to house temporary exhibitions, particularly the section at the north end of the first floor. Pick up a floor plan as you go in to check on the current arrangements.

Bear in mind that there is only one restaurant in the Prado, and it consequently gets very busy at peak times. The restaurant is inconveniently located in the basement at the south end, and frankly leaves a lot to be desired. You are not allowed to take bottles of water or other drinks into

the museum. Backpacks of any size must be checked into the cloakroom, but bags of any other shape are okay.

Romanesque & early Spanish art

Starting from the Puerta de Goya at the north end of the ground floor, stop in at **Room 51c** off the rotunda. The room contains 12th-century hunting scenes from the Mozarabic church of San Baudelio de Berlanga in Soria and Romanesque murals from the Santa Cruz chapel in Maderuelo in Segovia. In **Room 50,** don't miss the superb "St. Dominic of Silos Enthroned as Abbot" by Bartolomé Bermejo (circa 1405–1498), a masterpiece of Aragonese painting.

Paintings from Romanesque chapels around Spain have been transferred to the Prado to avoid deterioration in their original settings.

Early Italian painting

As you enter the long **Room 49,** look to your left to see the three panels by Sandro Botticelli (circa 1445–1510), portraying "The Story of Nastagio degli Onesti" (1483) from Boccaccio's *Decameron.* The fourth and final panel is in the Watney Collection in the United States. Opposite is the delicately painted "Annunciation" (circa 1435) by Fra Angelico (circa 1400–1455), which was transferred here from the Monasterio de las Descalzas Reales (see pp. 86–87). The series of paintings by Raphael (1483–1520) chart his evolution as an artist. The most striking is "Portrait of a Cardinal" (circa 1510), with the cardinal in a brilliant red robe.

15th- & 16th-century Spanish painting

Pedro de Berruguete (circa 1450–1504) is credited with moving Hispano-Flemish art forward by introducing Renaissance elements, as illustrated by the fascinating "Auto-da-fé presided over by St. Dominic" (circa 1490) in **Room 57b.** "The Last Supper" by Juan de Juanes (circa

First floor

Ground floor

Puerta de Goya

Puerta de Velázquez

1523–1579) in **Room 56** was painted for the altar of a church in Valencia and is considered to be one of the artist's best works.

Early Flemish & German art

Room 58 houses the exceptionally vivid "Descent from the Cross" by Rogier van der Weyden (1400–1464), which Felipe II inherited from his aunt, María of Hungary. The faces in the painting are brilliantly executed, and the composition leads the eye to the figures of Christ and Mary, whose robe was painted in lapis lazuli. Also in this room is Hans Memling's "Adoration of the Magi" (circa 1470) and "The Virgin and Child" (circa 1460) by Petrus Christus.

There are always crowds in **Room 56a**, which is dominated by the intriguing paintings of satirist Hieronymus Bosch (circa 1450–1516), whose passions ranged from the bawdy to the mystical. "The Garden of Earthly Delights" (circa 1505) depicts "Earthly Paradise" on the left and "Hell" on the right. "The Haywain" (circa 1510) was inspired by a Flemish proverb: "The world is like a haywain from which everyone takes whatever they can." Joachim Patinir's dreamlike landscape "Crossing the Styx" (circa 1515) portrays the Greek myth of Charon taking the dead to Hell.

The Prado's limited holdings of German art are exhibited in **Room 54,** which contains four masterpieces by Albrecht Dürer (1471–1528), including his magnificent "Self-Portrait" (1498) and the panels "Adam" and "Eve" (1507), which were all brought to Spain by Felipe IV.

Room 55b is devoted to

Puerta de Murillo

Italian painting 1300–1800

Spanish painting 1100–1850

Flemish painting 1430–1700

French painting 1600–1800

Dutch painting 1600–1695

German painting 1450–1800

Sculpture

Drawing and exhibition halls

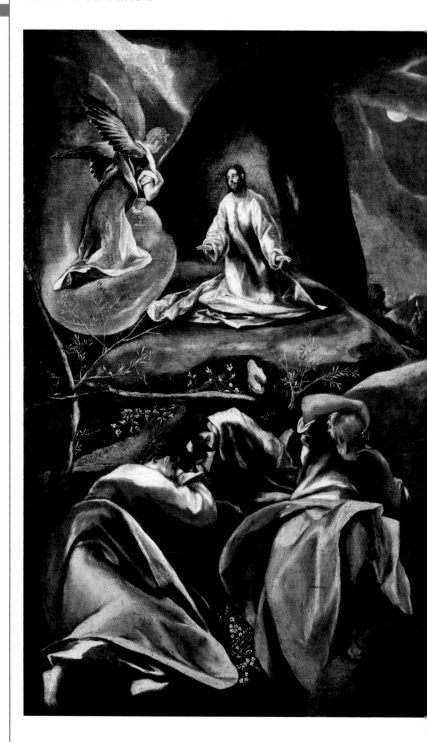

Anthonis Mor (circa 1519–1576), who was court painter to Felipe II. He painted the portrait of Mary Tudor (1554) for Carlos V; it was intended to impress Felipe II, who was considering marriage to Mary at the time. She subsequently became his second wife. Mor's "Pejerón, Jester of the Count of Benavente and the Duke of Alba" (1555) is believed to be the earliest pictorial representation of a jester.

Venetian school

Crossing the central concourse, you move into the south wing, where the next set of rooms is devoted to 16th-century Italian art. In the long **Room 75** is "Christ Washing the Disciples' Feet," also known as "El Lavatorio," by Jacopo Tintoretto (1518–1594), which is a masterpiece of perspective. Take a good look at it while standing to the right of the painting, letting your gaze wander from the figure of Christ across the canvas to the triumphal arch on the left. This painting was one of the many works acquired by Felipe IV from the collections of Charles I of England.

The painters of the Venetian school surpassed all other Renaissance artists with their masterful blending of color and light. Titian (circa 1490–1576) worked extensively for both Carlos V and Felipe II and is well represented in **Rooms 61–63.** "Charles V at the Battle of Mühlberg" (1548) is a brilliantly executed equestrian painting, commissioned to commemorate the emperor's victory over the Protestants in the 1547 battle. Carlos V is not depicted in a triumphant way, however, but rather with a reflective, resigned expression. Titian painted his

"Self-Portrait" late in life, when he was 80 years old. His fame during his lifetime rivaled that of Michelangelo, and it is said that Carlos V once did him the honor of picking up a paintbrush he had dropped.

El Greco

Rooms 60a–62a are devoted to El Greco (1541–1614), starting with early works and moving into his Spanish period when his figures lengthened and he became obsessed with the division between Heaven and Earth. Born in Crete, El Greco (Domenikos Theotokopoulos) spent the last four decades of his life in Toledo, where many of his best works are to be found (see pp. 214–217). "The Nobleman with his Hand on his Breast" (circa 1578), which was restored in the 1990s, depicts a knight of the realm making a solemn promise and has become an iconic image of 16th-century Spain. "The Resurrection," painted two decades later, features his trademark elongated figures and free brush strokes. (See pp. 38–42 for further discussion on Spanish painters.)

Classical and Renaissance sculpture takes up the rest of this floor, but unless this is a particular interest of yours, it is not a priority. Take the stairs at the south end up to the next level.

Goya

Rooms 19–23 and **35–39** at the south end of the first floor contain part of the Prado's superlative collection of works by Francisco de Goya. There is a further selection of his paintings in **Rooms 85** and **90–94** on the second floor, at the same end of the building. It makes sense to go up to see these works before continuing through the first floor.

Opposite: "Christ in the Garden of Olives" by El Greco features the flowing figures and soft tones that are typical of his style.

Goya's self-portraits depict his changing appearance over the years. This one dates from 1815, when he was 69 years old.

Goya was court painter to Carlos IV and painted many portraits of members of the royal family, often depicting them in a less than flattering way. One of his best known works is "The Family of Charles IV" (1800), in which the king looks melancholic, while the sharp-eyed Queen María Luisa is center stage, in charge of proceedings. The queen had 24 pregnancies but bore only 14 children, of whom only 7 survived. In a nod to Velázquez, Goya included himself on the left of the painting. His "Self-Portrait" (1815) is a very honest work, with no airs and graces, painted when he was 69 years old.

Two of Goya's most powerful paintings, "The Second of May, 1808, in Madrid: the Charge of the Mamelukes," and "The Third of May in Madrid: the Executions at Príncipe Pío" (both 1814), depict scenes from the Madrileños' desperate and ultimately unsuccessful efforts to free their city from French occupation (see pp. 204–205). These works have universal resonance, however, brutally conveying the unequivocal message of the absurdity and futility of war.

In the last decade of his life, during a period of deep depression caused by the deaths of his wife and son and by his own illness, Goya produced the perplexing "Black Paintings." Originally painted on the walls of his house by the Manzanares River, these disturbing works were later transferred to canvas and donated to the Prado in 1881. "Dog Half-submerged" seems extraordinarily modern today, with its composition of a dog's head against textured space.

Two canvases that always attract attention are "The Nude Maja" and "The Clothed Maja," which are often said to depict the Duchess of Alba, who was a close friend of Goya's. This attribution may not be true, but the strange position of the heads lends weight to the belief that they may have been added later, obscuring the real identity of the sitter.

Goya worked at the Real Fábrica de Tápices (see p. 172) for almost 20 years, producing a series of designs for tapestries that often depicted local festivals or portrayed the everyday folk of Madrid. "The Parasol" (1777) shows a young man shading a girl with a parasol, through which light filters down onto her face and clothes.

17th-century Spanish painting

Rooms 16–18a on the first floor contain a small selection of the fabulous holdings of Spanish art from the 17th century. If not occupied by a temporary exhibition, the long hall on this floor may also display works from this rich period. The many highlights include "The Holy Family of the Little Bird" by Bartolomé Esteban Murillo (1618–1682) from Seville, which is representative of his

(1591–1652), known as "El Españoleto," include four paintings of hermit saints, including "The Magdalen" (or "Saint Thais"), the sitter for which is believed to have been the artist's daughter. Also look for the ethereal light in "Christ Embracing Saint Bernard" by Francisco Ribalta (1565–1628). Ribalta was

gentle, sympathetic style. His depiction of children and religious figures in domestic settings helped people to identify with the subject matter and earned him enormous popularity both during his lifetime and in the following centuries.

The Prado exhibits only a few works by Francisco de Zurbarán (1598–1664), but all are masterpieces, including the sublime "Still Life," an astoundingly realistic depiction of jars and pots of different materials and textures in shades of cream and brown.

Works by José de Ribera

a key figure in Spanish baroque painting who trained in Madrid but worked mainly in Valencia.

Velázquez

The center of the first floor is devoted to Diego de Velázquez in **Rooms 12, 14, and 15.** The Prado has his best paintings, and the greatest of them all, "Las Meninas" ("The Maids of Honor" or "The Family of Felipe IV"), dominates the oval Room 12. Created circa 1656, it depicts a scene in Velázquez's studio in the Alcázar, when he was painting a portrait of Felipe IV and

Visitors take in the Prado's unparalleled collection of Goya's paintings.

his second wife, Mariana of Austria, who are reflected in the mirror at the back. Velázquez himself observes you from where he stands beside his easel, while the Infanta Margarita, attended by her maids and two dwarves, stares out of the canvas. José Nieto, a court chamberlain, oversees proceedings from the staircase leading down to the studio. If you are lucky enough to visit the Prado when the museum is not too crowded, spend some time looking at this remarkable painting from different angles, and new elements will jump out at you every few seconds.

"The Triumph of Bacchus," more commonly known as "The Topers" (circa 1629), depicts the mythological tale of Bacchus, but in Velázquez's version the god of wine is being worshipped by a group of decidedly unsavory-looking characters, such as might have been regular drinkers in the taverns of Madrid. "The Spinners," also known as "The Fable of Arachne," which was painted almost 30 years later in 1657, also uses ordinary people to portray a mythological subject. Look at the light falling on Arachne's neck and white blouse. Velázquez has managed to make the wheel seem as if it is spinning furiously, making the spokes disappear.

"The Surrender of Breda" (1634–1635), popularly known as "The Lances," was painted for the Hall of Realms of the Palacio del Buen Retiro, a building that is being remodeled to become part of the Prado (see p. 136). When the work is completed, the painting may be hung once again in its original location. It depicts the occasion in 1625 when the Spanish had triumphed over the Dutch at the Siege of Breda. The victor Ambrosio Spinola is shown humbly receiving the key to the town from Justin of Nassau, acknowledging the courage of his adversary.

17th-century Flemish & Dutch art

The north wing of the first floor is largely devoted to the Flemish school in **Rooms 7a–11,** with one work by the Dutch master Rembrandt (1606–1669) in **Room 7.** His renowned "Artemisa" (1634) shows the portly queen of Pergamon receiving the ashes of her husband. The sitter was probably Rembrandt's wife, Saskia. Look for the shadowy figure in the background.

The Prado has about a hundred works by Peter Paul Rubens (1577–1640), but only a small selection is on display. His masterpiece "The Three Graces" (circa 1635) in **Room 9** features the faces of his two wives and depicts companions of Venus who represent the sensual enjoyment of life. Rubens kept this painting in his own collection during his life; after his death it was acquired by Felipe IV.

Room 10a contains a number of portraits by Anthony Van Dyck (1599–1641), including "Sir Endymion Porter and Van Dyck" (circa 1635), in which the artist painted himself standing next to the nobleman.

French painting

The Prado's displays of French art are currently restricted to **Rooms 2–4** at the north end of the first floor. Nicolas Poussin (1594–1665) is represented by several works, some of which were bought to decorate the Palacio del Buen Retiro. These include his painting "Parnassus," which depicts the god Apollo surrounded by the nine muses.

Among the sublime landscapes by Claude Lorrain (1600–1682) is "Embarkation of St. Paula Romana at Ostia," in which the saint is setting off for the Holy Land on a misty early morning. Observe how the light seems to permeate the canvas from the back of the painting.

The Dauphin's treasure

The basement contains part of the collection of gems, crystal, and vessels that originally belonged to the Grand Dauphin Louis, the son of Louis XIV of France. The Grand Dauphin was the father of Felipe V of Spain, who inherited the treasure in 1712. One of the highlights of his collection is an onyx saltcellar decorated with a gold mermaid. There are crystal objects, goblets, and dishes adorned with diamonds, rubies, and emeralds; and other jewels. ■

"The Three Graces" by Rubens is a highlight of the Prado's Flemish and Dutch holdings.

Around the Parado

THE AREA BEHIND THE PRADO IS UNDERGOING GREAT change, with historic buildings being remodeled for new uses as part of the museum. It will be several years before the entire work is finished, but the new space will be well worth the wait.

The 15th-century Iglesia de los Jerónimos anchors the new development around the Prado.

Iglesia de los Jerónimos
✉ Calle Moreto 4
☎ 91 420 3578
🚇 Metro: Banco de España, Atocha

Real Academia Española
www.rae.es
✉ Calle Felipe IV 4
☎ 91 420 1478
🚇 Metro: Banco de España, Atocha

Casón del Buen Retiro
✉ Calle Alfonso XII 28
☎ 91 330 2800
🕐 Closed for restoration until 2008
🚇 Metro: Banco de España, Atocha

The linchpin of these new developments is the **Iglesia de los Jerónimos,** which has played a key role in the development of the area over the centuries. The church is a vestige of the monastery set up here in the 15th century for a community of Hieronymite monks. Carlos V chose the church to swear in his son, the future Felipe II, as the Prince of Asturias in 1528; heirs to the Spanish throne continued to be sworn in here until 1833. Carlos V and later monarchs also used to stay in the monastery's accommodations, which became known as the Buen Retiro, as it was a place for quiet contemplation and prayer. (Later, the grander Palacio del Buen Retiro was built for Felipe IV.)

Rafael Moneo has designed a spectacular extension to the Prado between the church and the Prado's main building. As part of this building plan, the church is being restored, but the 16th-century cloisters will be substantially altered to form part

of the new space, which will have an entrance designed by leading Spanish sculptor Cristina Iglesias. The project's $150,000,000 budget will no doubt increase before it is finished.

Next to the church is the redbrick **Real Academia Española,** or Spanish Royal Academy, a neo-Greek structure designed by Miguel Aguado de la Sierra and completed in 1894. The Academy was founded in 1714 by Felipe V with the aim of protecting and promoting the Spanish language and publishes the *Diccionario de la Lengua Española,* Spain's official dictionary. It is a great honor to be elected as an academician, a privilege usually reserved for renowned writers and poets.

Walking up Calle Felipe IV, you come to the **Casón del Buen Retiro,** which was originally the ballroom of the Palacio del Buen Retiro. The building was designed in 1637 by Alfonso de Carbonell and embellished in 1695 with a vaulted ceiling, on which Lucas Jordán painted "The Allegory of the Golden Fleece." When the restoration work is completed, it will be a study and research center for the museum.

One block farther north, on Calle Méndez Núñez, is the surviving section of the **Palacio del Buen Retiro** (*Calle Méndez Núñez 1, closed for restoration until 2008),* which until 2005 housed the Army Museum. The building will provide administrative space for the Prado. ■

Inside the
venerable
Palace Hotel,
a monument
of elegance

Along the Paseo del Prado

THE NORTHERN HALF OF THE PASEO DEL PRADO, BETWEEN
Plaza de Neptuno and Plaza de Cibeles, was conceived as a public
leisure area. The southern section, from Plaza de Neptuno down to
Atocha, was devoted to science, medicine, and learning, flanked by
the natural history museum (now the Prado), the Botanic Gardens,
and the San Carlos hospital (now the Reina Sofía).

Paseo del Prado
Map p. 125

Back in the 18th century, this
stretch was the eastern edge of the
city and the closest most ordinary
Madrileños got to the countryside.
Known as the Salón del Prado,
the promenade was designed by
engineer José de Hermosilla and

architect Ventura Rodríguez, under
the supervision of the Conde de
Aranda, Carlos III's senior minister.
Hermosilla was responsible for
landscaping the area, while Ventura
Rodríguez was in charge of decorat-
ing the boulevard. The layout is

Palace Hotel

www.starwoodhotels.com

✉ Plaza de las Cortes 7

☎ 91 360 8000

🚇 Metro: Banco de España

Congreso de los Diputados

www.congreso.es

✉ Plaza de las Cortes

☎ 91 390 6000

🕐 Guided tours Sat. a.m., except Aug. & special events

🚇 Metro: Sevilla, Banco de España

Hotel Ritz

www.ritzmadrid.com

✉ Plaza de la Lealtad 5

☎ 91 701 6767

🚇 Metro: Banco de España

typical of the baroque urban style prevalent at the time. It is thought that the arrangement of the fountains (see pp. 142–143) may have been inspired by Piazza Navona in Rome, as Hermosilla had studied there.

Just north of the Prado museum is the junction officially known as Plaza Cánovas del Castillo, after a leading politician who was assassinated in 1897. The square is marked by the Neptune fountain, and in fact is more commonly known as **Plaza de Neptuno.** The southwest corner of the square is occupied by the grand Parisian-style building of the **Palace Hotel** (see p. 249), which opened in 1912 by Alfonso XIII and has a white stuccoed facade decorated with garlands. Designed by Belgian architect Léon Monnoyer, the hotel features a spectacular circular lobby, La Rotonda. The hotel has always been popular with politicians, bullfighters, actors, writers, and artists. Guests over the decades have included Hemingway, Picasso, Dalí, and Madonna.

Just above the hotel is the triangular **Plaza de las Cortes,** with a 19th-century statue of Miguel de Cervantes by Antonio Solá. On the opposite side of the square is the **Congreso de los Diputados,** which houses the Spanish Parliament, known as Las Cortes. Standing on the site of a monastery, the building was designed by Narciso Pascual y Colomer and constructed between 1843 and 1850. The bronze lions on the steps were cast from cannon in 1866. The main door is used only for the State Opening of Parliament, a ceremony presided over by King Juan Carlos. The ceiling of the semielliptical debating chamber,

which was painted by Carlos Luis de Ribera, depicts Isabel II flanked by prominent figures in Spain's history, including Columbus, Cervantes, and Velázquez. An undulating glass extension was built alongside the building in 1990 by the architectural studio of Clos, Rubert de Ventós y Parcerisa.

As you return to the Paseo del Prado, on the left is the **Museo Thyssen-Bornemisza** (see pp. 146–151). Crossing the boulevard, you arrive at the semicircular **Plaza de la Lealtad.** In the center of the square is the **Monumento a los Caídos por España,** a cenotaph with a gran-

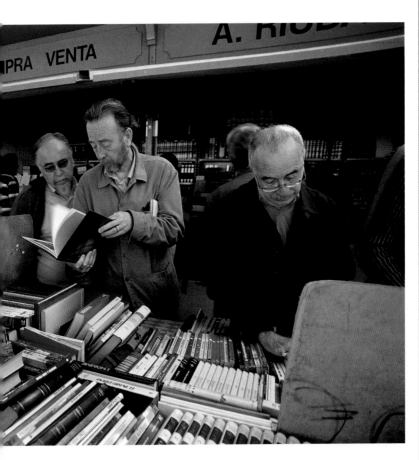

ite obelisk that commemorates those who lost their lives in the battle against French troops on May 2 and 3, 1808 (see pp. 204–205). Some of the worst fighting actually took place on this spot. Completed in 1840, the monument was designed by Isidro González Velázquez. It now also serves as the Tomb of the Unknown Soldier.

On the southeast corner is the sumptuous **Hotel Ritz** (see p. 249), which was designed in 1908 by the French architect Charles Mewes, architect of the Ritz hotels in Paris and London. Until then, the Hotel Paris in the Puerta del Sol had been the most fashionable place to stay in Madrid. The luxurious carpets were handmade at the Real Fábrica de Tápices (see p. 172), which sends expert craftsmen to repair them when necessary. During the Civil War the hotel was used as a hospital. The bar is a soothing place for a drink after a day in the museums, and the terrace is a popular meeting place in summer.

The north side of Plaza de la Lealtad is dominated by the con-cave neoclassic facade of the **Bolsa de Comercio** (Stock Exchange), which was designed by Enrique María Repullés y Vargas and built between 1884

Book-lovers spend hours browsing the stands of used books on the Paseo del Prado.

Bolsa de Comercio
www.bolsamadrid.es/ing /portada.htm
✉ Plaza de la Lealtad 1
☎ 91 589 2264
🚇 Metro: Banco de España

Museo Naval
www.museonavalmadrid
.com

✉ Paseo del Prado 5

☎ 91 379 5299

🕐 Closed Mon., &
Tues.–Sun. p.m.
Guided tours 11
a.m. Sat. & Sun.

🚇 Metro: Banco de
España

**The figure of
Apollo, god of
beauty and the
arts, crowns an
ornate fountain
on the Paseo
del Prado.**

and 1893. The building looks enormous from the front, but the site is triangular, with surprisingly little space behind the facade. The trading floor features an arcaded gallery and an iron and stained-glass vaulted roof.

MUSEO NAVAL

As you walk north up the Paseo del Prado, on the right you'll see the Museo Naval, which specializes in Spain's seafaring history.

In **Room 1,** which deals with the reign of the Catholic Monarchs at the end of the 15th century, you will find documents written by Christopher Columbus on his arrival in Santo Domingo. **Room 5** contains the bronze cannon that were used

in the Siege of Gibraltar (1780–1783), and **Room 7** charts the events of the Battle of Trafalgar in 1805. A model of one of the ships that took part in the battle, the *Santa Ana,* is in the **Central Patio. Room 8** contains nautical instruments, including compasses and sextants. Also in this room is a model of the submarine designed by Isaac Peral (1851–1895) in 1888. **Room 16** is devoted to General Franco and King Juan Carlos. Exhibits include the curiously small uniform that Franco wore as commander-in-chief of the armed forces and a model of the aircraft carrier *Príncipe de Asturias,* which is the flagship of the Spanish fleet.

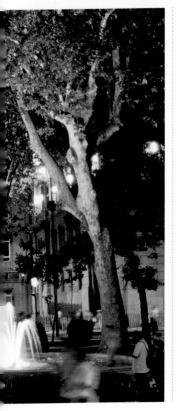

The highlights of the museum are found in **Room 17,** which deals with Spain's principal voyages of discovery from the 15th to the 18th centuries. The museum's most important exhibit is a parchment map that was the first document to show the New World. It was drawn in 1500 by Juan de la Cosa in El Puerto de Santa María near Cádiz, probably for the Catholic Monarchs. It shows places discovered by Columbus in 1492, 1493, and 1498. The Mediterranean is depicted fairly accurately, and Africa shows the latest Portuguese discoveries. The Asian continent and its archipelagos, however, are incomplete and only vaguely drawn.

Also in this room are two globes made by Coronelli in the late 17th century and an astronomical pendulum made in the 18th century by John Ellicott. **Room 18** is devoted to nautical sciences and contains an interesting collection of quadrants and astrolabes from the 16th to the 19th centuries. ■

The elegant Stock Exchange, built at the end of the 19th century, experiences an unusually quiet moment.

The Paseo's fountains

Eight *fuentes* (fountains) adorn the Paseo del Prado, all part of the original plan to develop the boulevard as an area of leisure in the late 18th century. The scheme was instigated by Carlos III, who was astonished by the lack of sophistication in Madrid when he arrived from Naples to take the throne. Ventura Rodríguez, the king's favorite architect, devised the overall concept for the fountains, which were made by leading sculptors of the day. The fountains are linked by a broad promenade that soon became popular with the Madrileños as a place to see and be seen.

The splendid **Fuente de la Cibeles,** crowned by the figure of Cybele, goddess of nature, punctuates the Paseo del Prado's north end; she is riding in a chariot drawn by two lions. One of Madrid's most important symbols, the monument symbolizes the fertility of the surrounding land. The fountain was made in the late 18th century by Francisco Gutiérrez and Robert Michel, but the cherubs were added at the end of the 19th century.

Originally Cybele faced south down the boulevard, but she was moved in 1891 to look toward the Puerta del Sol. As part of the Prado-Recoletos development plan, the fountain will be moved again. It is a place of pilgrimage for supporters of the Real Madrid soccer team; they congregate there after important wins and jump in the fountain.

Halfway down the center of the Paseo you reach the **Fuente de Apolo,** almost concealed among the trees, with a circular pool on each side of the central spray. The figure of Apollo, god of beauty and the arts, was sculpted by Manuel Álvarez and Alfonso Giraldo Bergaz. Four figures representing the seasons surround Apollo. Completed in 1802, the fountain has been restored several times, as the porous stone used to make it, from Redueña east of Madrid, erodes easily.

The Paseo del Prado is divided in two by Plaza de Cánovas del Castillo, more usually known as Plaza de Neptuno because of its

Fuente de Neptuno. Sculpted in marble by Juan Pascual de Mena, José Arias, and José Rodríguez between 1780 and 1786, it is a tribute to Spain's colonies and the Navy. Neptune, god of the sea, stands on a horse-drawn chariot shaped like a shell, holding a trident.

At the south end of the Prado museum is **Plaza de Murillo,** where there are four fountains of nymphs and water gods playing with dolphins. They were made between 1777 and 1782 of Colmenar stone by Robert Michel, Francisco Gutiérrez, Narciso Aldeb, José Rodríguez, and Alfonso Giraldo Bergaz. The fountains are a bit lost in their current location between the Prado and the Royal Botanic Garden, but should regain importance when they are moved as part of the remodeling.

The end of the Paseo del Prado is marked by the **Fuente de la Alcochofa** (Artichoke fountain) in the Glorieta de Atocha. This is a replica; the original was moved to the Parque del Retiro (see pp. 164–167) in 1880. It was sculpted in 1781 by Alfonso Giraldo Bergaz and Antonio Primo. Water flows from the bronze artichoke at the top of the fountain, which is supported by four cherubs. The artichoke is an allegory of the way wisdom must be discovered by gradually peeling away outer layers. It also represents life and health, as it is situated between the Reina Sofia museum, originally a hospital, and the Royal Botanic Garden. ■

The Neptune fountain (above) pays homage to the sea, while Cybele (left) represents the fertile land around the city. The Artichoke fountain (below) is a symbol of the many layers of wisdom.

Plaza de Cibeles

Plaza de Cibeles
🅐 Map p. 125

**Casa de América
(Palacio de
Linares)**
www.casamerica.es
✉ Entrance at Paseo
de Recoletos 2
☎ 91 595 4800
🕐 Closed Sun. p.m. &
Mon.
Ⓜ Metro: Banco de
España

PLAZA DE CIBELES IS THE PLACE WHERE MADRID'S NORTH-south and east-west thoroughfares meet. Because the plaza is a major traffic hub, it is currently difficult for pedestrians to get a decent view of the grand buildings surrounding it, let alone get anywhere near the grand fountain of the goddess Cybele (see pp. 142–143) in the center. When the area is redone in 2008, however, pedestrians will be able to get around the square more comfortably.

The southwest corner is occupied by the enormous **Banco de España,** the facades of which stretch down the Paseo del Prado and up Calle Alcalá. Founded in the mid-19th century, the bank moved to this landmark site, in what was then the new commercial district, in 1891. The trading floor, added in 1929–1930, was inspired by Roman baths. The ornate corner section facing Plaza de Cibeles was originally the main entrance and is decorated with sculptures by Jerónimo Suñol. The bank, which unfortunately is not currently open to the public, has a formidable art collection, including works by Goya and Zurbarán as well as leading contemporary artists.

In contrast to the forbidding Banco de España, the **Palacio de Comunicaciones** on the southeast corner is an exuberant example of the architecture of Antonio Palacios, who designed many of the signature buildings in this area. Curving around the crossroads, the ornate white structure looks like a cathedral, but it was actually built to be the city's main post office at the beginning of the 20th century. It operated as such for nearly a hundred years, and it is now slated to become the City Hall, which will move its headquarters from the present site in Plaza de la Villa (see p. 56). Although this is regarded as the architect's masterpiece, the

Palacio was one of his first buildings, designed with his partners Julián and Joaquín Otamendi. The three successfully combined Spanish style with new ideas from Chicago, New York, and Paris.

The **Palacio de Linares,** on

the other side of Calle Alcalá on the northeast corner, was built as a private residence for the Marquis of Linares in the second half of the 19th century. It is now part of the **Casa de América** cultural center, which stages exhibitions and other activities, usually related to Latin America, in the section at the rear.

Designed by Carlos Colubi and Adolphe Ombrecht, the neobaroque palace has a lavish interior, but this is not currently open to the public. The layout inside is unusual, as the marquis found out from his dying father that his wife was actually his half-sister.

The marquis then devised the residence as two separate apartments, so that the couple could live in the same house, but not as man and wife. The palace was closed up for many years, during which time there were quite a few sightings of ghosts.

An even grander palace is set back on landscaped grounds on the corner between the Paseo de Recoletos and Calle Alcalá. Currently housing the General Army headquarters, the **Palacio de Buenavista** (closed to the public) was built for the Duke of Alba by Juan Pedro Arnal in the late 18th century. ∎

Plaza de Cibeles is dominated by the majestic Palacio de Comunicaciones, the city's main post office for almost a century.

Museo Thyssen-Bornemisza

Museo Thyssen-Bornemisza
www.museothyssen.org

⚐ Map p. 125

✉ Palacio de Villahermosa, Paseo del Prado 8

☎ 91 420 3944

🕐 Closed Mon.

💲 $$

🚇 Metro: Banco de España

THE DISPLAYS AT THIS OUTSTANDING MUSEUM REPRESENT the best of Western art from the past 800 years. Begun in the 1920s by Baron Heinrich Thyssen-Bornemisza and consolidated by his son, Hans Heinrich, the collection is considered one of the best in the world. In 2004, the museum took in the Carmen Thyssen-Bornemisza Collection, which specializes in landscape painting.

The artworks were originally kept at the family home, Villa Favorita, in Lugano, Switzerland, but after expanding the collection with hundreds of modern paintings, Baron Hans Heinrich Thyssen-Bornemisza looked for a venue where they could be put on public view. Several countries vied for the prestigious collection, but the baron decided on the Palacio de Villahermosa in Madrid, a grand 18th-century neoclassic mansion on the Paseo del Prado. After the building was remodeled by Rafael Moneo, the collection was installed in 1992. Since the baron's death in 2002, the museum has been overseen by his widow.

VISITING THE MUSEUM
The displays comprise about a thousand exhibits, the majority of which are paintings, but the museum also contains sculptures, tapestries, and decorative objects. Displays are exhibited chronologically on three floors, starting on the second floor and working down to the ground floor. The museum has an excellent café and restaurant in the basement and a good store on the ground floor.

Early art
Starting on the second floor, work your way around counterclockwise. **Room 1** contains Italian primitives, among them "Christ and the Samaritan

Woman" by Duccio di Buoninsegna (1278–1319), the only artist known to have signed his work at this time. **Room 3** displays early Flemish art. Be careful not to miss the tiny panel by Petrus Christus from Bruges called "Our Lady of the Dry Tree" (circa 1465), which is one of the highlights of the museum. It portrays a story from the Old Testament about the Virgin Mary bringing new life to the chosen people. Also in this room is "The Annunciation," a diptych by Jan van Eyck, which looks like carved stone, and the intricate "Enthroned Madonna" by Rogier van der Weyden (1400–1464). In **Room 4**, look for "The Resurrected Christ" by Milanese artist Bramantino, a seminal work of the Italian Quattrocento.

Room 5 contains some exceptional Renaissance portraits. One of the best known works in the museum is Domenico Ghirlandaio's "Portrait of Giovanna Tornabuoni" (1488), a representation of perfection. The Latin epigram on the portrait is from the first-century poet Martial and says "Art, if only you could portray character and moral qualities, there would not be a more beautiful painting in the world." Hans Holbein the Younger's masterly "King Henry VIII," which depicts the English monarch looking coolly regal, is

Opposite:
The portrait of King Henry VIII by Hans Holbein the Younger, dating from 1536, depicts the monarch in a confident mood.

The museum showcases an outstanding collection of Derick Baegert's work, representing the best of late 15th-century art of the Rhineland.

one of the most valuable paintings in the collection. There is also a delightful portrait of Catherine of Aragón, Henry's first wife, by Juan de Flandes.

16th-century German & Italian art

You now enter the long **Room 6,** the Villahermosa Gallery, which displays "Portrait of a Young Man" by Raphael (1483–1520). Rooms 7–12 run alongside. The highlight in **Room 7** is Vittore Carpaccio's "Young Knight in a Landscape" (1510), which is thought to be one of the earliest full-length portraits.

The German paintings in **Rooms 8 and 9** include "Jesus among the Doctors" (1506) by Albrecht Dürer (1471–1528), which portrays Christ as a young man surrounded by inquisitive old men and draws the eye to the hands at the center. There are also several works by Derick Baegert (circa 1440–1515), including a triptych of Christ's Crucifixion.

In **Room 10,** the "Reclining Nymph" by Lucas Cranach the Elder (1472–1553) has a superbly painted transparent veil. Artists of the Venetian school, including Titian, Tintoretto, and Bassano, are displayed in **Rooms 11 and 12.** Titian's "St. Jerome in the Wilderness" (circa 1575) was painted at the end of his life. El Greco appears here because he

The final section on this floor, **Rooms 19, 20, and 21,** contain Flemish and Dutch paintings, including superlative works by Van Dyck, Brueghel, and Rubens, especially his "Toilet of Venus." Don't miss Rembrandt's penetrating "Self-Portrait" in **Room 21.**

17th-century Dutch & Flemish painting

Going down to the first floor, the first section, **Rooms 22–27,** contains some elegantly composed scenes of daily life, interiors, and landscapes by artists including Frans Hals and Pieter de Hooch. The still lifes in **Room 27** include an intriguing work by Willem Claesz Heda (circa 1593–circa 1680), which shows a magnificent array of silverware and glass beside a half-eaten pie.

19th-century American & European painting

Rooms 29 and 30 contain landscapes by artists of the Hudson River school. There are several seascapes by Fitz Lane and Martin Johnson Heade, pioneers of the Luminist school.

Room 31 marks an abrupt change of style to European Romanticism, with a wall of Goya, Géricault, and Delacroix, followed by Courbet and Constable. The Impressionists are in **Rooms 32 and 33.** Highlights include Renoir's "Woman with Parasol" (1873) and two exquisite pastels on paper by Edgar Degas: "Swaying Dancer" and "At the Milliner's." Vincent van Gogh's "Les Vessenots" (1890), in thick impasto, was painted shortly before he committed suicide.

Modernism

The modern art collection begins in **Room 34** with André Derain

began his working career in Italy. An early Caravaggio canvas, "St. Catherine of Alexandria" (circa 1597), shows Flemish influences.

17th- & 18th-century baroque

Rooms 13–18 contain early baroque works, including "San Sebastián" and "La Piedad" by Bernini (1598–1680). Francisco de Zurbarán's (1598–1664) "Santa Casilda" (circa 1630) depicts the saint as a serious young woman, set against the artist's trademark dark background. There are also splendid views of Venice by Canaletto (1697–1768) and Francesco Guardi (1712–1793).

(1880–1954) and the other fauves ("wild beasts"), so called because they seemed to break all the rules. **Rooms 35–40** display the museum's superlative collection of German expressionists. The Dresden-based group known as Die Brücke is represented by Emil Nolde, Karl Schmidt-Rottluff, and Ernst Ludwig Kirchner. The Blaue Reiter artists emerged from the magazine of the same name, founded in 1912 in Munich. There are works here by several of its members, including Franz Marc (1880–1916) and Wassily Kandinsky (1866–1944). The last room on this floor contains more objective and realistic works, including "Metropolis" by Georg Grosz (1893–1959) and "Hugo Erfurth with a Dog" by Otto Dix (1891–1969).

On the ground floor, **Rooms 41–44** are devoted to the experimental avant-gardes, with examples of cubism, futurism, constructivism, dadaism, and surrealism. There are works by Braque, Léger, and Juan Gris; Picasso is represented by "Man with a Clarinet" and "Head of a Man." Geometrical abstraction is represented by Moholy-Nagy, El Lissitzky, Schwitters, and Mondrian. The United States rules in **Room 46,** with abstract expressionism by Rothko, O'Keeffe, and De Kooning.

The final section, **Rooms 47 and 48,** rounds things off with surrealism, figurative tradition, and pop art, with works by artists including Salvador Dalí, David Hockney, Francis Bacon, Edward Hopper, R.B. Kitaj, James Rosenquist, and Yves Tanguy.

CARMEN THYSSEN-BORNEMISZA COLLECTION

Two buildings adjoining the Palacio de Villahermosa were remodeled to house the collection of the baroness, which includes about 200 works. The displays are arranged over two floors, which are accessed from the second floor of the main building. The ground floor of the area is used for temporary exhibitions. This collection was begun in the 1980s and ranges from 17th-century Dutch painting to examples of the 20th-century avant-garde.

Rooms A and B contain early Flemish and Italian art. "The Judgment of Solomon" by Lucas Jordán shows the influence of Caravaggio. There is an exquisite "Christ on the Cross" by Van Dyck, and Brueghel the Elder is represented by "The Garden of Eden." **Room C** is a long gallery that charts the development of landscape painting over four centuries. Look for Constable's "The Lock," which is one of the masterpieces of the collection. There is an interesting section devoted to the 18th-century vogue for architectural urban views, as well as superb works by Corot and van Gogh.

There is more 18th-century work in **Room D,** with examples of the rococo influences on French and Italian art, illustrated by the paintings of Boucher, Fragonard, and Piazzetta.

The North American 19th-century landscapes in **Rooms E and F** include work by such luminaries of the genre as Martin Johnson Heade, Sandford Robinson Gifford, and Frederic Edwin Church. **Room G** exhibits work by artists from the Barbizon school in France and the Hague school in Holland, both of which introduced a more naturalistic approach to landscape paintings. Artists include Courbet, Corot, Rousseau, and Boudin. **Room H** deals with early Impressionism, featuring work by Degas, Monet, Pissarro, Renoir, and Sisley.

The displays continue downstairs on the first floor in **Room I,** which is devoted to Auguste Rodin (1840–1917). The marble sculptures there were commissioned by August Thyssen in 1905 and are considered to be among the best examples of Rodin's work. Other pieces from this group are distributed throughout the exhibition rooms. This space is unusual in that it is an original room from the Palacio de Goyeneche, one of the two buildings that were converted to create this new part of the museum.

Room J shows how American art was influenced by European Impressionism in the last two decades of the 19th century, with works by Sargent, Metcalf, and Frieseke. The exhibits of late Impressionism in **Room K** include several masterpieces. Look for Monet's "Charing Cross Bridge" and Gauguin's "Orchard below Bihorel Church." More works by Gauguin can be found in **Room L,** including the superb "Allées et Venues, Martinique" and "Mata Mua." Also in this room are paintings by Bonnard and Vuillard. **Room M** moves onto Post-Impressionism, illustrated by Toulouse-Lautrec, Nolde, and Munch.

German expressionism is well represented in **Room N,** with excellent paintings by Kokoschka, Kandinsky, and Kirchner. Don't miss Erich Heckel's sublime "The House at Dangast." The emergence of fauvism in the beginning of the 20th century is addressed in **Room O,** with works including "The Midi Canal" by Matisse and "Harbor at L'Éstaque" by Braque. **Room P** is devoted to cubism, illustrated by Picasso's "The Harvesters" (1907), "Seated Woman" by Juan Gris, and "Still Life with Bananas" by Raoul Dufy. ∎

The Carmen Thyssen-Bornemisza Collection is displayed in an extension to the museum's original building.

Real Jardín Botánico

THE ROYAL BOTANIC GARDEN WAS FOUNDED IN 1755 BY Fernando VI on the banks of the Manzanares River. It was transferred here by Carlos III in 1781 as part of his plans to create a science hub along the lower part of the Paseo del Prado. The garden contains more than 30,000 plant species from all over the world and is a soothing place to stroll after a morning in the Prado.

A neoclassic entrance gate leads to the three levels of the Real Jardín Botánico.

Real Jardín Botánico
www.rjb.csic.es

- Map p. 125
- Plaza de Murillo 2
- 91 420 3017
- $
- Metro: Atocha

The design of the project was begun by Francesco Sabatini, who died before completing the project. It was continued by Juan de Villanueva with the collaboration of the botanist Casimiro Gómez Ortega. Their aim was to create a research center for the cultivation of species brought to Spain by the botanic expeditions of the late 18th century.

As you go in, take a look at the elegant neoclassic entrance gate, the **Puerta de Murillo,** which was designed by Juan de Villanueva in 1789 and is flanked by two sets of Doric columns. The garden is arranged across three levels, with a pavilion at the top where temporary exhibitions are held.

The lower level is called the **Terraza de los Cuadros** and is divided into 16 beds. In **Bed C3** there is a beautiful pomegranate tree that is thought to be 200 years old. At 23 feet (7 m), it is seven feet taller than these trees normally grow. The pomegranate was brought to Spain by the Arabs, who planted it extensively in the Nasrid kingdom of Granada, which took its name from the tree.

Beds C5 and C6 contain medicinal plants, which have

been cultivated here since the garden was founded and are given out free to the public. Originally, these plants were grown to provide supplies for the neighboring Hospital General de San Carlos, which is now the Reina Sofía museum.

Between **Beds C7 and C10,** which hold old varieties of roses, the Paseo de Carlos III leads down to the **Puerta Real,** a granite entrance arch that was designed by Sabatini and commemorates Carlos III. **Bed C12** contains a small selection of the one thousand species of plants that grow only in Spain. Many of these species are found in very few areas of the country and are in danger of extinction. **Bed 13** is laid out as a market garden with plants that are traditionally grown for food. Many of them were brought back from the botanic expeditions to the New World in the 18th century.

The second level is the **Terraza de las Escuelas Botánicas,** which contains plants and trees from different botanical schools. One of the most distinctive examples is an elm known as "Pantalones" because its trunk is divided into two branches that resemble a pair of pants. The tree is 200 years old and 112 feet (34 m) high with a diameter of 8 feet (2.4 m). There are several sequoias as well, evergreens that can grow taller than 100 feet (30 m) and live for several thousand years.

The next level, the **Terraza del Plano de la Flor,** was remodeled in the mid-19th century. It is arranged around an oval pond with a bust of the pioneering Swedish botanist Karl von Linné (1707–1778), who devised the binomial nomenclature used to classify plant species.

The pond is surrounded by beautiful trees, including a hundred-year-old Canarian palm.

Behind it is a neoclassic **pavilion** designed by Villanueva in 1781. This was originally intended as a hothouse for the cultivation of the most delicate species brought from America at

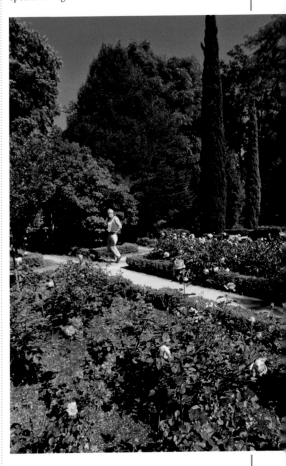

that time. The central space, which was added in 1794, houses a lecture theater named after Antonio José Cavanilles, one of the many renowned botanists who taught there. Restored in the 1980s, it is now used for temporary exhibitions. ∎

The gardens feature many older varieties of rose.

Museo Reina Sofía

Museo Reina Sofía
www.museoreinasofia.es

- Map p. 125
- Calle Santa Isabel 52
- 91 467 5062
- Closed Sun. p.m. & Tues.
- $. Free Sat p.m. & Sun. a.m.
- Metro: Atocha

THIS VAST MUSEUM (KNOWN OFFICIALLY AS THE MUSEO Nacional Centro de Arte Reina Sofía) is undergoing a far-reaching expansion program aimed at strengthening its position in the contemporary art world. Its collections of Spanish 20th-century art include works by Salvador Dalí, Joan Miró, Jorge de Oteiza, and Antoni Tàpies, but the undisputed highlight of the museum is Picasso's masterpiece "Guernica," which draws visitors from around the world.

The museum's international collections include works by artists of the caliber of Julian Schnabel, Donald Judd, Gerhard Richter, and Anish Kapoor. At least three temporary shows are usually running, and the museum also sponsors interesting cultural activities and concerts.

The Reina Sofía occupies the former Hospital de San Carlos, the monumental bulk of which is reminiscent of the monastery at El Escorial (see pp. 228–231). Although it was designed by José de Hermosilla in the mid-18th century, much of the construction was overseen by Francesco Sabatini in the reign of Carlos III. The hospital most innovative chefs in Spain.

The museum plans to remodel the original building so that the permanent collection can be displayed on four floors. The work will take place in stages, beginning in 2007 and lasting four years. The collection will be displayed chronologically, charting the artistic developments of the 20th century as exemplified by such Spanish masters as Picasso, Miró, Dalí, Juan Gris, José Gutiérrez Solana, and Sorolla. The increased exhibition space will also allow some of the museum's extensive holdings of video art, photography, contemporary design, and decorative arts to be displayed.

VISITING THE MUSEUM

The permanent collection is currently exhibited on two floors, with about 500 works on display. The visit begins on **Floor 2,** which you reach via a glass elevator. The 17 rooms on this floor contain artworks dating from the end of the 19th century to the period immediately after World War II.

At the turn of the 20th century in Spain, artists were particularly active in the Basque country and Catalunya. Work by leading artists from these two regions is exhibited in **Room 1.** Artists include Ignacio Zuloaga, Francisco Iturrino, Hermenegildo Anglada-Camarasa, Santiago Rusiñol, and María Blanchard. Madrid produced the more experimental Solana, who has **Room 2** to himself. Solana was a key figure in the *tertulia* discussion groups that formed an essential part of Madrid café society in the first decades of the 20th century (see pp. 118–119). The members of one of the most influential groups are portrayed in "The Gathering at the Café Pombo" (1920), which features

Left: Picasso's "Guernica," which protests Franco's atrocities against the civilian population in a Basque village, is considered modern art's most powerful antiwar statement.

remained open until 1965, but then deteriorated to such an extent that there was talk of demolishing the building. Owing to its historical interest, however, it was decided to renovate and remodel it to create a permanent home for the Spanish collection of contemporary art. The Museo Reina Sofía opened in 1986.

In 2005, a spectacular extension designed by renowned French architect Jean Nouvel added two new spaces for temporary exhibitions, as well as a library, research center, bookstore, and two auditoriums. Together these areas form a triangle around a central atrium under a red metal roof. There is also a café and restaurant run by Sergi Arola, one of the best and writer Ramón Gómez de la Serna and Solana himself.

Room 3 takes you through constructivism and cubism. Keep an eye out for the striking colors of Robert and Sonia Delauney, who visited Spain during World War I, as well as the geometrical forms of Joaquín Torres García (1874–1949). The cubist artist Juan Gris (1887–1927), who was born in Madrid and lived in Paris, occupies **Room 4** with a series of superb works including a portrait of his wife, "Josette" (1916), and "The Guitar in Front of the Sea" (1925), painted at the end of his life. The twisting bronze and iron sculptures of Pablo Gargallo, including "The Great Prophet" (1933), are displayed in **Room 5** at the end of this wing.

Picasso

Room 6 is devoted to Pablo Picasso (1881–1973), the most influential artist of the 20th century. In this room you are confronted by the shocking canvas of "Guernica" (1937), revealed in all its tortured, monochromatic splendor. Painted in less than two months for the Spanish Pavilion at the 1937 Paris World's Fair, it was a protest against the bombing of the Basque town of Gernika-Lumo by German aircraft on the orders of General Franco during Spain's Civil War (1936–1939). There was worldwide outrage when photographs of the attack appeared in newspapers, and the images affected Picasso so deeply that he was driven to produce the painting that would become a universal symbol of the brutality of war.

Also in this room are preparatory sketches for the painting, as well as other works including "The Woman in Blue," painted during a stay in Madrid in 1901 when Picasso was 20 years old.

Miró & González

Room 7, which runs parallel to the Picasso gallery, gives a wonderful overview of the career of the seminal Catalan artist Joan Miró (1893–1983). Among the colorful paintings are "Snail, Woman, Flower, Star" (1934) and "Portrait II" (1938). Miró's delightful sculptures, which include "Moon Bird" (1966), a huge black bronze of a horned creature, are in **Room 16.**

Room 8 features Julio González (1876–1942), trained as a welder and known for his use of iron. One of his wittiest sculptures is the self-portrait "Head Called 'The Rabbit' " (1930).

Surrealists

Development in Salvador Dalí's art is traced in **Room 10,** where works by the archsurrealist include "Cenicitas" (1928) and "The Great Masturbator" (1929), which was painted in the year he filmed the seminal movie *Un Chien Andalou* with Luis Buñuel. The range of his artistic style is illustrated by the realism of an earlier work, "Girl at the Window" (1925). His "Portrait of Joella" (1933) in **Room 11** is an oil and plaster sculpture that he made with the collaboration of Man Ray. **Room 12** is devoted to the pioneering surrealist filmmaker Luis Buñuel (1900–1983). You can see screenings of his films, which are regarded as some of the most important creative works of 20th-century Spain.

1920s–1940s

The final stretch on this floor contains pieces by artists working in Spain in the period until just after the Civil War. One of the strangest paintings is "Accidente" by Alfonso Ponce de León in **Room 13.** It was painted in 1936, a few months before the artist was killed in a car accident at the age of 36. Spookily, the painting shows a sharply dressed man in a blue suit, clutching a bloodstained handkerchief to his head after being ejected from a car. Also worth a look in this section is the work of neo-cubist Benjamín Palencia (1894–1980), whose works appear again in **Room 15** with sculptures by Alberto Sánchez from the period around World War II.

Postwar

Take the elevator to **Floor 4,** where **Room 18** concentrates on Spanish art after the Civil War and **Room 19** displays figurative work and early canvases by Antoni Tàpies (born 1923),

Spain's greatest living artist. Tàpies was a founding member of the influential Dau al Set group, which began in Barcelona in 1948. The collection then focuses on the genesis of abstract art in Spain in **Rooms 20–23.** The exuberant canvases of José Guerrero contrast with the geometric iron sculptures of Basque artist Jorge de Oteiza.

International artists reappear in **Room 24** with powerful works by Francis Bacon, Henry Moore, Graham Sutherland, Pierre Alechinsky, and Asger Jorn, culminating in an excellent display of pieces by the brilliant French artist Yves Klein (1928–1962). His Italian counterpart Lucio Fontana (1899–1968), the master of slashed, perforated, monochrome canvases, has good coverage in **Room 26.**

Schoolchildren learn about the bold colors and abstract shapes used by the Catalan artist Joan Miró in his "Mujer, párajo y estrella" (1970).

The large spaces in the Reina Sofía are particularly suitable for exhibiting installation work.

The energetic brush strokes of Antonio Saura (1930–1998) are prominent in **Room 29,** next to international artists Jean Dubuffet, Yves Klein, and Mark Tobey in **Room 30. Room 32** features Pablo Palazuelo's outstanding steel sculptures. The leading figures of the arte povera movement, including Mario Merz and Jannis Kounellis, are represented in **Room 33.**

The American abstract expressionist Robert Motherwell (1915–1991) appears in a large section dedicated to Antoni Tàpies in **Rooms 34–35.** The fusion of sculpture and painting pioneered by Tàpies is well illustrated by the superb piece "Superposition of Gray Material" (1961). This work is an excellent example of his trademark *matèrica* technique of layering different textures, often using clay, earth, and sand.

Rooms 37–39 contrast Eduardo Arroyo's bold narrative pictures with the issue-conscious pop art of the Equipo Crónica partnership and its Spanish contemporaries. Also in these rooms look for the figurative paintings of Guillermo Pérez Villalta, one of Spain's most interesting contemporary artists.

The adjacent **Room 44** is devoted to video art, with installations by Jordi Colomer, Carles Congost, and Susy Gómez.

Room 41 contains some superlative American minimalist art from the 1960s and '70s, with work by such internationally renowned figures as Dan Flavin, Ellsworth Kelly, Barnett Newman, Bruce Nauman, Robert Mangold, and Donald Judd, who is represented by a group of open-sided cubes. Don't miss the stunning steel, iron, and alabaster sculptures of Basque artist Eduardo Chillida (1924–2002), one of the leading creative figures of the 20th century, in **Rooms 42–43.**

The final section of this floor, **Rooms 40 and 45,** contains a wide range of Spanish and international art from the last two decades of the 20th century, including works of sculpture and photography. Artists include Miquel Barceló, Ferrán García Sevilla, Juan Muñoz, Cristina Iglesias, Thomas Ruff, Anish Kapoor, Jean Marc Bustamente, and Günther Förg. ∎

Picasso's "L'Hombre del Cordero" sculpture ("Man with a Sheep," 1943) and other works showcased at the museum represent the Catalan's variety of styles.

More places to visit around the Paseo del Prado

CAIXAFORUM

This 19th-century electricity plant just off the Paseo del Prado is being converted into an art venue for the prestigious Fundación La Caixa (see pp. 183–184), run by Catalunya's largest savings bank. Designed by leading Swiss architects Herzog & de Meuron, the building is scheduled to open in 2007. La Caixa has a distinguished collection of Spanish and international contemporary art, part of which is installed in its flagship museum in Barcelona. This building will show selections from the permanent collection as well as stage temporary exhibitions and other cultural activities. Located between the Prado and the Reina Sofía, it will add strength to the already powerful artistic punch of Madrid's museum mile. www.lacaixa.es 🗺 Map p. 125 ✉ Calle Almadén & Calle Cenicero ☎ 902 223 040 🚇 Metro: Atocha

LA FÁBRICA GALERÍA

Top international artists such as Sol LeWitt exhibit at this lively space, which also runs a program of cultural activities and art events, including dance, theater and other performances once a month on Monday nights. It specializes in photographic shows and video installations, and is one of the main venues during the PhotoEspaña festival in June and July. La Fábrica also publishes art books and magazines. www.lafabricagaleria.com 🗺 Map p. 125 ✉ Calle Alameda 9 ☎ 91 360 1325 🕐 Closed Sun. & Mon. 🚇 Metro: Atocha

MUSEO DEL FERROCARRIL

The Estación de las Delicias, an elegant late 19th-century ironwork railroad station, has been converted to house a railway museum. A good place to take children, it features exhibits including steam engines, model railways, and station clocks. Displays illustrate all the different elements that make up a railroad network and how they work. www.museodelferrocarril.org 🗺 Map p. 125 ✉ Paseo de las Delicias 61 ☎ 902 228 822 🕐 Closed Mon. & Aug. 💲 $. Free Sat. 🚇 Metro: Delicias

MUSEO POSTAL Y TELEGRÁFICO

The museum charts the development of postal services beginning in the 13th century, when mail was delivered by messengers on horseback, to the creation of a railroad mail system in the second half of the 19th century. Displays include Spain's first postage stamp, produced in 1850, along with machines and materials used to make stamps. The extensive stamp collections feature many first-day issues from all over the world, and 19th-century examples from Cuba, the Philippines, and Puerto Rico. One section deals with the history of telecommunications, including a model of the Hispasat satellite. www.correos.es 🗺 Map p. 125 ✉ Calle Montalbán ☎ 91 396 2679 🕐 Closed Sat. p.m. & Sun. 🚇 Metro: Banco.

PALACIO DE FERNÁN NÚÑEZ

This sumptuous mansion was built in the mid-19th century for the Duke and Duchess of Fernán Núñez and is now occupied by Renfe, the Spanish railway network. Although used as a stronghold by republicans in the Civil War, the palace is incredibly well preserved with a series of lavish reception rooms decorated with antiques and handmade carpets from the Real Fábrica de Tápices (see p. 172). The most extraordinary space is the rococo ballroom, with gold-plated walls, plush yellow silk seating, elaborate chandeliers, and ornate mirrors. 🗺 Map p. 125 ✉ Calle Santa Isabel 44 ☎ Tours: 91 527 1812 🚇 Metro: Atocha, Antón Martín

REAL MONASTERIO DE SANTA ISABEL

Felipe II founded this enormous Augustinian convent at the end of the 16th century. It later benefited from the patronage of Queen Margarita de Austria, wife of Felipe III, who also established the Real Monasterio de la Encarnación (see pp. 84–85). The church, which is open only during services, was designed by Gómez de Mora. The convent contains a rich collection of artistic treasures, but these are not currently on public display; the situation is likely to change in the future. www.patrimonionacional.es 🗺 Map p. 125 ✉ Calle Santa Isabel 48 ☎ 91 527 3183 🚇 Metro: Atocha, Antón Martín ∎

Once the grounds of a royal palace, the city's most popular green space is a place to jog, skate, or simply sit at one of the many cafés under the trees and watch the world go by.

Parque del Retiro & around

A granite artichoke, peeled open to reveal its heart, tops the Fuente de la Alcachofa in Parque del Retiro.

Parque del Retiro & around

IN A CITY AS DENSELY PACKED AS MADRID, THE PARQUE DEL RETIRO (Retiro Park) provides an essential breathing space. After the cultural onslaught of the museums along the Paseo del Prado, a stroll around the lake is a great way to clear your head. If you feel like even more artistic stimulation, however, there are usually two or three exhibitions running in the park itself.

The park was originally the gardens of the Palacio del Buen Retiro, built in the 17th century for Felipe IV. Only one wing and the ballroom of the palace remain on the hill behind the Prado, where they are extensions of the museum.

The palace gardens were first opened to the public in the mid-18th century, although at that time strict rules governed who could enter—to prevent the riffraff from concealing their identities and sneaking in, lace mantilla headscarves were forbidden for women, while men could not wear capes or hats.

These days, you can do more or less anything in the park, which means that the quieter areas are perhaps best avoided. It is generally very safe, however. .

For two weeks in June, the road running through two sides of the park is transformed with the installation of hundreds of stands for the city's annual international book fair. Visitors to the fair come not only to buy books but also to attend talks by leading writers and publishers.

The residential area of Los Jerónimos, which occupies the hill west of the park, was also part of the Buen Retiro palace. It is now one of the most prestigious neighborhoods in the city. The Museo Nacional de Artes Decorativas (National Museum of Decorative Arts) is housed here and contains fascinating displays of furniture and ceramics.

Like the Paseo del Prado, the area south of the park will be transformed into a friendly pedestrian area in the next decade as part of the plan to turn this part of Madrid into a cultural hub. A little off the beaten track, a visit to the Real Fábrica de Táouces (Royal Tapestry Factory) is like stepping back a couple of centuries and well worth the short walk to get there. ■

The park's monument to Alfonso XII provides a dramatic backdrop for a soccer game.

PASEO RECOLETOS

CALLE RECOLETOS

CALLE SERRANO

CALLE LAGASCA

CALLE VELÁZQUEZ

Príncipe de Vergara

RECOLETOS

VILLANUEVA

CALLE ALCALÁ

O'DONNELL

IBIZA

Palacio Marqués de Salamanca

CALLE COLUMELA

Puerta de Alcalá

Retiro

Retiro

Puerta de Madrid

Montaña Artificial

CALLE
DOCTOR CASTELO

co España

CALLE ALCALÁ

PLAZA INDEPENDENCIA

Puerta de Independencia

Puerta de Hernani

Casita del Pescador

Puerta de América

CALLE MENORCA

PLAZA CIBELES

Palacio de Comunicaciones

AVENIDA MÉJICO

Fuente de Galápagos

Casa de Vacas

PASEO COLOMBIA

PASEO REPÚBLICA DOMINICANA

Puerta de la Reina Mercedes

Ibiza

C. IBIZA

CALLE NARVÁEZ

PASEO PRADO

Museo Nacional de Artes Decorativas

CALLE ALFONSO XII

PLAZA MAESTRO VILLA

PLAZA NICARAGUA

PASEO SALÓN DEL ESTANQUE

GLORIETA SARDANA

Monumento a Alfonso XII

Puerta de Sáinz de Baranda

AVENIDA MENÉNDEZ PELAYO

Santísimo Sacramento

JERÓNIMOS

PASEO ARGENTINA

Puerta de España

Estanque

PASEO VENEZUELA

Jardines del Arquitecto Herrero Palacios

Area of map detail

Puerta de Felipe IV

PASEO PARTERRE

Fuente de Alcachofa

PLAZA HONDURAS

Palacio de Velázquez

RETIRO

PARQUE DEL RETIRO & AROUND

PASEO SAN PABLO

Palacio de Cristal

PASEO DUQUE DE FERNÁN NÚÑEZ

Jardines de Cecilio Rodríguez

Museo Nacional del Prado

C. ESPALTER

Puerta de Murillo

PARQUE **DEL** **RETIRO**

PLAZA MURILLO

La Chopera

PASEO REPÚBLICA DE CUBA

PASEO PRADO

PASEO PRADO

REAL JARDÍN BOTÁNICO

CALLE ALFONSO XII

Monumento al Ángel Caído

PASEO URUGUAY

La Rosaleda

CUESTA

CLAUDIO MOYANO

Puerta del Ángel Caído

Ministerio de Educación y Ciencia

Viveros Municipales

PASEO DUQUE DE FERNÁN NÚÑEZ

CALLE REYES MAGOS

Atocha

Ministerio de Agricultura

Atocha

CALLE POETA

ESTEBAN

VILLEGAS

AVENIDA MENÉNDEZ PELAYO

Observatorio Astronómico Nacional

C. AGUSTÍN QUEROL

CALLE GUTENBERG

Atocha Renfe

Museo Nacional de Antropología

PLAZA MARIANO DE CAVIA

Antigua Estación de Atocha

Atocha Renfe

CALLE ANDRÉS

PASEO INFANTA

ISABEL

PASEO REINA CRISTINA

TORREÓN

AVENIDA MEDITERRÁNEO

AVENIDA CIUDAD

Panteón de los Hombres Ilustres

Real Fábrica de Tapices

PACÍFICO

CALLE JUAN DE URBIETA

PASEO DELICIAS

Estación de Atocha

Real Basílica Nuestra Señora de Atocha

DE BARCELONA

Menéndez Pelayo

CALLE GRANADA

CALLE MÉNDEZ ÁLVARO

Menéndez Pelayo

CALLE DELICIAS

0   300 meters

0   300 yards

Parque del Retiro

Parque del Retiro

- Map p. 163
- 91 588 6318
- Metro: Retiro, Ibiza

A VISIT TO RETIRO PARK TAKES IN HISTORY, ARCHITECTURE, botany, and usually some art, too. Perhaps most interesting, however, is seeing all the different activities going on there. Some people practice tai chi or play chess under the trees, while others strum guitars or play drums. On weekends, Madrid's various foreign communities, particularly Latin Americans, congregate in different parts of the park for picnics, while Catalans perform their traditional dance in the Glorieta de la Sardana.

Light floods into the Palacio de Cristal, which was originally a hothouse and is now an exhibition space.

All these activities seem mild compared with the extravagant events that took place there when the Buen Retiro palace opened in 1635. The park, which was then the palace gardens, hosted fireworks displays, jousting tournaments, and concerts. Plays by Calderón de la Barca, Lope de Vega, and other leading figures of the golden age were performed on a floating stage on the lake.

The gardens were developed during a dramatic downturn in Spain's fortunes, when the country was floundering economically after a period of great prosperity following the discovery of America. Felipe IV was so delighted with his new palace and its grounds, however, that he lost touch with what has happening to his empire—which was exactly what his adviser, the Count-Duke of Olivares, had intended when he ordered the construction of the complex.

The rectangular space covers 292 acres (118 ha) and is planted with 15,000 trees. Although it has changed greatly over the centuries, mostly as a result of wartime damage, the layout is more or less the same and some original features have survived.

The most popular entrance is at the northwest corner, by the Puerta de Alcalá (see p. 168). The main path, the Avenida de Méjico, leads diagonally up to the **Fuente de Galápagos,** a fountain adorned with turtles, frogs, and dolphins. Designed by Francisco Javier de Mariátegui in 1831, the fountain was commissioned by Fernando VII to celebrate his daughter Isabel's first birthday.

Immediately south of the fountain is the huge rectangular **Éstanque** (lake), which was dug out when the palace gardens were created in the 17th century. It was used not only for theatrical performances but also for elaborately staged mock battles. In 2003, a new boathouse and moorings were built. The lake is dominated by the **Monument to Alfonso XII,** which was designed by José Grases Riera and completed in 1922. The bronze equestrian statue of the king by Mariano Benlliure is flanked by a semicircular colonnade.

The promenade along the lake, known as the **Salón del Éstanque,** is usually lined with buskers, mime artists, tarot readers, and puppeteers. On the right is the path known popularly as the Paseo de las Estatuas, but officially as **de Argentina.** It is flanked by 18th-century statues intended for the Palacio Real.

The end of the Salón del Estanque, on the lake's southwest corner, is marked by the **Fuente de la Alcachofa,** designed by Ventura Rodríguez in the 18th century. The Artichoke Fountain will return to its original location at the end of the Paseo del Prado, where there is now a replica, during the development over the next decade.

If you turn right here, toward the city center, you come to the

Lucifer tumbles backward on his journey to Hell on the Monument to the Fallen Angel.

Fallen angel

Madrid claims to have the only statue in the world to celebrate the devil. Serenely situated in the Parque del Retiro, the **Monumento el Angel Caído** (Monument to the Fallen Angel) was created in 1878 by Ricardo Bellver and depicts Lucifer's descent into Hell. The winged bronze figure crowns a fountain surrounded by gargoyles of monsters. ∎

Parterre, which was inspired by Versailles. It was created in the 18th century in the reign of Felipe V as part of an unfulfilled plan to build a new palace. Although the garden has been replanted several times, it contains some of its original trees, including a Mexican cypress more than 400 years old and believed to have been brought to Spain by conquistador Hernán Cortés (1485–1547).

From the Artichoke fountain, the Paseo de la República de Cuba heads south. In the area to the left are two pavilions, both designed by Ricardo Velázquez Bosco in the 1880s. The **Palacio de Velázquez,** a palace that

Palacio de Velázquez

www.museoreinasofia.es

☎ 91 573 6245

🕐 Closed Tues.

Ⓜ Metro: Ibiza, Retiro

Palacio de Cristal

www.museoreinasofia.es

☎ 91 574 6614

🕐 Closed Tues.

Ⓜ Metro: Ibiza, Retiro

features colored bricks, enameled tiles, and arches, was built for a mining exhibition in 1883. It is used for various shows.

A short distance to the south, the **Palacio de Cristal** is an elegant glass-and-iron structure inspired by London's Crystal Palace and the Palm House at Kew Gardens. It was built in 1887 to exhibit plants and flowers from the Philippines. The pavilion overlooks a lake where black swans glide through the water. Both buildings are now used as exhibition spaces under the auspices of the Reina Sofía museum

(see pp. 154–159).

South of the pavilions, along the Paseo de Uruguay, is the elliptical **Rosaleda,** a delightful rose garden that was designed by Cecilio Rodríguez in 1915. The rose bushes came from the most famous gardens in Europe, but the Rosaleda had to be replanted in the 1940s after being destroyed in the Civil War.

This part of the park used to be occupied by the Royal Porcelain Factory, which Carlos III had built in 1760. Porcelain produced there is on display in the Palacio Real (see pp. 72–77)

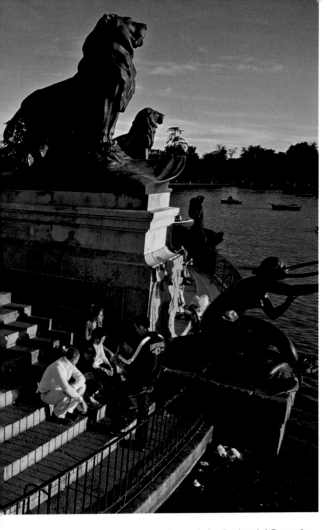

The steps in front of the Monument to Alfonso XII by the lake are a coveted spot for enjoying the sunshine.

and in the palace in Aranjuez (see p. 220). The building was demolished after being damaged during the War of Independence.

The **Jardínes de Cecilio Rodríguez,** on the park's east side, commemorate the gardener who made such a great contribution here and in the Parque del Oeste (see pp. 202–203). Classical music concerts are occasionally held here in the summer.

The broad Paseo del Duque de Fernán Núñez heads north alongside the gardens. Near the end of the road there is a little pavilion on the right in the middle of a pond, the **Casita del Pescador,** which is now an information center. Behind it is a hill known as the **Artificial Mountain,** built in the 1820s for Fernando VII. Water pumped around the structure flows down the the hill like a mountain stream. The ruins nearby are the remains of a 13th-century Romanesque church brought from Ávila.

Turning back toward the lake along the Paseo de Colombia, you will see the **Casa de Vacas** on the right. This exhibition building originally housed cows, kept to provide fresh milk for visitors. ■

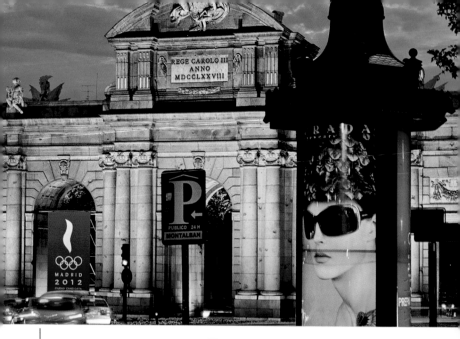

Puerta de Alcalá

ONE OF MADRID'S MOST IMPORTANT SYMBOLS, THE Puerta de Alcalá is a grandiose triumphal arch built to commemorate the first 20 years of the reign of Carlos III. The monument was the point of entry to the city for visitors from Barcelona and France, and it was also close to the Buen Retiro palace.

Puerta de Alcalá

 Map p. 163

Metro: Retiro

The arch stands in the center of Plaza de la Independencia, a circular crossroad between the grand avenues of Alcalá, Alfonso XII, and Serrano surrounded by elegant 19th-century apartment buildings. Nowadays traffic roars around the arch, making it rather difficult to reach on foot.

The neoclassic granite monument, 70 feet (21 m) high, was designed by Francesco Sabatini, the favorite architect of Carlos III, and completed in 1779. It comprises three semicircular arches. The central one is larger than the other two, as it was originally used by royal entourages, while the others were for carriages. Smaller flat arches at each end were for pedestrians.

Above the arches are reliefs featuring horns of plenty, a reference to the healthy economic situation in the reign of Carlos III. The entablature and attic are decorated with Italianate baroque sculptures by Robert Michel and Francisco Gutiérrez in white Colmenar stone. If you manage to get close to the monument, look up at the capitals on the Ionic columns on the outer side, which are decorated with bat heads.

Calle Alcalá formed part of the authorized route for the seasonal migration of sheep across Spain, an event that took place every year for centuries. To this day, if sheep farmers want to stage a protest, they consider it their right to drive their flocks along the street and through the gate to Plaza de Cibeles. ∎

Museo Nacional de Artes Decorativas

THE NATIONAL MUSEUM OF DECORATIVE ARTS CONTAINS extensive collections of furniture, ceramics, textiles, jewelry, glassware, fans, and Oriental art. The exhibits are displayed over five floors in a palatial late 19th-century residence, which is interesting in its own right. Some of the exhibits appear in rooms that re-create how Spanish aristocratic families lived in different centuries.

Details of 18th-century life are revealed on hand-painted tiles of a Valencia kitchen in the Museo Nacional de Artes Decorativas.

If you are on your way to the Parque del Retiro, it is worth stopping here to see the reconstruction of an 18th-century Valencian kitchen, which is decorated with about 1,500 hand-painted tiles. Unfortunately, the kitchen is on the museum's top floor, which is sometimes closed—particularly on weekends—owing to staff shortages. Other floors may also be closed, so call ahead to check. The museum's collection of 20th-century design is not currently on display.

The kitchen was transferred to the museum from a mansion in Valencia. In the 18th century, it became traditional on Spain's east coast to cover surfaces with tiles depicting popular themes. In this kitchen we see the servants preparing hot chocolate, pies, and cakes for the lady of the house. The tiles display typical foods such as sausages, onions, and salt cod, as well as traditional cooking utensils of the period.

Several rooms on the second floor have coffered wooden ceilings, including a 15th-century example brought from León. Displays include Flemish tapestries and Spanish carpets from the 16th century, when Spain's carpet industry was the most important in Europe. The museum has an excellent collection of furniture from the Gothic to the baroque periods, including several elaborate *bargueño* cabinets from the 16th and 17th centuries.

The ceramic collection, on the third floor, comprises more than 4,000 items, the oldest of which is an 11th-century vat from Toledo. The displays include examples from all the major Spanish centers of ceramic production, including Talavera, Teruel, and Manises. The great European producers—Meissen, Sèvres, and Capodimonte—are also well represented. Glass displays include Greco-Punic, Roman, and Visigothic pieces and more recent exhibits from Limoges and La Granja.

The collection of Oriental art, begun by Carlos III, includes ceramics, costumes, musical instruments, and paintings from the Ming (1368–1644) and Qing (1644–1912) dynasties. ∎

Museo Nacional de Artes Decorativas

http://mnartesdecorativas.mcu.es

🅰 Map p. 163

✉ Calle Montalbán 12

☎ 91 532 6499 or 91 532 6845

🕐 Closed Tues.–Sun. p.m. & Mon.

💲 $. Free Sun. a.m.

🚇 Metro: Banco de España, Retiro

South of Parque del Retiro

The Museo
Nacional de
Antropología
displays objects
brought to Spain
from remote
cultures in the
19th and 20th
centuries.

South of Parque del Retiro

🗺 Map p. 163

Observatorio Astronómico Nacional

www.oan.es

✉ Calle Alfonso XII 3

☎ 91 527 0107

🕐 Guided visits Fri.

🚇 Metro: Atocha Renfe

THE AREA SOUTH OF THE PARQUE DEL RETIRO IS PART OF the far-reaching development plan for the Paseo del Prado (see p. 136). The new, pedestrian-friendly layout will make the museums and other points of interest much more accessible, as at present you have to tackle a series of broad avenues choked with traffic to get from one place to the next. The slope between the park and Atocha station is set to be landscaped and become a hub of science-related museums and attractions. While this will be a massive improvement, it is well worth making the effort to visit this area now.

The development should restore the neoclassic **Observatorio Astronómico Nacional** to a position of prominence. Located just off the southwest corner of the Parque del Retiro, this superb building stands on the highest point in the area, with panoramic views across the city. Designed by Juan de Villanueva in 1790 and restored by Narciso Pascual y Colomer in 1845, it was part of Carlos III's Paseo del Prado scheme (see p. 124). Its cruciform structure features a central hall with a rotunda surrounded by Ionic columns. Work is under way on a museum of astronomy, scheduled to be completed in 2007.

The **Cuesta de Claudio Moyano,** which leads down the side of the Real Jardín Botánico (Royal Botanic Garden) from Calle Alfonso XII to the Paseo del Prado, is lined with wooden kiosks selling new, secondhand, and antique books. As part of the development, the hill will become more accessible to pedestrians and the kiosks will be moved from the side to the center. On the other side of the hill is the rear of the **Ministry of Agriculture,** built in the 1890s as the Ministry of Development. Designed by Ricardo Velázquez Bosco, it features his trademark elements of tiles and colored bricks.

Next to the ministry, with a grand neoclassic entrance, is the **Museo Nacional de Antropología,** designed by the Marquis of Cubas in the late 19th century. The museum was founded by the scientist Pedro González Velasco to exhibit his collections from distant cultures. The displays include mummies of Guanches, the original inhabitants of the Canary Islands, and finds from expeditions to Equatorial Guinea undertaken by Spanish explorers in the late 19th and early 20th centuries. A section devoted to North Africa displays objects from the Tuareg and Berber cultures. The American collections include Inuit sculptures and sculptures from Peru.

The round redbrick structure opposite is the new part of **Estación de Atocha,** Atocha station, designed by Rafael Moneo and completed in 1992. On March 11, 2004, a devastating terrorist attack killed 192 people arriving at the station on commuter trains. There are plans to install a monument to the victims from the street-level entrance to the concourse below.

The original section of the station was designed by Alberto del Palacio at the end of the 19th century. It is now a hothouse with palm trees and tropical plants taking the place of plat-

forms. Travelers relax there while waiting for trains, a world away from the station noise.

A five-minute walk along the Paseo de la Infanta Isabel, which becomes the Paseo de Reina Cristina, brings you to the **Panteón de los Hombres Ilustres.** Designed at the end of the 19th century by Fernando Arbós y Tremanti, the pantheon was intended to be a cemetery for important figures in Madrid's history. As the city has been so lax over the centuries with the remains of its most illustrious citizens, many of the most obvious candidates, including Velázquez

Museo Nacional de Antropología

http://mnantropologia.mcu.es

✉ Calle Alfonso XII 68

☎ 91 530 6418

🕒 Closed Sun. p.m. & Mon.

💲 $

🚇 Metro: Atocha Renfe, Atocha

Each level of the Museo Nacional de Antropología deals with a different part of the world.

Dyed yarns are used to create tapestries at the Real Fábrica de Tápices.

Panteón de los Hombres Ilustres

✉ Calle Julián Gayarre 3
☎ 91 454 8800
🕐 Closed Sun. p.m.
Ⓜ Metro: Atocha Renfe, Menéndez Pelayo

Real Fábrica de Tápices

✉ Calle Fuenterrabia 2
☎ 91 434 0550
🕐 Closed Sat., Sun., Mon.–Fri. p.m., Aug.
💲 $. Guided tour
Ⓜ Metro: Menéndez Pelayo, Atocha Renfe

and Cervantes, could not be found. You can, however, see the elaborate tombs of several 19th-century politicians, sculpted by leading artists of the time, including Mariano Benlliure and Agustin Querol.

Next to the pantheon is the **Real Basílica de Nuestra Señora de Atocha,** an uninspiring neo-baroque structure that was built after the Civil War when the original church was destroyed. This is the site of one of Madrid's oldest and most important legends, which describes how the figure of Our Lady of Atocha healed and protected a nobleman's family during the Moorish invasion. Many Madrileños are more devoted to Our Lady of Atocha than they are to the Almudena (see pp. 78–79).

Around the corner is the fascinating **Real Fábrica de Tápices** (Royal Tapestry Factory). Founded by Felipe V at the beginning of the 18th century, the factory has been in this building since 1889. Francisco de Goya worked at the original factory, where he produced preparatory paintings and sketches for tapestries, often depicting popular festivals and scenes from everyday life. Known as cartoons, many of these are now in the Prado museum.

Today, weavers painstakingly make tapestries on 18th-century looms that would have been familiar to Goya. About 75 people work there now, compared with 250 in its 18th-century heyday, when Bourbon monarchs provided plenty of business. Every royal residence in Spain is decorated with tapestries and carpets made then. The factory is now a foundation, with workshops where students train in this intricate craft. It takes three to four months to make a square yard of the costly tapestry. ■

Cutting through the city like a fast-flowing river, Madrid's north-south axis is defined by the Paseo de la Castellana, a grand boulevard flanked by flagship buildings that chart the city's architectural development over the last century.

La Castellana & Salamanca

A marble sculpture in the Nuevos Ministerios area commemorates Spain's 1978 Constitution.

La Castellana & Salamanca

RUNNING NORTH FOR 4.5 MILES (7.25 KM) FROM PLAZA DE COLÓN TO Plaza Castilla, the Paseo de la Castellana is one of the most prestigious commercial streets in the city. Although streaming with ten lanes of traffic at all hours of the day, the central boulevard is worth a visit if you want to get an idea of the modern city. To the east of the Paseo de la Castellana is the upscale area of Salamanca. In this district, marked by elegant residences, leading designers such as Armani and Prada have their boutiques. Salamanca is also known for its venues for contemporary art.

Madrid's smartest boutiques are sprinkled throughout the Salamanca district.

The Paseo de la Castellana is divided into three distinct sections. The first, which covers about half a mile (0.8 km) from Plaza de Cibeles to Plaza de Colón, is known as the Paseo de Recoletos and dates from the second half of the 19th century. The second stretch of 2 miles (3.2 km) ends at Plaza San Juan de la Cruz and was developed between the late 19th century and the 1930s Civil War. The third section, up to Plaza de Castilla, was built mainly in the second half of the 20th century. A fourth stage beyond Plaza de Castilla is currently taking shape.

As it extends northward, therefore, the street is like a museum of modern architecture, with a chronological progression of styles. Signature high-rise buildings mark it as Madrid's business and financial hub.

The Salamanca district was developed between 1860 and 1920 by the maverick Marquis of Salamanca and comprises a grid of tree-lined broad streets flanked by stylish apartments and shops. Madrid's bullring, Plaza de Toros de las Ventas, is located on the area's eastern fringe. It is worth visiting even if you do not want to see a bullfight. An interesting museum and good guided tours help give an insight into this most ingrained of Spanish traditions.

Other museums in this part of town include the Museo Arqueológico Nacional, which explores ancient civilizations as well as Spanish history; the Museo Nacional de Ciencias Naturales, the Museum of Natural Sciences; and the Museo Lázaro Galdiano, with its excellent art collections; and the Museo Sorolla, displaying paintings of a Valencian artist in his own house. ■

Creating new waxwork figures at the Museo de Cera

Paseo de los Recoletos

FOR MADRILEÑOS, THE PASEO DE RECOLETOS IS inextricably associated with the beloved custom of sitting at outdoor cafés, a tradition that began more than a century ago. The name "Recoletos" comes from an Augustinian Recollect monastery that was located on the right of the street until the mid-19th century. A change in the law at that time allowed foreign investors to operate in Spain, which led to rapid development along the boulevard.

After the monastery was demolished, the land was snapped up by the Marquis of Salamanca (1811–1883), a larger-than-life character who built himself a sumptuous residence on the site. The palace is now the headquarters of the **Banco Bilbao Vizcaya Argentaria,** which holds temporary art exhibitions in the covered courtyard on the first floor. If the building is open, it is worth going in just to have a look at the interior, particularly the grand staircase to the right of the entrance.

Almost hidden on the left of the Paseo is the rebuilt **Iglesia de San Pascual,** a vestige of the convent that stood there until the 19th century. To the right of the altar there is a figure of Santa Clara. It is revered by people working in show business, who often pop into the church to ask her to help find their next job.

A little farther up is the **Café Gijón** *(Paseo de Recoletos 21, tel 91 521 5425),* founded in 1888 and one of the few remaining traditional cafés in Madrid (see pp. 118–119). With its marble tables and velvet banquettes, this is a good place to spot famous actors and writers. In warm weather, its outdoor tables are ideal for people-watching. At the end of the Paseo on the left is the **Museo de Cera** *(Paseo de Recoletos 41, tel 91 319 2649, $$$),* a wax museum where exhibits range from Cervantes to Bart Simpson. ■

Plaza de Colón

THINGS ARE ON THE MOVE IN PLAZA DE COLÓN, AS A MAJOR remodeling scheme gets under way in late 2006 to spruce up this major junction. The square commemorates Christopher Columbus and the discovery of America, which the new arrangement aims to make more coherent by repositioning its key features.

The neo-Gothic column crowned by a figure of Columbus, designed by Jerónimo Suñol and Arturo Mélida in the late 19th century, is set to move from the sidelines to its original location in the middle of the crossroads. On the right, the **Centro Cultural de la Villa** is also getting a face-lift. This theater and exhibition venue has been hidden below ground, but it will now have a more obvious entrance on the **Jardines del Descubrimiento.** The large landscaped area commemorates Columbus with three large blocks that represent his ships, each featuring inscriptions and reliefs relating to his voyages. The airport bus terminal is located under the square.

The southeast corner of the square is taken up by the enormous 19th-century building that houses the **Biblioteca Nacional** at the front and the **Museo Arqueológico Nacional** (see pp. 180–182) at the rear. The **book museum** on the first floor is not currently open to the public, but there is usually at least one temporary exhibition running at any given time.

The towers on the northwest side, which seem to be joined by a pistachio-colored hat, are the Torres de Jerez, popularly known as the **Torres de Colón.** Built between 1967 and 1976 by Antonio Lamela, they were altered by the same architect in the 1990s. The towers were built from the top down by slotting the stories onto concrete pillars. ■

The neoclassic Biblioteca Nacional houses Spain's prestigious literary heritage.

Plaza de Colón
Map p. 175

Centro Cultural de la Villa
www.munimadrid.es
Plaza de Colón
91 480 0300
Closed Sun. p.m. & Mon.
Metro: Colón, Serrano

Biblioteca Nacional
www.bne.es
Paseo de Recoletos 20–22
91 580 7805 or 91 580 7823
Exhibitions: 91 580 7894
Closed Sun. & Sat. p.m.
Metro: Colón, Serrano

Terrazas

Outdoor cafés, known as *terrazas,* are an integral element of Madrid summers, opening after Easter and closing when the temperature drops to wintry levels in late October. Some provide a shady spot for watching the world go by on a lazy afternoon, while others are more like nightclubs, with throbbing music and a glamorous clientele.

Terrazas are not a modern phenomenon, however, having been a ubiquitous feature of the city for more than a hundred years. In the 19th century, the Paseo de Recoletos was adorned with gardens and fountains and was such a pleasant place to relax that it became known as Recoletos Beach. A string of kiosks—the precursors of today's cafés—sold refreshments, and people went there to cool down with a lemonade after midday Mass at the San Pascual church or to take a pre-dinner stroll in the evening.

In the 1980s, the terrazas along the Paseo de Recoletos became fashionable, a trend that spread up the Paseo de la Castellana over the years, until the boulevard became a nocturnal promenade stretching for miles. In the 1990s, late-night terrazas moved away from residential areas to bigger spaces where noise was not a problem. Now, some of the hippest places to be seen in the summer are the terrazas flanking the Príncipe Pío commercial center near the Manzanares River, which provides a pleasant, cooling breeze.

The more traditional terrazas offer a range of typical drinks. *Granizado de limón* is crushed ice, sugar, and lemon juice, while *granizado de café* is the same thing with coffee. The thick, creamy liquid that you see some people drinking through a straw is *horchata,* made with *chufas,* which are tubers from the sedge plant and are sometimes called tiger nuts or earth almonds. When crushed with sugar and ice, the chufas acquire a flavor and texture that is unlike anything you are ever likely to have tasted, so give it a try.

The Paseo del Pintor Rosales, by the Parque del Oeste (see pp. 202–203) on the western edge of the city, is a good place for a quiet drink, and being just outside the center with views to the mountains means the temperature is a few degrees lower too. This is one of the few places in Madrid where you can still find *leche merengada,* which, if made properly, is a mix of cream, milk, and egg whites, flavored with lemon and cinnamon. You might also come across *blanco y negro,* which is coffee topped with leche merengada, or sometimes just regular vanilla ice cream.

For more of a neighborhood feel, sit at one of the many terrazas in the octagonal Plaza de Olavide, which is popular with families who share tapas while the kids and dogs run around the gardens. Perhaps the most traditional terraza of all is Las Vistillas *(Calle Bailén),* with fabulous views of the Palacio Real and the Guadarrama mountains beyond. ∎

By day or night, El Espejo (opposite, above, and below), one of the popular outdoor cafés on the Paseo de Pecoletos, offers a leisurely place to relax over a drink with friends.

Schoolchildren sketch ancient exhibits (above). The sculpture known as the Dama de Elche is a masterpiece of Iberian art (below).

Museo Arqueológico Nacional

THIS IS ONE OF SPAIN'S MOST IMPORTANT MUSEUMS. IT contains not only archaeological finds but also religious sculpture, jewelry, ceramics, and architectural fragments. While part of the collection is devoted to ancient civilizations, there are also extensive exhibits that provide a fascinating insight into Spain's history and culture. Unfortunately, information panels are currently in Spanish only. You need at least three hours to get around the museum, but may want to go in just to see the fabulous Iberian exhibits, or perhaps the section that charts the development of Islamic Spain.

The displays begin in the basement with prehistory and the origins of humanity. There are some exceptional pieces in **Rooms 5 and 6,** which deal with the Bronze Age. Look for the copper-and-gold Guadalajara sword, which is a rare example of weaponry from the period (second millennium B.C.), and the bowls from Axtroki in the Basque country, made of hammered gold with geometric patterns that suggest a cult of sun worship. **Rooms 7–9,** devoted to the Iron Age, contain a beautiful collection of gold Celtic torques (collars) and Celtiberian silver.

Rooms 10–11 deal with the ancient cultures of the Balearic and Canary Islands. While we may now think of these places as holiday resorts, the Balearics were inhabited as far back as 5000 B.C. The Guanches were definitely living in the Canaries by 2500 B.C. and were probably in the islands a lot earlier than that.

Room 13, a large space in the south wing, is devoted to ancient Egypt and Nubia from 4000 B.C. up to the Roman Conquest. The sarcophagus of Amenemhat (circa 1000 B.C.), from Thebes, is exquisitely decorated over its entire surface with myths related to the afterlife. The exceptional collections of Greek pottery in **Rooms 14–16** include a cup painted by Aison, one of the great artists of fifth century B.C., which depicts the exploits of Theseus.

On the first floor, start with the Iberian and Phoenician works in **Rooms 19–20** and follow the exhibits clockwise. One of the first things you see is the Pozo Moro monument, a huge structure of carved sandstone blocks that looks as if it belongs in a museum of contemporary art. This is actually a reconstruction of a funerary monument from the end of the sixth century B.C. that was found in the province of Albacete. Also look for the Dama de Galera, a small alabaster Phoenician sculpture from the seventh century B.C. The feminine figure, flanked by two sphinxes, is holding a bowl that was filled with perfume in funeral rituals. Another extraordinary exhibit is the Aliseda Treasure from Cáceres in western Spain. Made by Tartessians in the seventh century B.C., it includes exquisite earrings and bracelets.

The museum's highlight is the Dama de Elche, the Lady of Elche, a beautiful Iberian sculpture from the fourth century B.C. Found in 1897 in the city of Elche in eastern Spain, this bust of a wealthy woman has a tiara, an elaborate headdress, and impressive coils of hair curling around each side of her face. An indentation at the back was prob-

ably intended for the deposit of ashes, and the sculpture is thought to have been a funerary urn.

Afterward, see the Dama de Baza, a painted, carved figure of a woman also from the fourth century B.C. The life-size, seated sculpture comes from an Iberian necropolis and has a cavity for ashes. The richly adorned woman, still retaining traces of color, represents the goddess of death, a concept that developed from the Mediterranean tradition of worshiping the Mother God, as represented in Greek mythology by Demeter.

Rooms 21–26 display the Roman collections, which include a mosaic floor from Zaragoza, dating from the second century A.D., that depicts the Triumph of Bacchus. The rooms contain several bronze tablets engraved with regulations, including the Malacitanian Law, which dates from the first century A.D. and was originally displayed in a public building. A marble seated figure of Empress Livia, originally from Paestum in Italy, is swathed in superbly carved draped clothing.

Museo Arqueológico Nacional
www.man.es

🔲 Map p. 175
✉ Calle Serrano 13
☎ 91 577 7912
🕐 Closed Sun. p.m. & Mon.
💲 $. Free Sat. p.m. & Sun. a.m.
🚇 Metro: Serrano, Retiro, Colón

A bronze sculpture graces the entrance to the Museo Arqueológico Nacional.

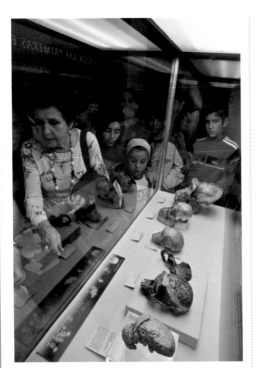

Visitors to the Museo Arqueológico Nacional examine a collection of skulls and bone fragments.

enamel. Made in Córdoba, the cylindrical box is decorated with gazelles, peacocks, pinecones, and roses.

A gilded earthenware urn, which was made in the 14th century at the Cartuja de Jerez de la Frontera, is an excellent example of the work of the Nasrid craftsmen who decorated the exquisite Alhambra. The carvings on an ivory crucifix, donated by King Fernando I and Queen Sancha to the church of San Isidro in León in the 11th century, feature the risen Christ above the crucified figure, which suggests that the craftsman who made the piece was influenced by the art of central Europe.

You enter **Room 32** through a 12th-century decorated arch that came from the monastery of San Pedro de Arlanza in Burgos. The Romanesque displays include a 12th-century polychrome Madonna from Santa Maria de Taull in Catalunya.

Room 33 contains superlative displays of Romanesque, Gothic, and Mudejar art. The 12th-century choir stalls from Santa María de Gradefes in León are a fine example of Mudejar craftsmanship, with vestiges of red and green decoration depicting heraldic lions. Also here is a 14th-century crozier in silver and enamel that belonged to Pope Benedict XIII.

The **second floor** contains the 16th- to 19th-century collections, as well as extensive displays of coins, but these rooms are frequently closed. Temporary exhibitions are also held on this floor. Outside the entrance, steps lead to an underground space where there is a replica of the Altamira caves on Spain's north coast, which are covered with fascinating Paleolithic paintings. ■

The outstanding exhibit in **Rooms 27–29,** which are devoted to Visigothic Spain, is the Guarrazar Treasure from Toledo (seventh century A.D.). It contains votive crowns, crosses, and fragments of various other pieces, the highlight of which is the gold crown of King Recceswinth (*R*.649–672), adorned with garnets, pearls, and sapphires.

Rooms 30 and 31 trace the development of the Islamic empire in Spain and the emergence of Romanesque art. Exhibits include 11th-century decorative friezes from the Alfajería palace in Zaragoza and a 14th-century lamp from the Alhambra palace in Granada, the final base of the Moors in Spain. There is a perfectly preserved tenth-century canister from Zamora, which is finely worked in ivory, silver, and

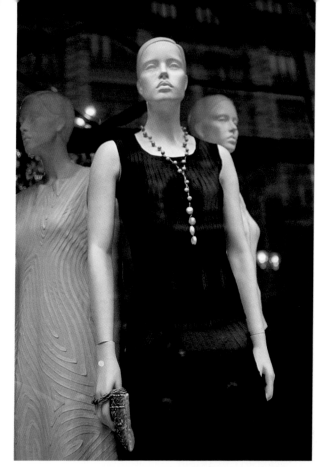

At Adolfo
Domínguez, one
of Spain's best
known designers

Calle Serrano & around

MOST OF MADRID'S MOST FASHIONABLE SHOPS ARE located on Calle Serrano and the surrounding grid of streets in the Salamanca district. Walking up and down these grand avenues, which are also lined with upscale residences, you feel as though you are in a different city, a world away from the crowded, narrow streets of the Old Town. While you could easily spend all day popping into boutiques and drinking coffee at chic cafés, there are a few cultural surprises in the area that are definitely worth a look.

Calle Serrano gets its name from Francisco Serrano (1810–1885), who held the title of Duke of la Torre and was an influential politician and military man. Along with General Prim, he led the revolution that dethroned Isabel II in 1868.

This area features Spanish designers such as Loewe, Adolfo Domínguez, and Amaya Arzuaga, as well as international names including Armani, Chanel, Prada, and Versace. The most interesting boutiques are at the bottom of Calle Serrano, particularly along Calle Jorge Juan.

As you walk up Calle Serrano, on the right you will see the

Calle Serrano
🅐 Map p. 175

Fundación La Caixa
www.lacaixa.es
✉ Calle Serrano 60
☎ 91 426 0202
🕐 Closed Tues. & Sun. p.m.
🚇 Metro: Serrano

Fundación Juan March

www.march.es

- ✉ Calle Castelló 77
- ☎ 91 435 4240
- 🕐 Closed Sun. p.m. & Aug.
- 🚇 Metro: Núñez de Balboa

Residencia de Estudiantes

www.residencia.csic.es

- ✉ Calle Pinar 21–23
- ☎ 91 563 6411
- 🕐 Closed Sun. p.m.
- 🚇 Metro: Gregorio Marañón, República Argentina

Salvador Dalí and Federico García Lorca spent time at the Residencia de Estudiantes.

Little luxuries

The apartment blocks in the Salamanca neighborhood were the first in Madrid to have elevators and coal-fired stoves. The city's bourgeoisie had been reluctant to move away from the center, but were eventually tempted by these innovations. The deciding factor were bathrooms with hot running water and toilets with flushing mechanisms. ■

Fundación La Caixa, an art venue that stages excellent contemporary exhibitions. La Caixa, a Catalan savings bank, is building a new museum near the Reina Sofía (see p. 160) and may close this center when the new building is completed in 2007.

Just off Calle Serrano, occupying the block between Calle Ayala and Calle Lagasca, is the **Mercado de la Paz** *(tel 91 431 7725),* one of the best food mar-

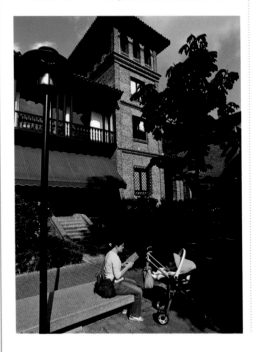

kets in the city, with fantastic charcuterie and cheese stands. A few minutes' walk farther down, look for **Teatriz** *(tel 91 577 5379)* at Calle Hermosilla 15 on the corner of Calle Claudio Coello. This former theater was transformed by Philippe Starck and Javier Mariscal into a restaurant, bar, and café. It is a good place to take a break and observe the well-groomed locals.

Only a few of the palaces and mansions from the 19th century still survive, but there is a fine example on the corner of Calle Lagasca and Calle Juan Bravo. Now the Italian Embassy, this neo-baroque structure was originally the **Palacio de Amboage,** built for an aristocratic family between 1914 and 1918 by Joaquín Rojí. Walk around to Calle Velázquez to get a view of the incredible gardens.

A couple of blocks farther east is the **Fundación Juan March,** which was created in 1955 by financier March and organizes a prestigious program of exhibitions, concerts, and lectures. Its first-class art collection is divided between this center and the museums of contemporary art in Cuenca and Palma de Mallorca.

One of Madrid's cultural institutions, the **Residencia de Estudiantes** is hidden away off the top of Calle Serrano but will become more accessible after a garden is created between the building and the Museo Nacional de Ciencias Naturales (see p. 187). Founded in 1910, the Residencia was originally a liberal teaching center. It soon became a magnet for artists, writers, and scientists. Students over the years included Lorca, Dalí, and Buñuel; Ravel, Stravinsky, and de Falla all performed there. It now hosts exhibits and other events and has a good café and restaurant, as well. ■

Museo Lázaro Galdiano

Museo Lázaro Galdiano

www.flg.es

🅰 Map p. 175

✉ Calle Serrano 122

☎ 91 561 6084

🕐 Closed Tues.

💲 $. Free Wed.

🚇 Metro: Gregorio Marañon, Rubén Darío

THE GRAND HOME OF PUBLISHER AND BUSINESSMAN JOSÉ Lázaro Galdiano (1862–1947) houses his impressive collection of Spanish and European paintings, which includes important works by Goya. The extensive exhibits also contain sculpture, jewelry, miniatures, ceramics, enamels, and weaponry. Galdiano and his wife, Paula Florido, were patrons of the arts and played an active role in the cultural life in Madrid in the first half of the 20th century.

The displays are arranged over all four floors of the mansion, which is itself of considerable interest, particularly the *piano nobile* on the second floor. The many notable exhibits include a bronze pitcher from the sixth century B.C. and the late 17th-century cup of Emperor Rudolph II.

A selection of Spanish art ranging from the 15th to the 19th centuries is displayed chronologically on the **first floor.** Early works include "La Virgen de Mosén Sperandeu de Santa Fé" (1438–1439) by Blasco de Grañén and the Castillian "San Jerónimo en su Escritorio" (circa 1480–1490) by the Maestro del Parral. Among the exceptional works from the 16th and 17th centuries is "San Francisco de Asís" (1577–1580) by El Greco.

The most outstanding of the eight Goya paintings are the terrifying "El Aquelarre" and "El Conjuro," which belonged to the Dukes of Osuna. The former depicts a coven of haggard witches casting a spell, while the latter shows the devil as a goat, appearing before women who have killed their children.

The **second floor** is devoted to European art, with Italian, Flemish, Dutch, French, and English paintings. In this rich collection, of particular interest is "El Salvador Adolescente" (circa 1490–1495), a panel attributed to Giovanni Antonio Boltraffio, a disciple of Leonardo. The Flemish paintings include "Meditaciones de San Juan Bautista" by Hieronymus Bosch. In the English collection are works by Joshua Reynolds, George Romney, and John Constable. ∎

Medieval stained glass in the Sala de Musica is just one of the many treasures of the Museo Lázaro Galdiano.

Museo Sorolla

THE PAINTER JOAQUÍN SOROLLA (1863–1923), WHO WAS born in Valencia, lived in this house from 1911 until his death. Obsessed with the portrayal of light, he is best known for his languid beach scenes, many of which have been reproduced on greeting cards and posters. Coveted by European and American collectors during his lifetime, his work was exhibited in London in 1908 and in Boston and New York a year later.

Museo Sorolla

http://museosorolla.mcu.es

🅰 Map p. 175

✉ Paseo General Martínez 37

☎ 91 310 1584

🕐 Closed Mon. & daily p.m.

💲 $

🚇 Metro: Iglesia, Rubén Darío, Gregorio Marañón

The first three rooms you visit were his **offices** and **studio,** which are decorated and furnished just as they were in Sorolla's day. Some of his best known paintings are displayed in this section, including the sun-dappled "Pink Bathrobe" (1916) and "Strolling Along the Sea Shore" (1909), which show his skill at re-creating the luminosity of the Mediterranean coastline.

Upstairs, the original bedrooms now contain works from his stays in northern Spain, often depicting his wife and daughters by the seaside. **Room 6** displays some of the paintings he produced between 1912 and 1919 for the Hispanic Society of America in New York, which show people from all the provinces of Spain in traditional dress.

Back downstairs, a few rooms have been left as they were when the family lived there. Sorolla decorated the dining room with an elaborate border of flowers and fruit, featuring portraits of his wife and daughters.

Sorolla also designed the stunning gardens, inspired by the Reales Alcazares in Seville and the Alhambra in Granada. Don't miss the Cordoba-style courtyard off the gardens, which is decorated with tiles from Talavera. Rooms around the courtyard contain Spanish ceramics and drawings of scenes from New York. ■

Museo Nacional de Ciencias Naturales

THE NATURAL SCIENCE MUSEUM GREW FROM THE ROYAL Natural History Office founded by Carlos III in 1772. The imposing building, completed in 1887, houses both permanent displays and at least two temporary exhibitions at any time.

The museum's displays are divided between two iron-and-glass pavilions either side of a central dome. You start in the **Biology Zone,** on the left as you face the building. **Mediterranean Nature and Civilization** trace the development of landscapes and life-forms in the region. Displays discuss livestock migration and endangered animals such as the Iberian lynx and the brown bear. A room devoted to the Mediterranean has models of lobsters, crabs, and a giant squid.

Downstairs, a circular room re-creates the **Royal Natural History Office** and explains the origins of the museum. In the **Ecology Zone,** at the other end of the building, the **History of the Earth and Life** section contains the skeleton of a megatherium, a giant slothlike creature found in Argentina in 1788, which is believed to be 1.8 million years old. This and other skeletons on display were found during the many Spanish expeditions to South America at the end of the 18th century. The museum also has a life-size reproduction of a diplodocus skeleton that was found in Wyoming and given to Alfonso XIII by Andrew Carnegie.

Upstairs, exhibits cover evolution from primates to modern humans. A section on geology highlights Spain's deposits of sulfur, marble, and mercury. ■

Museo Nacional de Ciencias Naturales
www.mncn.csic.es
Map p. 175
Calle José Gutiérrez Abascal 2
91 411 1328
Closed Mon. & Sun. p.m.
$
Metro: Gregorio Marañon, Nuevos Ministerios

Skeletons of dinosaurs and other animals show the size of long-extinct species at the Natural Science Museum.

Nationalist leader José Calvo Sotelo is commemorated in front of the leaning towers of Puerta de Europa in Plaza Castilla.

Nuevos Ministerios to Plaza Castilla

DEVELOPMENT OF THIS STAGE OF THE PASEO DE LA Castellana began in the 1920s, but really got going after the Civil War. General Franco wanted to create not only a new gateway to the north, but also a space for military parades and political rallies. The No. 27 bus runs the length of this route and is a good way of seeing the various flagship buildings without getting too exhausted.

Nuevos Ministerios to Plaza Castilla

🅰 Map p. 175

🚇 Metro: Nuevos Ministerios, Santiago Bernabéu, Cuzco & Plaza Castilla

Nuevos Ministerios exhibition center

✉ Paseo de la Castellana 67

☎ 91 597 5132

🕐 Closed Sun. p.m. & Mon.

🚇 Metro: Nuevos Ministerios

It is difficult to believe now, but a century ago this was open countryside with a racecourse at the start of the stretch. Now the land is occupied by the massive white granite structure known as **Nuevos Ministerios,** which was begun in the 1930s and houses several government ministries. The original architect, Secundino Zuazo, had in mind a kind of bureaucratic version of Juan de Herrera's monastery at El Escorial (see pp. 228–231), with the various sections separated by courtyard gardens. An exhibition venue under the white arches specializes in architectural shows.

Beyond the ministries on the left, on the other side of Calle Raimundo Fernández Villaverde, is another huge complex, this one devoted to shopping and business. It is known as **AZCA,** from Asociación Zona Comercial A. Dominated by a massive El Corte Inglés department store, the concrete buildings have not stood the test of time.

The brown high-rise block next to it at Paseo de la Castellana 79–81 is the **Banco**

Bilbao Vizcaya, designed by one of Spain's top 20th-century architects, Francisco Javier Sáenz de Oiza, and completed in 1978. He won several awards for this building, designed to rust with age.

Next up on the left, past AZCA, is the **Torre Picasso** *(Plaza Pablo Ruiz Picasso),* which has 43 stories and stands 515 feet high (157 m), with a white aluminum casing. It was designed in the early 1980s by Minoru Yamasaki—architect of the World Trade Center in New York—in the last years of his life and completed in 1988.

On the corner of Avenida General Perón is the **Palacio de Congresos y Exposiciones** *(Paseo de la Castellana 99, tel 91 337 8101),* a conference and exhibition center built in 1964. A dramatic mosaic by the Catalan artist Joan Miró provides a welcome splash of color in this commercial area.

Across the street is the **Estadio Santiago Bernabéu,** the home of Real Madrid soccer club, which holds a crowd of 72,000. Stadium tours take you to the locker rooms, presidential box, tunnels, and the field itself.

At the end of this stretch is **Plaza de Castilla,** a junction dominated by the sloping twin towers known officially as the Torres Puerta de Europa but more usually as the **Torres Kio.** The granite, glass, and metal structures were designed by Philip Johnson and John Burgee and completed in 1998. ∎

Estadio Santiago Bernabéu

www.realmadrid.com

🅰 Map p. 175

✉ Avenida de Concha Espina 1

☎ 91 398 4300. Ticket sales: 902 324 324

💲 Guided tours: $$$

🚇 Metro: Santiago Bernabéu

Soccer lingo

The white strip usually worn by the Real Madrid soccer team has given rise to the nickname *merengues* ("meringues"), applied to both the players and their supporters. Top players are called *galácticos,* owing both to their extraordinary talents and to the exorbitant amounts paid to bring them to the club. ∎

Estadio Santiago Bernabéu, home to the Real Madrid team, is a place of pilgrimage for soccer fans from around the world.

Contemporary art

Madrid's lively contemporary art scene is finally becoming more organized after three decades of varying fortunes. Most of the city's galleries were established following the death of General Franco in 1975, when severe restrictions on cultural expression were lifted after nearly 40 years of dictatorship.

One of the key figures in the contemporary art scene is Juana de Aizpuru, who runs galleries in Seville and Madrid and shows painting, sculpture, and photography by leading Spanish and international figures. Her artists include Sol LeWitt, Mike Kelley, Albert Oehlen, and Franz West, as well as Spanish photographers Alberto García Alix and Cristina García Rodero.

Juana de Aizpuru's greatest contribution to the Spanish art scene, however, was setting up ARCO *(Parque Ferial Juan Carlos I, tel 91 722 5800)*, Madrid's contemporary art fair, in 1982. By inviting leading artists, gallerists, and collectors from all over the world, the fair opened up the Spanish art market. In its early years, ARCO gained a reputation as a "fun" art fair. While this undoubtedly attracted audiences, it was only when the fair was put on a more professional footing in the 1990s that sales started to increase. It takes place for a week every year in February and is now an essential event for anyone in Spanish art.

The main areas for galleries are Chueca, Chamberí, the lower blocks crossing Calle Claudio Coello in the Salamanca district, and the streets around the Reina Sofía museum, particularly Calle Doctor Fourquet. The galleries in each area coordinate their opening evenings, which are detailed on leaflets available in the galleries. If your stay coincides with one of these dates, when galleries are open until midnight, it is an entertaining way to see Madrid's art world at play.

In Chueca, one of the most interesting galleries is Moriarty *(Calle Almirante 5, tel 91 531 4365)*, which started in 1981 by showing work from artists emerging from Madrid's cultural explosion, a phenomenon that became known as *la movida madrileña*. The gallery still represents key figures from the movement, but shows work by renowned international artists, too.

Soledad Lorenzo, a revered figure in the

Galería Moriarty (left and above), founded in 1980, is one of the most exciting venues in Chueca, where more than a dozen galleries are located. Here the work of Chema Madoz is featured in a recent show.

art world, always has excellent exhibitions at her large space in Chamberí, a few blocks north of Chueca. The gallery *(Calle Orfila 5, tel 91 308 2887)* shows work by Spanish artists of the caliber of Miquel Barceló, José María Sicilia, and Guillermo Pérez Villalta, as well as international artists, including Julian Schnabel and Louise Bourgeois.

The area around the Reina Sofía looks set to become the most interesting gallery area. The opening of Jean Nouvel's extension to the museum has helped to consolidate the neighborhood as Madrid's contemporary art hub, a situation that will be strengthened by the new CaixaForum space nearby, slated to be completed in 2007 (see p. 160). ∎

Plaza de Toros de las Ventas

LAS VENTAS IS THE LARGEST BULLRING IN SPAIN AND THE second biggest in the world after the one in Mexico City. Dubbed the "cathedral of Bullfighting," the ring opened in 1934 and holds almost 24,000 spectators. Bullfights are held from March to October, and the spectacular setting is also occasionally used for concerts, opera, and theatrical performances.

Plaza de Toros de las Ventas

www.las-ventas.com

- ⚑ Map p. 175
- ✉ Calle Alcalá 237
- ☎ 91 356 2200. Ticket sales: 902 150 025
- 🕐 Closed Nov.–Feb.
- 🚇 Metro: Las Ventas

Museo Taurino

- ☎ 91 725 1857
- 🕐 Closed Mon., Sat., & daily p.m.
- 💲 Guided tours: $$

Designed by José Espeliú, the red-brick structure is a good example of neo-Mudejar architecture, with horseshoe arches and ceramic decoration featuring the coats of arms of all the provinces in Spain. Outside the ring there is a monument to Dr. Alexander Fleming, whose discovery of penicillin saved many bullfighters' lives.

The arena, which has a diameter of 200 feet (60 m), is surrounded by ten sections of seats, divided into stands, boxes, and upper galleries. The ticket prices, which range from $2 to $300, are based on whether the seat is in the sun or the shade, and also on

the proximity to the action. The cheapest, therefore, are in the sun in the upper galleries, while the most expensive are in the shade and either in the boxes or in the rows close to the ring. Stand 7, in the sun, is notorious for having the most critical fans, who sing and chant throughout the fight. The band sits in Box 29 and only plays at the end, when the bull has been killed. The Royal Box is painted white, with intricate arabesque decoration, and has its own elevator and bathroom.

The key figure at a bullfight is the Presidente, who is usually a chief of police and orchestrates proceedings from the presidential box, advised by two experts. If a bullfighter has performed very well, he may be awarded one or two of the bull's ears; for a superlative fight, he receives the tail. The Presidente signals this by waving a white handkerchief. When the crowd thinks the bull-fighter deserves an ear, they will shout and wave handkerchiefs. If they are sufficiently vociferous, the Presidente is obliged to bow to their wishes. A bullfighter awarded two ears may be carried by his team through the gateway known as the Puerta Grande, used only for this purpose.

If you are not attending a bull-fight but want to take the guided tour or visit the museum, enter via the **Patio de Caballos** on the east side of the ring. This is where the horses are kept, and there is also a Mexican-style chapel, where the matadors, dressed in their suits of lights, pray before going into the ring. Next to it is a surgery with two operating theaters.

The fascinating **Museo Taurino** contains portraits with information in English that gives the background of important matadors and explains how each one contributed to bullfighting. The museum has a series of engravings by Goya from 1814–1816, based on a letter about the origin and develop-ment of bullfighting in Spain. Other exhibits include the blood-stained suit of lights worn by the famous bullfighter Manolete, who was gored to death in 1947 in Andalucía. ■

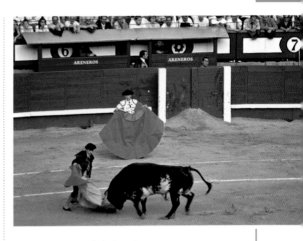

The matador and his team flourish their capes to make the bull charge (above). Bullfighting aficionados wait to meet their friends outside the bullring (below).

Abstract sculptures by 20th-century artists enliven the space beneath the Juan Bravo flyover.

More places to visit in la Castellana & Salamanca

MUSEO CASA DE LA MONEDA

The museum at Spain's Royal Mint, which produces coins and stamps, charts the development of the institution from its origins in the 18th century. The displays detail the different kinds of money used over the centuries, and the coin collection includes Greek, Roman, Visigothic, and Moorish examples. Other sections deal with stamps, lottery tickets, and tools and machinery. www.fnmt.es �ï Map p. 175 ✉ Calle Doctor Esquerdo 36 ☎ 91 566 6544 🕐 Closed Sat. & Sun. p.m. & Mon. 🚇 Metro: O'Donnell, Goya

MUSEO DE ESCULTURA AL AIRE LIBRE DE LA CASTELLANA

Under the Juan Bravo overpass on the Paseo de la Castellana are several sculptures by leading Spanish artists of the 20th century. The engineers of the overpass worked with artist Eusebio Sempere to make the most of this rather inhospitable outdoor space, which contains works by such sculptors as Joan Miró, Julio González, Pablo Palazuelo, and Martín Chirino. The highlights are Eduardo Chillida's suspended sculpture "Stranded Mermaid" and Andreu Alfaro's steel "A World for Children." www.muni madrid.es/museoairelibre ⚏ Map p. 175 ✉ Paseo de la Castellana 41 ☎ 91 588 8672 🚇 Metro: Rubén Darío

MUSEO DE LA CIUDAD

Madrid's development from its origins to the present day is charted in this modern museum. The Museum of the City contains reconstructions of important buildings and models of key places in the city's history, such as the Palacio Real, Plaza de la Villa, Paseo de la Castellana, and the Las Ventas bullring. One floor of the museum is devoted to Madrid's infrastructure and urban development, with displays on the public transportation system and the water supply. www.munimadrid.es ⚏ Map p. 175 ✉ Calle Príncipe de Vergara 140 ☎ 91 588 6599 🕐 Closed Sat. & Sun. p.m. & Mon. 🚇 Metro: Cruz del Rayo ■

MUSEO GEOMINERO

More than 6,000 fossils and 3,500 minerals are featured in the permanent displays at this museum dedicated to geology and mining. The collections are housed in the Escuela Superior de Ingenieros de Minas, which was designed by Ricardo Velázquez Bosco and is decorated with ceramic friezes, arches, columns, and statues. Ask at the museum's entrance if you can also take a look at the building's magnificent Gothic-style library. www.igme.es ⚏ Map p. 175 ✉ Calle Ríos Rosas ☎ 23 91 349 5759 🕐 Closed p.m. 🚇 Metro: Ríos Rosas ■

Characterized by grandiose architecture from the era of General Franco, the city's western edge is bordered by leafy parkland, which sprawls down the hillside toward the Manzanares River.

Plaza de España & western Madrid

Suits of armor at the Museo Cerralbo

Plaza de España & western Madrid

THE AREA TO THE WEST OF PLAZA DE ESPAÑA HAS A DISTINCTIVE character, quite different from that of the dense downtown streets. Here you can easily appreciate how Madrid is set higher than the surrounding countryside, with clear views to the Sierra de Guadarrama in the northwest. The breeze blowing in from the mountains, together with the proximity to the river, cools the air and reduces pollution, making this a popular residential area. Students from the university campus in Moncloa pack the streets of the district of Argüelles, which is a lively area full of shops and bars.

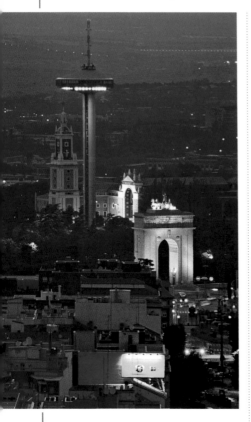

The Faro de Madrid rises up behind the Arco de la Victoria.

Plaza de España is flanked on two sides by signature skyscrapers that testify to Franco's illusions of grandeur. Back in the 18th century, the hill to the east of the square was earmarked as the site for the new royal palace. The idea never came to fruition, and instead of a palace, a huge barracks, the Cuartel del Conde Duque, was built between 1714 and 1720 on the hill, which is now a cultural center.

Calle de la Princesa leads off Plaza de España toward Argüelles, an area developed in the second half of the 19th century. The stretch between the Argüelles and Moncloa metro stations is lined with shops, which suddenly give way to the huge redbrick complex of the headquarters of the Spanish air force. Beyond this is a triumphal arch, the Arco de la Victoria, built to commemorate Franco's victory in the Civil War.

The futuristic Faro de Madrid (Faro observation tower) is located just in front of the Museo de América, one of Madrid's most important museums, which has outstanding collections from the different cultures of Latin America. A short walk away is the Museo del Traje, an excellent new museum devoted to all aspects of fashion and clothing over the centuries.

Beyond Plaza de España to the northwest is the leafy oasis of the Parque del Oeste. Now a pleasant place to stroll or picnic, the park has a dark past as the scene of wartime fighting. A cable car links it to the Casa de Campo park across the river, with its zoo and amusement park. ■

CAMINO ZARZÓN

Zoo Aquarium

0   400 meters

0   400 yards

Casa de Campo

◁6

C. SINESIO DELGADO

CALLE FRANCOS RODRÍGUEZ

DEHESA
DE LA VILLA

Francos
Rodríguez

M30

A6

CARRETERA DEHESA DE LA VILLA

AVENIDA COMPLUTENSE

QUINTA
DE LOS PINOS

◁5

Alvarado

MONCLOA

AVENIDA PUERTA DE HIERRO

Manzanares

CARRETERA EL PARDO

PASEO JUAN XXIII

C. RAMIRO DE MAEZTU

AVENIDA PABLO VICTORIA

Metropolitano

AVENIDA REINA IGLESIAS

Cuatro
Caminos

PARQUE
BOTÁNICO

Guzmán
el Bueno

AVENIDA COMPLUTENSE

Ciudad
Universitaria

C. ISAAC PERAL

PASEO SAN FRANCISCO DE SALES

CALLE BRAVO MURILLO

◀ Palacio
de la Moncloa

PASEO SAN FRANCISCO DE SALES

◁4

CARRETERA CASTILLA

M30

Universidad Complutense

PASEO SAN FRANCISCO DE SALES

CALLE CEA BERMÚDEZ

Museo del Traje ◀

PLAZA
CRISTO REY

CALLE GUZMÁN EL BUENO

CALLE VALLEHERMOSO

Canal

Museo de América ◀

Islas Filipinas

CALLE

CALLE OBISPO TREJO

Faro de Madrid ◀

GLORIETA
QUEVEDO

AVENIDA SÉNECA

Arco de la
Victoria

PASEO MORET

Moncloa

Quevedo

CAMINO GARABITAS

PARQUE
DEL
OESTE

**Cuartel General
del Ejército del Aire** ◀

PASEO MARQUÉS DE MONISTROL

ARGÜELLES

Argüelles

C. ALBERTO AGUILERA

GLORIETA
RUIZ JIMÉNEZ

CAMINO VALDEZA

**La Rosaleda
de Ramón Ortiz** ◀

PASEO PINTOR

C. MARQUÉS DE URQUIO

CALLE PRINCESA

Palacio de Liria ◀

CASA
DE
CAMPO

PASEO PIÑONEROS

Manzanares

Cementerio ◀

ROSALES

Ventura
Rodríguez

**Centro
Cultural del
Conde Duque** ◀

◁3

**Estación Salida
Teleférico** ◀

Noviciado

Teleférico

**Iglesia de
San Antonio
de la Florida** ◀

**Templo
de Debod** ◀

**Torre de
Madrid** ◀

**Iglesia
de San Marcos** ◀

CARRETERA TELEFÉRICO

PASEO PLÁTANOS TORRECILLA

Museo Cerralbo ◀

Montaña del
Príncipe Pío

PLAZA
ESPAÑA

Edificio España ◀

Plaza de España

GRAN VÍA

**Terminal
Teleférico** ◀

Príncipe Pío ◀

**Convento de los
Padres Carmelitas
Descalzos** ◀

PASEO CASTAÑOS

Lago Casa
de Campo

GLORIETA
SAN VICENTE

Príncipe
Pío

Santa
Domingo

Callao

C. BAILÉN

Lago

AVENIDA ÁNGEL

Palacio Real

Ópera

CAMPO
DEL
MORO

PASEO VIRGEN DEL PUERTO

**Catedral de
la Almudena** ◀

◁2

CARRETERA BATÁN

**Parque de
Atracciones** ◀

AVENIDA PORTUGAL

Puerta
del Ángel

M30

C. SEGOVIA

É

PASEO EXTREMADURA

Alto de
Extremadura

PARQUE
DE CARAMUEL

**PLAZA DE ESPAÑA
& WESTERN MADRID**

Batán

E90

◁I

△
D

Manzanares

NV   Lucero

△
C

Area of map detail

Plaza de España

THE SPACE NOW OCCUPIED BY PLAZA DE ESPAÑA WAS known as Leganitos meadow back in the 17th century and features in *Don Quijote de la Mancha*. The site was later occupied by a convent, which was demolished unfinished in 1789, and then by a barracks, which met the same fate in 1908. The current plaza took shape in the mid-20th century, after the victory of General Franco's Nationalists in the Civil War. The square was developed as a symbol of national greatness, its imposing buildings intended to show how Spain was becoming part of the modern world.

Plaza de España
- Map p. 197
- Metro: Plaza de España

The top of the square at the Gran Vía end is dominated by the massive bulk of the **Edificio España,** one of Madrid's signature buildings. Designed by Joaquín and Julián Otamendi, the tiered structure in brick and limestone with neo-baroque decoration has 25 stories and 32 elevators. When it was completed in 1953, it was the tallest building in Spain at 384 feet (117 m).

The revolutionary building was intended to be a self-contained urban complex, containing offices, apartments, restaurants, stores, a hotel, and a rooftop swimming pool. The hotel, which occupies a third of the building, is now part of the Crowne Plaza group.

The **Torre de Madrid,** on the west side of the square, became Madrid's tallest building, and the world's tallest concrete structure, when it was built in the 1950s. The work of the Otamendi brothers, measuring 466 feet (142 m) high with 34 stories, it's called the "Giraffe" by Madrileños owing to its tall, slender shape. It was the tallest building in Madrid for four decades until the construction of the Torre Picasso in 1988 (see p. 189).

In the center of the square, there is a monument to Miguel de Cervantes, designed and built between 1925 and 1930 by the architects Rafael Martínez Zapatero and Pedro Muguruza, and sculpted by Lorenzo Coullaut Valera. A stone figure of Cervantes, seated and holding a book, presides over the monument, with bronze figures of Don Quixote on his horse and Sancho Panza on his donkey in front of the great writer.

The mosaic dome at the bottom of the square belongs to the church of the **Convento de los Padres Carmelitas Descalzos.** Designed in 1916, its facade features neo-medieval decoration. ■

The Cervantes monument in Plaza de España (above and right) features Don Quixote and Sancho Panza, with Cervantes behind.

Museo Cerralbo

Museo Cerralbo
http://museocerralbo
.mcu.es

🅰 Map p. 197

✉ Calle Ventura
Rodríguez 17

☎ 91 547 3646 or
91 547 3647

🕓 Closed p.m. & Mon.

💲 $. Free Wed. &
Sun.

🚇 Metro: Plaza de
España, Ventura
Rodríguez

THE MARQUIS OF CERRALBO, ENRIQUE DE AGUILERA Y Gamboa (1845–1922), was an eccentric maverick who led a rich and varied life. As well as being active in politics, he was an avid archaeologist, traveled widely, and collected art and artifacts from all over the world. His palatial home gives an intriguing insight into how the nobility lived in the late 19th and early 20th centuries.

His collections include paintings, armor, fans, clocks, lamps, swords, ceramics, and archaeological finds, among other items displayed throughout the mansion. Highlights of the painting collection include "The Ecstasy of St. Francis" by El Greco, as well as works by other 17th century artists including Titian, Tintoretto, Zurbarán, José de Ribera, and Alonso Cano.

As you walk around the second floor, peek into the **bathroom,** which has an enormous marble tub. Separate bathrooms were a luxurious novelty at the time, as running water had only just become available in Madrid. This floor was where the family lived and contains bedrooms, sitting rooms, and a dining room. Perhaps the most surprising is the **music room,** which is dominated by an enormous lamp made of colored Murano glass in the shape of a gondola.

The grand staircase is decorated with the coat of arms of the Cerralbo family as well as 17th-century tapestries. The third floor was used principally for entertaining, and the rooms are correspondingly grander. The exception is the austere, galleried library, which contains 12,000 books. Exhibits on this floor include the armor worn by the second Marquis of Cerralbo in 1592 defending La Coruña against the English fleet led by Francis Drake. The **ballroom** is the most astounding room in the house, with opulent marble, stucco, and silk decoration.

Don't miss the **basement,** which contains a fascinating collection of photographs and memorabilia related to the family's travels and social life. ■

Templo de Debod

WHEN THE ASWAN DAM WAS BUILT IN LOWER NUBIA IN Egypt in the 1960s, many temples and monuments were in danger of being lost in the floodwaters. The Debod temple was actually underwater, visible only when the dam was opened in the summer and the water level dropped. A team of Spanish archaeologists and engineers helped save the temples of Abu Simbel, and in recognition of their efforts this temple was donated to Spain in 1968. One of the few Egyptian monuments outside the country, it was rebuilt in the Parque del Oeste and opened to the public in 1972.

Templo de Debod
www.munimadrid.es
/templodebod

Map p. 197

Parque del Oeste, Paseo Pintor Rosales

91 366 7415

Closed Sat. p.m., Sun. p.m., & Mon.

Metro: Ventura Rodríguez, Plaza de España

The construction of the temple began at the beginning of the second century B.C. on the orders of King Adikhalamani of Meroe. Various Ptolemaic pharaohs continued the work, building a series of rooms around the original nucleus. After Egypt was annexed to the Roman Empire, the temple was completed by the emperors Augustus, Tiberius, and possibly Hadrian, who added courtyards, the entrance pathway, and a landing quay on the Nile River.

Dedicated to the gods Amun and Isis, the temple contains a series of chapels, the most interesting of which is dedicated to King Adikhalamani. An audiovisual exhibit re-creates the visit of French archaeologist Jean François Champollion in 1829 to decipher its inscriptions.

The red granite *naos* (inner chamber) was built by Ptolemy XII in 80–51 B.C. and was the most sacred place in the temple. The god Amun was believed to live there, and only priests were allowed to enter. Upstairs, a model shows the location of Abu Simbel and other temples. ∎

The ancient Debod temple was brought to Spain from the banks of the Nile.

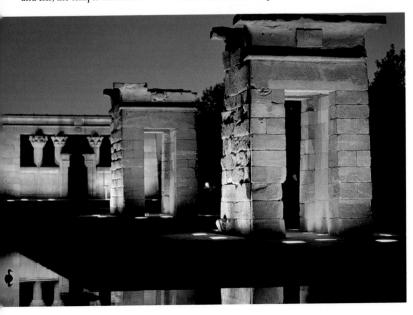

Madrid's western parks

Madrid's western parks

Map p. 197

Parque del Oeste

Avenida del Arco de la Victoria & Paseo del Pintor Rosales

Metro: Moncloa

Reindeer at the Zoo-Aquarium live in a spacious enclosure.

MADRID'S TWO WESTERN PARKS FORM A SUBSTANTIAL green space that stretches for miles toward the Sierra de Guadarrama. Separated by the Manzanares River, they have very different characters. The Parque del Oeste is ideal for walks in the fresh air or a picnic on the grass, as it is a shady space with sandy paths leading through landscaped gardens. The Casa de Campo, while wilder with more scrubland, offers a wealth of leisure activities, including cycling, boating, and swimming in huge outdoor pools.

One of Ernest Hemingway's favorite spots in Madrid, the **Parque del Oeste** was designed by landscape gardener Cecilio Rodríguez in 1906. Just three decades later, however, it was virtually destroyed during the Civil War and had to be rebuilt in the 1940s. The sloping L-shaped space stretches from Plaza de España up to the university campus in Moncloa and down to the Manzanares River in the west. One of the most beautiful parts of the park is **La Rosaleda de Ramón Ortiz,** a rose garden that hosts a competition for the best blooms each spring.

The southern end, toward Plaza de España, is known as the Montaña del Príncipe Pío and is the highest part of the park, with sweeping views across the city. There used to be a large barracks here, near where the Templo de Debod is now (see p. 201), a stronghold of General Franco's troops at the start of the Civil War. This area is also where 43 Madrileños were executed by French soldiers on May 3, 1808 (see pp. 204–205). The victims are buried in a small **cemetery** in the center of the park, on Calle Francisco y Jacinto Alcántara. The cemetery opens to the public

only on May 2 and 3 each year.

There are several sidewalk cafés by the park on the Paseo del Pintor Rosales. They are pleasant places to stop off for a cool drink or ice cream. Near the cafés is the station for the **Teleférico** cable car *(tel 91 541 7450 or 91 541 1118,*

$), which will take you over to the **Casa de Campo.** The park was originally a hunting ground, created by Felipe II in the mid-16th century to link his residence at the Alcázar with the hunting lodge at El Pardo (see p. 232). It became known as the Royal Wood and was extended over the centuries by other monarchs. In the Civil War, Franco's army used this site to attack the city, and trenches still exist in the park.

The recently modernized **Zoo-Aquarium** houses about 6,000 animals on 50 acres (20 ha) of landscaped grounds. The 500 different species include gorillas, koalas, and white tigers. The sharks and dolphins are the highlight of the aquarium. Next to the zoo is the popular **Parque de Atracciones** amusement park, which has 40 rides, as well as restaurants and an outdoor arena for summertime concerts. ■

Casa de Campo
✉ Avenida de Portugal
☎ 91 479 6002
Ⓜ Metro: Lago, Batán, Casa de Campo
Bus: 33

Children visiting the zoo are encouraged to help feed the exotic birds.

Zoo-Aquarium
www.zoomadrid.com
✉ Casa de Campo
☎ 91 512 3770
$ $$$
Ⓜ Metro: Batán, Casa de Campo; Bus: 33

Parque de Atracciones
www.parquedeatracciones.es
✉ Casa de Campo
☎ 91 463 2900 or 91 463 6433
$ $$$
🕐 Closed a.m.
Ⓜ Metro: Batán
Bus: 33, 65

Patriotic uprising

May 2 is a public holiday in the Madrid area and marks the start of three weeks of festivities. It is the day when Madrileños celebrate everything that is good about the city, but the events that led to this date of commemoration were anything but happy.

In March 1808, King Carlos IV was in Bayonne in France with his son Fernando, who wanted his father to abdicate so that he could succeed to the throne. After Manuel Godoy, his powerful prime minister, was ousted by a popular uprising in Aranjuez (see p. 220) on March 17, the ineffectual Carlos gave in to his son's wishes and Fernando briefly became king.

On March 23, the French army entered Madrid under Marshal Murat, ostensibly as part of an alliance formed between Carlos IV and Napoléon Bonaparte in order to attack Portugal. Ten thousand soldiers came into the city itself, with another 20,000 in the surrounding villages. Fernando VII was still in Bayonne, where, many Madrileños believed, he was being held prisoner. They suspected that the entire royal family was planning to flee to France, abandoning them to Napoléon's troops.

On the morning of May 2, crowds gathered in front of the Palacio Real, as it was rumored that Prince Francisco de Paula, the youngest son of Carlos IV, was leaving Madrid to join his family. As the people became increasingly agitated, French troops started shooting indiscriminately into the crowds, and the situation soon deteriorated into widespread violence.

There were about 8,600 Spanish soldiers in Madrid, most of whom performed ceremonial duties at the Royal Palace and did not have any combat experience. When the trouble began, their commander, Francisco Javier Negrete, ordered his men to remain in their barracks, reasoning that they were underarmed and drastically outnumbered,

and therefore unable to resist the French attack. Many managed to escape, however, to fight alongside the citizens of Madrid. A fierce battle took place in the Puerta del Sol, where Madrileños, many of them women, fought against the Mamelukes, a squadron of Egyptian soldiers renowned for their brutality. The battle was later commemorated by Goya in the painting "The Second of May, 1808, in Madrid: the Charge of the Mamelukes," which is on display in the Prado museum.

The desperate Madrileños resolved to arm themselves with weapons stored at the Monteleón artillery barracks, located where Plaza Dos de Mayo is now (see p. 107). Two young army captains, Pedro Velarde and Luis Daoíz, took charge of the crowd and armed them with swords. Savage fighting then ensued in the surrounding streets, which led to thousands more French troops being sent to the area to try to gain control of the barracks. Both Velarde and Daoíz died in the battle, in which at least 800 French soldiers were killed.

The French military authorities were incensed at suffering such losses at the hands of a mainly civilian force and ordered their troops to capture and shoot anyone found on the streets with weapons. These executions were carried out at several locations around the city, but the place that will always be remembered is the Montaña del Príncipe Pío. These shootings, which took place in the early hours of May 3, were depicted by Goya in his seminal painting "The Third of May, 1808, in Madrid: Executions on Príncipe Pío Hill," which is also in the Prado museum.

Despite their heroic resistance, the Madrileños eventually had to admit defeat. Napoléon installed his brother Joseph as king of Spain, leading to the Spanish War of Independence. The exact number of casualties was never known, but, surprisingly, more French than Spanish died. According to the official figures, about 2,000 French soldiers were killed, but only about 150 Madrileños lost their lives. ■

Goya's painting depicting the executions of Madrileños on May 3, 1808, is a haunting image of the brutality of war.

Ermita de San Antonio de la Florida

THIS NEOCLASSIC CHURCH HAS A RATHER PLAIN exterior, but often the most unpromising places hold the greatest riches. This is certainly the case here, as the dome is decorated with astonishing frescoes by no less an artist than Francisco de Goya.

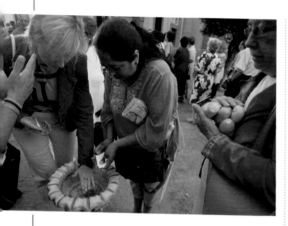

On St. Anthony's day, unattached women visit the font at San Antonio de la Florida to help bring romance their way.

Ermita de San Antonio de la Florida

- Map p. 197
- Glorieta de San Antonio de la Florida 5
- 91 542 0722
- Closed Sat p.m., Sun p.m., & Mon.
- Metro: Príncipe Pío

The Greek-cross church, which was designed by Italian architect Filippo Fontana, was completed

Romantic ritual

On June 13, hundreds of women come to San Antonio de la Florida to take part in a ritual that they hope will improve their romantic prospects in the following year. The tradition, which was started by seamstresses, involves dropping 13 pins into the font, then putting the palm of your hand on top to see how many stick to it. You do this three times, and the number of pins that stick indicates the number of boyfriends you can expect to come along. Nowadays, women of all ages form a winding line to the font, which is moved to the garden outside the church for the occasion. ∎

in 1798. Goya, who was then 52 years old and had become deaf, took only four months to paint the dome. The frescoes depict a miracle said to have been performed by St. Anthony of Padua after his father, Martín de Bulloes, had been accused of murder. The saint brought the man back from the dead to name the real killer and thereby absolve his father. The scene shows a group of people gathered around a circular railing, using light and color to shape the form of the figures. If you look at each of them individually, you see that they all have very definite expressions and features. Some look like rather unsavory characters, while others have kind faces, but above all these are real people, such as you might encounter today.

The church's location so close to the Manzanares River, together with the perishable paint that Goya used, meant that cracks appeared in the walls and the paint gradually deteriorated. In the 1920s, it was decided to try to prevent further damage by building a replica church alongside for parish services. The original building is now also known as the **Museo y Panteón de Goya.** The restoration of the frescoes, which did not begin until 1989, was completed in 2005, just in time for the popular street festival that takes places every year on the weekend closest to June 13, St. Anthony's day. ∎

Moncloa's museums

THE MONCLOA AREA HOUSES THE SPRAWLING CAMPUS OF the Universidad Complutense, Madrid's main university. Among the facilities are two major museums: one devoted to Spain's former colonies in Latin America and the other to fashion and costume. Also worth visiting is the observation tower known as the Faro de Madrid, which provides panoramic views of the city.

The Museo del Traje displays fashions by leading designers as well as regional costumes.

MUSEO DEL TRAJE

The Museo del Traje, which opened in 2004, has extensive collections of historical costumes and contemporary fashion. The development of clothing is traced from the late 16th century to the present day, with examples of regional costume from all over Spain. One section is devoted to leading Spanish designers from the 20th century, including Mariano Fortuny, Paco Rabanne, and Pertegaz, who designed Letizia Ortiz's dress for her marriage to Crown Prince Felipe in 2004. A room is devoted to Balenciaga, the renowned Basque designer. The textile section includes lace and embroidery, as well as examples of Coptic and Hispano-Muslim designs. The displays are exhibited on a rotating basis to avoid deterioration from excessive exposure to light.

The building, which previously housed the Spanish Museum of Contemporary Art, was designed in the late 1960s by Ángel Díaz Domínguez and Jaime López de Asiaín and won the National Prize for Architecture. It has a good gift shop, as well as an excellent café and a formal restaurant.

FARO DE MADRID

The Faro tower, designed by Salvador Pérez Arroyo in 1992, is 302 feet (92 m) high and is used primarily for telecommunications and traffic supervision. It is also open to visitors, who zoom up to a circular observation deck in a glass elevator. You can see across Madrid with stunning views of the Guadarrama mountains. Information panels on the deck help to identify key buildings around the city.

Museo del Traje
http://museodeltraje.mcu.es
- Map p. 197
- Avenida Juan de Herrera 2
- 91 550 4700
- Closed Sun. p.m. & Mon.
- $. Free Sat. p.m. & Sun. a.m.
- Metro: Moncloa, Ciudad Universitaria Bus: 46, 82, 83, 84, 132, 133

Faro de Madrid
- Map p. 197
- Avenida de los Reyes Católicos
- 91 544 8104
- Closed Mon.
- $
- Metro: Moncloa

MUSEO DE AMÉRICA

This museum, which explores the cultures of Spain's former colonies in Latin America, contains unrivaled collections of artworks, ceramics, and weaponry. The exhibits, which range from the pre-Columbian period to the present day, were either brought to Spain during the centuries of

of America in 1892, including the Quimbayas Treasure from Colombia, one of the highlights of the museum.

The displays are organized in five sections on the second and third floors and are arranged thematically rather than geographically or chronologically. **Area 1** begins with the myths that arose

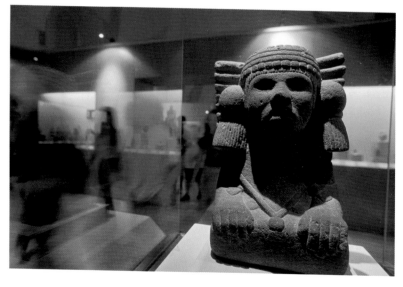

A sculpture of Aztec goddess Chalchiutlicie is on display in the Museo de América.

Museo de América
http://museodeamerica. mcu.es

- Map p. 197
- Avenida de los Reyes Católicos 6
- 91 549 2641 or 91 543 9437
- Closed p.m. & Mon.
- $. Free Sun.
- Metro: Moncloa, Islas Filipinas

Spanish rule or donated by Latin American governments. The museum is particularly strong on the ancient civilizations of Colombia, Peru, and Mexico.

Although the museum has been open in its current form only since 1994, it has its origins in the 16th century, when Felipe II took steps to found a museum for objects brought back from America. In the 18th century, finds from scientific expeditions were added to the collections, which were first exhibited in the Museo Arqueológico Nacional (National Archaeological Museum). Important donations were made to commemorate the fourth centenary of the discovery

about America in Europe over the centuries, then explains how more accurate information started to come through from Spanish chroniclers and as a result of expeditions. Exhibits include fascinating maps, Amazonian feathered hats, Diquis gold from Costa Rica, and an extraordinary 18th-century feathered cape from Hawaii.

Area 2 covers the geography and landscapes of Latin America and charts how the mix of races and cultures came about from Paleolithic times to the present day. Exhibits include letters and logs written by Christopher Columbus.

Area 3 deals with the way different indigenous populations, from tribal communities to complex societies, organized their everyday lives. Ceremonies to mark rites of passage, such as childbirth, puberty, and marriage, are illustrated by feathered headdresses, jewelry, and ornaments. Exhibits include Olmec jades, Incan objects, ceramics from Ecuador, and basketware by Hopi and Chumash Indians. This section continues on the next floor, where there is a reconstruction of a Maya house.

Some of the most precious pieces in the museum are in **Area 4,** which focuses on religious beliefs. There are rooms devoted to funeral rites, fertility symbols, and sacred objects. A highlight is the limestone Madrid Stele, which dates from A.D. 600–800 and shows a Maya god. Inscribed with hieroglyphics, the stone originally supported a throne in the palace in Palenque, Mexico. It was found in 1785 by archaeologist Antonio del Río, who was sent to excavate the ruined palace by Carlos III. Also here is the amazing pre-Columbian Quimbayas Treasure, which Colombia would now like to have back in its own country. Discovered in 1819, the 125 objects in the Treasure include crowns, musical instruments, and figures of caciques, mainly in gold and silver. They date from A.D. 500–1000.

The final section, **Area 5,** explores the themes of language and communication. The key exhibit is the Tro-Cortesian codex, one of only four Maya manuscripts in the world, thought to date from the 15th century. It comprises 56 pages covered with scenes from Maya life as well as hieroglyphics that link activities such as harvesting and hunting to specific dates. Probably made for a spiritual leader, it is packed with religious and magical references.

Also of great interest is the 16th-century Tudela codex, which was made at an art school set up by Franciscan monks in Mexico. Its 125 pages contain paintings by an indigenous artist and texts in Spanish written by a missionary. ■

Arches crown the Natural History Room at the Museo de América (top). A restorer works on an 18th-century tapestry (above).

The Palacio de Liria was built in the 18th century for the third Duke of Berwick.

More places to visit in Plaza de España & western Madrid

CENTRO CULTURAL DEL CONDE DUQUE

Originally the barracks for the Royal Guard, this massive building was designed by Pedro de Ribera in 1717. It has been extensively restored and refurbished for its current use as a lively exhibition center and concert venue. It also houses the Municipal Museum of Contemporary Art, which has rotating displays of works by artists including Ouka Lele, Ceesepe, and Javier de Juan. www.muni madrid.es/museoartecontemporaneo 🅰 Map p. 197 ✉ Calle Conde Duque 9–11 ☎ 91 588 5928 or 91 588 5861 🕐 Closed Sun. p.m. & Mon. 🚇 Metro: Noviciado, San Bernardo, Ventura Rodríguez, Plaza de España

CUARTEL GENERAL DEL EJERCITO DEL AIRE

The vast headquarters of the Spanish Air Force were designed in the 1940s by Luis Gutiérrez Soto, who was advised by Hitler's architect, Albert Speer. With its granite and redbrick facade, slate roofs, and slender spires, it emulates the Habsburg architecture of the 17th century. General Franco wanted to create a style for the architecture of his dictatorship that would link him to Spain's period of greatest splendor, and this building certainly reflects his desire for architectural grandeur. 🅰 Map p. 197 ✉ Calle Romero Robledo 8 ☎ 91 549 0700 🚇 Metro: Moncloa

IGLESIA DE SAN MARCOS

Designed by Ventura Rodríguez in the mid-18th century, the interior of this elegant church features five overlapping ellipses, a device used to overcome the problem of the narrow building site. It was constructed to commemorate the victory of Felipe V at the Battle of Almansa in 1707. The dome is decorated with frescoes by Luis González Velázquez, and there is a polychrome figure of St. Mark by Juan Pascual de Mena on the altarpiece. 🅰 Map p. 197 ✉ Calle San Leonardo 10 ☎ 91 547 1079 🚇 Metro: Plaza de España, Ventura Rodríguez

PALACIO DE LIRIA

The Palacio de Liria, which is the home of the Duchess of Alba, was designed by Ventura Rodríguez and Sabatini in the second half of the 18th century. After being damaged by fire in the Civil War, it was restored by Sir Edwin Lutyens. The palace was built for Jacobo (James) Fitz-James Stuart, the third Duke of Berwick. It contains an impressive art collection, including works by such major painters as Rembrandt, Titian, El Greco, Velázquez, and Goya. Unfortunately, the palace is open to the public only by reservation, and viewing is strictly limited. 🅰 Map p. 197 ✉ Calle de la Princesa 20 ☎ 91 547 5302 🕐 Guided tours Fri. a.m. 🚇 Metro: Ventura Rodríguez ■

The area around Madrid is dotted with historic towns, royal palaces, monasteries, hilltop castles, dramatic mountains, and medieval villages, all of which make memorable day trips. The undisputed highlight is the monumental city of Toledo.

Excursions

The fairy-tale castle of the Alcázar in Segovia

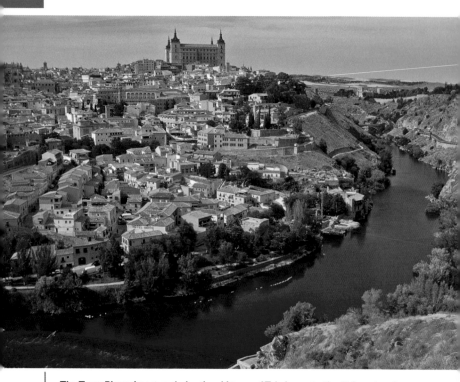

The Tagus River almost encircles the old town of Toledo, protecting it from invaders.

Excursions

THERE IS A HUGE VARIETY OF PLACES TO VISIT AROUND MADRID, AND MOST of them are easy to reach in an hour or so, whether by public transportation or by car. You can choose from historic sites such as Toledo, El Escorial, Segovia, or Aranjuez for your excursion or go for a more leisurely look around the countryside, with a break for a hearty lunch at a traditional restaurant. Keep in mind that the locals love escaping on weekends, too, particularly to the villages in the mountains around the city, which means heavy traffic jams returning to Madrid on Sunday evenings.

There are good train and bus services in and out of Madrid, but a car is useful if you want to combine several places in one day. For many first-time visitors to Madrid, Toledo is the essential day out. After the largely 19th-century appearance of central Madrid, the wealth of medieval monuments lining the narrow lanes of Toledo is quite a contrast. Also high on most people's lists is the massive 16th-century monastery at El Escorial, which encapsulates the spirit of the Habsburg realm.

Nearer Madrid, the university town of Alcalá de Henares is packed with fascinating monuments and is famous as the birthplace of writer Miguel de Cervantes. After a few days in the hectic, noisy capital, however, you may just feel like driving south of Toledo across the plains of La Mancha to see some of the places mentioned in *Don Quixote.* Or, for an even quieter getaway, you can head up to the hills in the Sierra de Guadarrama for a hike through the pine forests in the pure mountain air. ■

Toledo

ONE OF SPAIN'S GREAT HISTORIC CITIES, TOLEDO IS spectacularly situated on a granite hill, almost surrounded by the Tagus River. Its winding lanes are particularly atmospheric in the evening when the tourist buses have departed, making an overnight stay a rewarding experience if you have time. There is a tremendous amount to see—the entire city center has National Monument status—so plan carefully if you have only one day.

Inhabited since prehistoric times and settled by the Romans, Toledo became the capital of Visigothic Spain in A.D. 554. When the Moors arrived in 712, they allowed the Christian and Jewish communities to remain in the city and carry on their lives as usual, creating a flourishing trading and cultural center. After Alfonso VI gained control in 1085, Toledo became the capital of the kingdom of Castile and León. The three cultures continued to prosper and played an important role in the development of the Western world, particularly in the fields of astronomy, mathematics, medicine, music, and literature.

The Christian rulers gradually became less tolerant, however, and the Jews began to be persecuted and were eventually expelled in 1492. This was disastrous for the economy, and the situation worsened when Felipe II transferred the court permanently to Madrid in 1561. It was shortly after this, in 1577, that the Greek painter El Greco arrived in Toledo, living through the city's decline until his death in 1614. In the same year, the final Muslim descendants were expelled, which severely affected the manufacturing industry.

THE SIGHTS

Standing in the heart of the city, the extraordinary **Catedral** was begun 1226 and completed in 1493, standing on the site of a sixth-century temple founded by the Visigoths. The intricately carved choir stalls include battle scenes from the conquest of Granada. The altarpiece is a Flamboyant Gothic polychrome carving of the life of Christ. In the ambulatory behind the altar is the astounding Transparente (1732), which was designed by Narciso Tomé to allow light to penetrate from the ceiling and consists of marble figures from the Last Supper amid a riot of angels and saints. The Treasury contains a superb 16th-century monstrance by Enrique del Arfe. There are several paintings by El Greco in the **museum,** as well as works by Titian, Velázquez, and Goya.

West of the Catedral is a cluster of monuments including the **Iglesia de Santo Tomé** *(Plaza del Conde, tel 925 256 098, $),* which houses El Greco's masterpiece "The Burial of the Count of Orgaz." Nearby is the **Museo de El Greco** *(Calle Samuel Leví, tel 925 224 046, closed Sun. p.m. & Mon., $, free Sat. p.m. & Sun. a.m.),* which contains a good collection of his paintings, including "View and Map of Toledo" (circa 1614).

Opposite is the Sinagoga del Tránsito (Synagogue of the Transit), which is now the **Museo Sefardí.** Built in the mid-14th century for Samuel ha-Leví, who was treasurer to Pedro el Cruel of

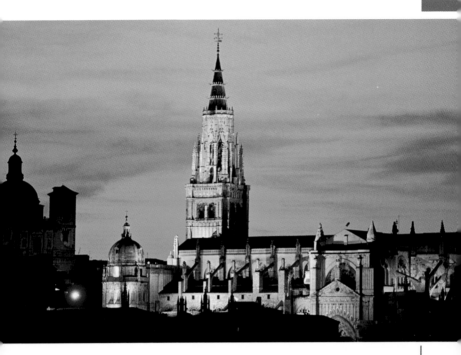

Castile, the interior features bands of Hebrew calligraphy and a spectacular cedarwood-coffered ceiling. The fascinating museum traces the history and culture of Sephardic Jews over the centuries.

The Moors built the **Sinagoga de Santa María la Blanca** *(Calle de los Reyes Católicos 4, tel 925 227 257, $)* for Jews in Christian times at the end of the 12th century. The white interior looks more like a mosque than a synagogue, with aisles divided by horseshoe arches. A little farther down the road is the **Monasterio de San Juan de los Reyes,** built for the Catholic Monarchs in the late 15th century. The church was designed by Juan Guas and combines Gothic, Mudejar, and Renaissance features. The cloister has delicate filigree carvings, with a Mudejar ceiling on the upper gallery.

At the top of the hill east of the Catedral stands the massive **Alcázar** *(Cuesta Carlos V 2, tel 925 223 038, closed for restoration until 2008)*, which dates from the 11th century but has often been rebuilt. A Nationalist stronghold in the Civil War, it was relentlessly besieged by the Republicans. When the restoration is completed, the building will house the Army Museum, which is being transferred from Madrid.

Nearby is the busy **Plaza de Zocodover,** which was a cattle market under the Arabs before Juan de Herrera remodeled it in the 16th century. Just off the square through an arch is the **Museo de Santa Cruz** *(Calle Cervantes 3, tel 925 221 036)*, a beautiful Renaissance structure that Cardinal Mendoza founded as an orphanage in the 16th century. Now a museum of art and archaeology, it contains paintings by El Greco and Goya as well as Roman mosaics, ceramics, and tapestries. ∎

Toledo presents a dramatic profile when twilight falls and the church towers stand out against the backlit sky.

Museo Sefardí
www.museosefardi.net
✉ Calle Samuel Leví
☎ 925 223 665
🕐 Closed Sun. p.m. & Mon.
💲 $. Free Sat. p.m. & Sun. a.m.

Monasterio de San Juan de los Reyes
✉ Calle San Juan de los Reyes 2
☎ 925 223 802
💲 $

Toledo's Catedral is a superb example of Spanish Gothic architecture.

A walk around Toledo

This walk takes you through steep, high-walled streets, stopping at intriguing churches, convents, and even a mosque. Toledo is full of fascinating corners, so remember to look down side alleys as you walk around, as well as to gaze up at the tiled balconies and into the plant-filled courtyards.

From Plaza de Zocodover, walk down the busy Calle Comercio, Toledo's main shopping street. When you reach a crossroad, continue down the hill along Calle del Hombre de Palo, then bear left down Calle Arco del Palacio and walk through the arch to reach the main door of the **Catedral** ❶ (see p. 214) on the triangular Plaza del Ayuntamiento.

Walk up the steps to the left of the **Palacio Arzobispal** (Archbishop's Palace) opposite, which lead to the pretty Plaza del Consistorio. Make a sharp right and walk up Cuesta del Ordenal. At the top, turn right and immediately left into the narrow Callejón de Jesús María. At the top turn right, where you will see the imposing baroque facade of **San Ildefonso.** Turn left beside the church into Calle de San Román, which leads to the church of **San Román** ❷; the entrance is around the corner on Calle San Clemente. Originally a Visigoth

church, this structure is Mudejar and was built in the 12th century. Inside there are Roman columns, Caliphal arches, Romanesque frescoes, and a Plateresque chapel. It now houses a museum of Visigothic culture, the **Museo de los Concilios y de la Cultura Visigoda** (tel 925 227 872, closed Sun. p.m. & Mon.). You can walk up the bell tower for views across the city and surrounding countryside.

On leaving the church, continue down Calle de San Román and turn left at the bottom into Plaza de Padilla. Cross the square diagonally to descend the steps, and then turn right to skirt the convent and church of **Santo Domingo el Antiguo** ❸ (tel 925 222 930, closed Sun. a.m.). This was Toledo's first convent, founded in 1085 by Cistercians, and it is today home to 12 nuns. The church, neoclassic inside, houses the tomb of El Greco and has three of his paintings. Two of these, "St. John the

Baptist" and "St. John the Evangelist," are part of the altarpiece; the third, the exceptional "Resurrection of Christ," is on the right. El Greco's modest tomb is in the crypt, visible through a glass pane in the floor. The magnificent choir and adjoining antechamber are also full of interest.

Walk down Calle de Santa Leocadia to Plaza Merced, dominated by the grand provincial council building. Turn right up Calle Merced, which becomes a typically narrow, high-sided lane, to Plaza de Capuchinas. Continue up Calle Tendillas and take the first left down Calle Algibes. This brings you to the baroque facade of **Santo Domingo el Real ❹**, one of several convents on the square. Walk through the *cobertizo* (a covered passageway), turn right up another, and continue along Calle Santa Clara until you skirt the apse of the 13th-century Mudejar church of **San Vicente.**

Turn left into Calle de los Alfileritos, and then take the third lane on your left, Calle del Cristo de la Luz. This brings you to the

- See area map p. 213
- ► Plaza de Zocodover
- ↔ 2.6 miles (4.2 km)
- ⏱ 2 to 3 hours
- ► Puerta de Bisagra

NOT TO BE MISSED
- Catedral
- Iglesia de San Román
- Convento de Santo Domingo el Antiguo
- Mezquita del Cristo de la Luz

Mezquita del Cristo de la Luz ❺ *(tel 925 254 191, $)*, a stunning mosque dating from A.D. 999.

Continue downhill through the arch and down the steps. Turn right and immediately left onto Calle Real de Arrabal, which leads to the Gothic-Mudejar **Iglesia Santiago de Arrabal ❻**, built in the 13th century. Just beyond the church you come to the **Puerta de Bisagra,** the city's main gate. ■

Don Quixote country

IT IS FOUR CENTURIES SINCE *EL INGENIOSO HIDALGO DON Quijote de la Mancha* (usually known to English-speaking readers as *Don Quixote*) was published in 1605. Written by Miguel de Cervantes (1547–1616), this great novel is set in the vast area south of Toledo, parts of which remain remarkably wild to this day. Don Quixote rides across this landscape with his faithful squire, Sancho Panza, encountering an array of colorful characters along the way. The adventures that they experience in the course of the book make for a fast-paced story, but the novel is also a satire of the social mores prevalent in Spain at the end of the 16th and beginning of the 17th centuries.

Think of Don Quixote, and images of castles, plains, and windmills spring immediately to mind. If you drive southeast from Toledo, you soon pass by a string of castles at Almonacid de Toledo, Mascaraque, Mora, Manzaneque, and the pretty village of Orgaz. Nearby is **Tembleque,** where Sancho Panza worked before joining Don Quixote on his quest to make the world—or at least La Mancha—a better place. Tembleque has a lovely town square, with wooden balconies and granite arcades.

To the east, amid a landscape of lakes and oak forests, is the village of **Villacañas,** founded by the Knights of the Order of St. John in the 13th century. Some inhabitants still live in underground caves. With lakes on either side of the road, you soon come to **Campo de Criptana,** where windmills stretch across the plains. In Don Quixote's illusory world, the windmills became giants who waved their elongated arms to fend off enemies.

Vineyards cover the fields along the road to **El Toboso,** which was home to the lovely Dulcinea. Her house has been reconstructed in 16th-century style with typical furnishings of the time and is now a museum. Nearby is the **Museo**

Cervantino, with many editions of the book. More windmills dot the landscape around **Mota del Cuervo,** on the road to the village of **Belmonte** to the east, which has an imposing 14th-century castle and whitewashed houses.

Perhaps the most impressive windmills are at **Consuegra,** south of Orgaz. The 11 mills, open to visitors, were used to grind wheat for flour. Each *molino* has a name, and the first one, "Bolero," is a tourist center. One of the most interesting is "Sancho," which has its original 16th-century equipment and still operates during the Saffron Rose Festival every October. From "Vista Alegre," near the fortress at the top of the hill, there are panoramic views across the plains. "Caballero del Verde Gabán" has been turned into a library, with editions of *Don Quixote* in various languages.

Heading south, you arrive at **Puerto Lápice,** a village mentioned several times in the novel and where a medieval atmosphere still prevails. The landscape changes as you cross the wetlands of the **Parque Nacional de las Tablas de Daimiel,** home to many species of aquatic birds.

Continuing south, you reach **Almagro,** a flourishing town in the 16th and 17th centuries. The well-preserved center revolves around its golden age theater, the **Corral de Comedias,** on the main square, where the International Festival of Classical Theater takes place in July. The arcaded **Plaza Mayor** is one of the most spectacular in Spain. With good restaurants, hotels, and shops, Almagro is a good choice for an overnight stop. ■

Almagro
www.ciudad-almagro.com
Visitor information
✉ Plaza Mayor 1
☎ 926 860 717

A newly married couple prepares for an atmospheric set of wedding photographs at Campo de Criptana.

Aranjuez

Aranjuez
www.aranjuez.com

📍 213 C3

✉ 30 miles (48 km) south of Madrid

🚗 By car: A-4 (direction: Córdoba) to exit 37, then M-305. By train: C-3 from Atocha station. By bus: AISA & SAMAR from Estación Sur

WITH A PRIVILEGED LOCATION BETWEEN THE JARAMA and Tagus Rivers, this elegant town developed around a royal palace built in the 18th century. Aranjuez is also renowned for the delicious strawberries and asparagus that grow in spring in the fertile fields alongside the rivers. The extensive gardens around the palace inspired Joaquín Rodrigo to compose the "Concierto de Aranjuez," and the town was also the setting of Schiller's play, *Don Carlos*. A visitor train *(tel 902 088 089)* links the various points of interest, which otherwise require walking several miles.

The Palacio Real's Arab Room reflects a warm Moorish style.

Visitor information

✉ Plaza San Antonio 9

☎ 91 891 0427

Note: From early April to mid-Oct., Sat. & Sun. only, the "Tren de la Fresa" steam train runs between Madrid and Aranjuez, with palace & museum admission included *(tel 902 240 202)*.

The **Palacio Real** *(Plaza de Parejas, tel 91 891 1344, closed Mon., $$)* was originally built as a spring and summer residence for Felipe II, but the structure was largely destroyed by fire in 1655. Felipe V asked Santiago Bonavía to design and build a new palace, which reflects the French tastes of the Bourbon monarchy. Highlights include the China Room, lined with porcelain tiles made at Madrid's Buen Retiro factory. Also impressive are the Rococo Throne Room and the Arab Room, inspired by the Alhambra in Granada.

The gardens around the palace are open on Mondays when the buildings are closed. The **Jardín del Príncipe** (Prince's Garden) has 371 acres (150 ha) planted with a surprising variety of trees, many of which grew from seeds brought from the Americas.

At the far end of the garden is the **Casa del Labrador,** a neo-classic mansion built for Carlos IV by Isidro González Velázquez in 1804. The most astounding of a series of lavish rooms is the **Gabinete de Platino,** where the walls are encrusted with gold, platinum, and bronze. Nearby is the **Museo de Falúas Reales,** a museum of leisure boats used by the royal family. ∎

Chinchón

Chinchón's medieval main square has been a lively marketplace for hundreds of years.

THERE ARE NOT MANY SIGHTS IN THE QUAINT LITTLE town of Chinchón, but people flock here on weekends to enjoy a hearty lunch at one of the restaurants on the porticoed main square, Plaza Mayor. Wooden balconies surround the irregularly shaped medieval space.

The square has been used for bullfights for the past 500 years, but nowadays they take place only during local festivals in July, August, and October. Concerts and theatrical performances are occasionally staged there, too, including a passion play at Easter. Shops around the square sell the local specialties, which include *anís,* a strong aniseed liquor made at several distilleries around the town, as well as chorizo sausage, garlic, and wine.

The hills around the square are a labyrinth of tiny streets lined with grand mansions displaying coats of arms and huge wooden doors. These include the **Casa de la Cadena,** south of the square, where Felipe V stayed in 1706 during the War of Spanish Succession.

Francisco de Goya's brother Camilo was a priest at the 16th-century **Iglesia de la Asunción,** just north of Plaza Mayor, which has a painting attributed to the artist on the altarpiece. Goya used to visit the town regularly, and he liked to paint in the square. The playwright Lope de Vega also used to come here, as his plays were often staged in a theater in the palace of the Counts of Chinchón. The **Teatro de Lope de Vega** now stands on the site, next to Iglesia de la Asunción.

In the 1960s, Orson Welles stayed in town while filming *Chimes at Midnight* and *The Immortal Story.* Chinchón is still a popular location when a director requires a medieval square. It is not unusual to come across a film crew on a weekday morning. ∎

Chinchón
www.ciudad-chinchon.com
🗺 213 C4
✉ 28 miles (45 km) south of Madrid
🚗 By car: A-3 to Puente de Arganda, then M-311, or A-4 to M-404 turnoff. By bus: La Veloz service 337 from outside Conde de Casal metro station (tel 91 409 7602)

Visitor information
✉ Plaza Mayor 6
☎ 91 893 5323

Street actors portray a scene from *Don Quixote*.

Alcalá de Henares

ALTHOUGH IT IS QUICK AND EASY TO REACH FROM Madrid, Alcalá de Henares gets relatively few visitors. Ugly industrial development on the outskirts means it looks unpromising as you approach, but there is plenty to see in this charming place once you venture into the center. An important Roman town, its university was founded in 1499 and Miguel de Cervantes was born there in 1547. Leading golden age writers studied in the town in the 17th century, and their plays were performed at a courtyard theater that still exists.

The theater, known as the **Corral de Comedias** *(tel 91 882 2442)*, is located in Plaza de Cervantes, the main square. Dating from 1601, the theater retains its original layout and has recently undergone restoration. At the time of writing, it was used only for occasional performances, but may open to visitors in the future. Ask at the tourist office, as it is really worth seeing.

The main building of the **University** *(Plaza San Diego, tel 91 885 6487)* is the 16th-century Renaissance-style **Colegio de San Ildefonso.** The **Patio Trilingüe** within the university got its name from the schools of Latin, Greek, and Hebrew that were originally located around the courtyard. The **Capilla de San Ildefonso,** completed in 1510, has a magnificent Mudejar coffered ceiling.

Leading off Plaza de Cervantes is the arcaded **Calle Mayor,** which is more than half a mile long (1 km). It leads to the **Museo Casa Natal de Cervantes** *(Calle Mayor 48, tel 91 889 9654, closed Mon.),* which is a reconstruction of the house where the great writer was born. Farther along Calle Mayor is the late-Gothic **Catedral Magistral** *(Plaza de los Santos Niños, tel 91 888 0930, closed Sat. & Sun., except during services),* built at the beginning of the 16th century. Its bell tower, like many in the town, hosts a stork's nest. ■

Alcalá de Henares

www.alcalaturismo.com

- 213 C4
- 21 miles (34 km) east of Madrid
- By car: A-2/N-2 (direction: Zaragoza). By train: C-1, C-2, & C-7A from Atocha station. The "Tren de Cervantes," with tourist information and guided tour, runs May–Oct. Sat.–Sun. By bus: Continental Auto service 233 from Avenida de América station (tel 91 356 2307)

Visitor information

- Callejón Santa María 1
- 91 889 2694

Ávila

THE WALLED TOWN OF ÁVILA IS A WORLD HERITAGE SITE, set high on a spur at an altitude of 3,609 feet (1,100 m) with panoramic views across the plains. It is often bitterly cold in winter, but during the rest of year it is a pleasant place to explore on foot. The medieval center is packed with churches and convents, many of them devoted to St. Teresa, the 16th-century mystic who became one of Spain's patron saints. Traditional restaurants in the town serve Iberian black beef from a local breed of cattle.

The walls, built at the end of the 11th century to fend off the Moors, have 88 cylindrical turrets and 9 gateways. At 39 feet (12 m) high and 10 feet (3 m) thick, they are the most substantial walls in the world, showing the impor-

tory, don't miss the tomb of Bishop Alonso de Madrigal, nicknamed "El Tostado" ("the toasted one") for his dark complexion. The **museum** in the sacristy contains a monstrance (1571) by Juan de Arfe.

Ávila
www.avilaturismo.com
⬛ 213 A5
✉ 70 miles (113 km) northwest of Madrid
🚗 By car: A-6 to Villacastín, then N501. By train: From Chamartín or Atocha stations By bus: Larrea (91 530 4800) from Estación Sur

Visitor information
✉ Plaza Pedro Davila
☎ 920 211 387

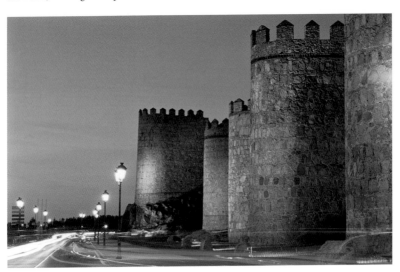

tance of the town after the Christian Reconquest. You can walk around them, a distance of 1.5 miles (2.5 km), starting from the Puerta del Alcázar.

The **Catedral,** begun in the 12th century, mixes Romanesque and Gothic styles. There are Plateresque carved stalls in the choir and paintings by Pedro Berruguete and Juan de Borgoña on the high altar. In the ambula-

The **Convento de Santa Teresa** *(Plaza de la Santa)* is a 17th-century baroque structure on the site where St. Teresa's house stood. A chapel in the room where she was born contains sculptures by Gregorio Fernández. The saint spent 27 years at the **Monasterio de la Encarnación** *(Paseo de la Encarnación, closed Tues.),* outside the walls, where a museum contains a reproduction of her cell. ∎

Ávila's 11th-century ramparts still surround the city.

Catedral
✉ Plaza de la Catedral
☎ 920 211 641
💲 Museum: $

Segovia's castle, cathedral, and churches are all built from golden sandstone.

Segovia

WITH ITS FAIRY-TALE CASTLE, ROMAN AQUEDUCT, AND strategic location on a limestone ridge between two rivers, Segovia is nothing if not dramatic. Despite its wealth of monuments, however, Segovia is not just a tourist town. It has a lively cultural scene, and historic buildings are being assigned new uses as galleries, museums, or schools. No trip would be complete without a meal of roast lamb or suckling pig at one of the town's excellent restaurants. At an altitude of 3,300 feet (1,000 m), it is always colder here than in Madrid, so bring an extra layer, even in summer.

Segovia

www.segoviaturismo.co

 213 B5

✉ 53 miles (85 km) NW of Madrid

🚗 By car: A-6 to Guadarrama, then the direct N603, scenic N601, or fastest (toll) AP-61 By train: C-8b from Atocha or Chamartín (local) By bus: La Sepulvedana (tel 91 530 4800) from Paseo de la Florida 11

Before Madrid was made capital, Segovia was one of the most important places in Castile, as borne out by the town's many Romanesque churches. The Castilian king Alfonso VI installed his court there and Isabella Católica was proclaimed Queen of Castile in the church of San Miguel in 1474. The town declined as Madrid gained in importance, but it enjoyed an

18th-century renaissance when Felipe V built a palace a few miles away at La Granja in the 1720s (see p. 232).

The area was inhabited as far back as 80 B.C., but it came to prominence under the Romans, who built the **aqueduct** at the end of the first century A.D. Made of granite blocks from the Guadarrama mountains, with no binding material to hold them together, it is 95 feet (29 m) high and 2,388 feet (728 m) long, with 166 arches. It was built to bring water from the Frío River, 12 miles (19 km) away, a function it fulfilled until the 1960s. Following restoration in the 1990s, it can now carry water again, but no longer supplies the town.

From **Plaza del Azoguejo,** in front of the aqueduct, **Calle Cervantes** leads up toward Plaza Mayor. On the right you pass the 15th-century **Casa de los Picos,** with a distinctive facade studded with pointed granite stones. The street later becomes Calle Juan Bravo, named after the hero of the Revolt of the Comuneros (1520–1521), when the inhabitants of Castile protested the unfair treatment they were receiving from Carlos V and the nobility. There is a statue of Bravo in **Plaza de San Martín,** next to the church of the same name, which has a Mudejar tower. Nearby is the square 15th-century **Torreón de Lozoya** *(open from 7 p.m.),* which belonged to one of the town's many noble families. Beside the tower is the **Museo de Arte Contemporáneo Esteban Vicente** *(Plaza de las Bellas Artes, tel 921 462 010, closed Sun. p.m. & Mon.),* which displays work donated by this abstract expressionist painter. The museum, in a 15th-century palace, also puts on temporary exhibitions.

Just off the semiporticoed **Plaza Mayor,** with its outdoor cafés, rises the vast, late-Gothic **Catedral,** which stands at the highest point of the town. The harmonious, golden sandstone structure was built in the 16th century by Juan Gil de Hontañón and his son Rodrigo. Near the entrance, in the Capilla de la Piedad, there is a polychrome altarpiece by Juan de Juni (1571). The cloister, by Juan Guas, was moved here from an earlier structure near the Alcázar. The high altar was designed by Francesco Sabatini and was added at the end of the 18th century. As well as tapestries and Romanesque and Gothic statuary, the **muse-**

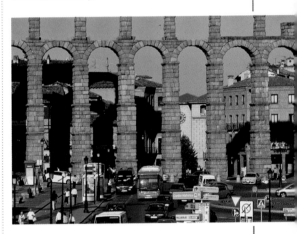

The towering Roman aqueduct was built to bring water to Segovia from the Guadarrama mountains.

um contains the tomb of the Infante Don Pedro, son of Enrique II, who fell to his death in 1366 from the Alcázar.

The **Alcázar,** on the edge of the ridge, looks like a ship that is about to set sail across the fields of Castile. Originally built by the Trastámara dynasty in the 13th century, the castle was extended by Felipe II, but had to be rebuilt after being largely destroyed by fire in the mid-19th century. With its turrets, spires, parapets, and ramparts, it looks the part of a fantasy castle, and it has featured in numerous movies. The Royal Artillery runs the **museum** inside, where weapons and suits of armor are displayed in rooms with beautiful Mudejar ceilings. If you walk up the 150 steps to the top of the tower, you are rewarded with sweeping views. ■

Visitor information

- ✉ Plaza Mayor 10
- ☎ 921 460 334
- ✉ Plaza del Azoguejo 1
- ☎ 921 466 720

Catedral

- ✉ Calle Marqués del Arco 1
- ☎ 921 462 205
- 💲 Cloisters, chapter house, museum: $

Alcázar

www.alcazardesegovia.com
- ✉ Plaza de la Reina Victoria Eugenia
- ☎ 921 460 759
- 💲 $. Free on Tues. for EU nationals

A drive around the Guadarrama mountains

The Sierra de Guadarrama, northwest of Madrid, is a range of granite mountains that runs between the plains of La Mancha and Castile. This drive takes you through some dramatic landscapes with plenty of places to stop and breathe the mountain air. Roads are good and well signposted, but check weather conditions in winter as there is sometimes heavy snowfall.

The Cuenca Alta del Manzanares nature reserve is popular with weekend hikers.

From central Madrid, head north up Paseo de la Castellana and take the M-607. Just after Colmenar el Viejo, turn onto the M-609, and, after 3 miles (5 km), take the M-608 toward Manzanares el Real. You drive through the Cuenca Alta del Manzanares nature reserve, a good place to stretch your legs, with the Santillana reservoir on the left and the craggy peaks of La Pedriza on the right.

As you approach **Manzanares el Real** ①, the village's 15th-century fairy-tale **castle** (tel 91 853 0008, closed Mon., $$$) appears before you. The restored structure was built for the powerful Mendoza family and has cylindrical towers and a gallery with fabulous views. There is also a museum inside that charts the castle's history.

Continue along the M-608, toward Cerceda, then turn onto the M-607 toward Navacerrada. The road starts to climb steadily as you drive past another reservoir on the left. **Navacerrada** ②, which has a 16th-century church, is popular with weekenders from Madrid and has several cafés

and restaurants. Turn right immediately after the village onto the M-601 up to the mountain pass of **Puerto de Navacerrada.** At 6,168 feet (1,880 m), this is a small ski resort on the border between the Madrid region and Segovia province, which stretches out below you as you reach the top immediately beyond the village. Turn right at the junction here onto the M-604 toward Cotos and Rascafría, with the valley on your left and the steep hillside covered in pine trees to the right.

After 10 minutes you reach **Puerto de Cotos** mountain pass at 6,004 feet (1,830 m), which used to be a ski station but has recently been turned into the Peñalara nature reserve. On the hillside above the café there is an information center where you can pick up a leaflet detailing well-marked walking routes.

Continue along the M-604 toward Rascafría. The road now winds down into the Lozoya Valley, dropping 2,300 feet (700 m). After 20 minutes, just before Rascafría, you reach the **Real Monasterio de Santa María de El Paular** (tel 91 869 1425, www.monasterioelpaular.com). Founded in 1390, the monastery is home to a small community of Benedictine monks. The 16th-century church has an altarpiece with Gothic tracery. Part of the monastery has been converted into the upscale **Hotel Santa María de El Paular** (tel 91 869 1011), which has two restaurants.

Rascafría ③, five minutes farther along the M-604, has a range of restaurants. From the village, take the M-611 toward Miraflores de la Sierra, which is 15 miles (24 km) away over the Puerto de Morcuera pass. After crossing the Lozoya River, the road climbs again with a series of sharp bends. The landscape here is gentler, however, with cattle grazing in the fields. As you drive over the Puerto de Morcuera pass at 5,892 feet (1,796 m), the plains of Castile open up before you, and the road winds down to **Miraflores de la Sierra** ④. The village, which is surrounded by oak forests and is very lively on weekends, is a pleasant place for a stroll and a coffee at an outdoor café.

To return to Madrid, follow the signs along the M-611, M-609, and M-607, passing Soto del Real and Colmenar el Viejo. As you approach Madrid, keep in the lane for the M-30, then take the Paseo de la Castellana/Plaza de Castilla exit. ∎

▲ See area map p. 213
▶ Madrid
↔ 110 miles (177 km)
⊕ 1 day, including stops
▶ Madrid

NOT TO BE MISSED
- Castillo de Manzanares el Real
- Real Monasterio de Santa María de El Paular

Bell towers flank the solemn basilica at the heart of El Escorial's complex.

El Escorial

San Lorenzo de El Escorial

www.sanlorenzoturismo.org

 213 B4

✉ 30 miles (49 km) northwest of Madrid.

🚗 By car: A-6 to Guadarrama, then M-600
By train: C-8a from Atocha or Chamartín. By bus: Herranz (91 896 9028) service 661 or 664 from Intercambiador de Moncloa station

THE PALACE-MONASTERY OF SAN LORENZO DE EL ESCORIAL was founded by Felipe II to provide a suitable resting place for his father, Emperor Carlos V, and future Spanish monarchs. The enormous granite structure symbolizes the glory of the Habsburg dynasty, the power of the Spanish Empire, and Felipe's firm commitment to the Catholic faith. The charming small town of San Lorenzo below the monastery has a range of cafés and restaurants. Although in the foothills of the Guadarrama mountains, El Escorial is at a height of 3,373 feet (1,028 m), providing stunning views across the landscape.

The name commemorates the Spanish victory over the French at the battle of St. Quentin in 1557, which took place on August 10, St. Lawrence's day. The structure has a parallelogram layout, which represents the gridiron on which the saint was burned to death. Built between 1563 and 1584, it was designed by Juan Bautista de Toledo. After Toledo's death in 1567, Juan de Herrera took over the project, which included not only the monastery, but also a palace, college, seminary, and library. The building is 673 feet (205 m) from north to south and 525 feet (160 m) from east to west. There are 2,673 windows, 1,200 doors, and 16 courtyards.

The original Hieronymite monks were forced to leave the monastery following the disentailment of religious property in 1836. A community of Augustinians moved into the monastery in 1885 and now run a school in the building.

VISITING EL ESCORIAL

The visit follows a set route, which is well signed with information panels in Spanish and English. You start in the **Sala de San Mauricio,** which contains the El Greco painting "The Martyrdom of St. Maurice and the Theban Legion" (1580–1582). Stairs lead down to the **Museo de Arquitectura,** a museum that charts the development of the building and the ways in which Herrera modified the original plans. Most of El Escorial's superlative art collection is now in the Prado, but the nearby **Museo de Pintura** still contains several Spanish, Flemish, and Italian masterpieces. These include works by Titian, Tintoretto, Veronese, Rubens, and José de Ribera. Look for the triptych by Michel Coxcie (1499–1592), "The Martyrdom of St. Philip."

Stairs lead to the **Palacio de Felipe II,** where the first rooms were occupied by his daughter, the Infanta Isabel Clara Eugenia. The **Sala de Retratos** contains portraits of Habsburg monarchs. The **king's bedchamber,** where he died in 1598, is surprisingly austere. The bed was angled so that Felipe could see the high altar of the church.

Regal grandeur soon returns as you descend to the baroque **Panteón Real,** an octagonal chamber adorned with gilt, red jasper, and black marble. The pantheon contains the tombs of nearly all the Spanish monarchs from Carlos I to Alfonso XIII. Nine adjoining chambers contain tombs of princes and princesses.

The vaulted chapter houses, the **Salas Capitulares,** contain more outstanding paintings by El Greco, Velázquez, and Titian. Don't miss "Christ Carrying the Cross" and "The Crown of Thorns" by Hieronymus Bosch.

The courtyard **Patio de los Evangelistas** is surrounded by a **cloister,** which is decorated with frescoes on the theme of the Redemption. In the courtyard's center is a small Doric temple.

The magnificent **Basílica** stands at the center of El Escorial, surrounded by 43 side chapels. It is crowned by a dome 302 feet (92 m) high and decorated with stunning frescoes by Lucas Jordán. The **Capilla Mayor,**

Visitor information

✉ Calle Grimaldi 2
☎ 91 890 5313

The gilded bronze altarpiece in the Capilla Mayor is the most important part of El Escorial's church.

The tombs of Spanish monarchs are traditionally kept in the Panteón Real at El Escorial.

Real Monasterio de San Lorenzo de El Escorial
www.patrimonionacional.es/escorial/escorial.htm

⚠ 213 B4

✉ Paseo de Juan de Borbón y Battenberg

☎ 91 890 5902 or 91 890 5903 or 91 890 5904

🕐 Closed Mon.

💲 $$. Free Wed. for EU nationals

which is the spiritual core of the entire building, is dominated by an altarpiece in gilded bronze and marble, flanked by sculptures of Carlos I and Felipe II and their families. One of the side chapels contains a monumental marble "Christ" sculpted by Benvenuto Cellini (1500–1571) in 1562.

Above the **Patio de los Reyes** (Courtyard of the Kings) on the west side of the structure is the barrel-vaulted **Royal Library,** which is 180 feet (55 m) long and contains more than 40,000 books and documents, including the diary of St. Teresa and Greek, Latin, Arab, and Hebrew manuscripts. Look up at the ceiling frescoes, which were painted by Pellegrino Tibaldi and represent Philosophy, Theology, Grammar, Rhetoric, Music, Arithmetic, Geometry, Dialectics, and Astrology. The books are stacked with the spines facing inward and the leaves outward, a technique that allows air to permeate the paper. Among several globes, the most intriguing is the pine **Armillary Sphere,** which was made about 1582 and shows the solar system as it was defined by the Greek astronomer Ptolemy, with the Earth in the center of the universe.

In the gardens around the monastery there are two pavilions that Juan de Villanueva designed during the reign of Carlos III.

Main entrance

College with four courtyards

Grand entrance

EL ESCORIAL

Opening times vary during the year, so ask at the monastery if you are interested in seeing the interiors.

Surrounded by magnolia, sequoia, and cedar trees in the **Jardínes del Príncipe** is the Italianate **Casita del Príncipe,** which was has a neoclassic facade and was built in 1772 for the future Carlos IV. Inside are tapestries, paintings by Lucas Jordán and Corrado Giaquinto, and a room covered with porcelain plaques made at the Buen Retiro factory in Madrid.

MORE SIGHTS

The town of San Lorenzo holds an elegant 18th-century theater, the **Real Coliseo de Carlos III.** A 20-minute walk along the Paseo de Carlos III brings you to the **Casita del Infante** (or Casa de Arriba; *Crta. de Robledo de Chavela, tel 91 890 5903, $*), a small hunting lodge that was home to King Juan Carlos when he was a student.

Three miles (5 km) up the hill south of the monastery is the **Silla de Felipe II,** a seat carved from rock where the king watched the building's construction. ■

Basílica

Museo de Arquitectura

Panteón Real (below church)

Museo de Pintura

Patio de los Evangelistas

Salas Capitulares

Monastery with four arcaded courtyards

Patio de los Reyes

More places to visit around Madrid

EL CAPRICHO DE OSUNA
This neoclassic palace and gardens near the Madrid airport were built in the 18th century for the Duke and Duchess of Osuna, a cultured couple who were friends of Goya's and leading figures in artistic circles. The gardens, which were designed by Jean-Baptiste Mulot, have islands, bridges, follies, streams, and a

Visitors stroll in the gardens of El Capricho.

lilac maze. Badly damaged during the Civil War, when the palace was a Republican stronghold, the complex has been meticulously restored in recent decades. 🅰 213 C4 ✉ Paseo de la Alameda de Osuna, 6 miles (10 km) east of Madrid center ☎ Information from Madrid Tourism Center, tel 91 588 1636 ⏱ Closed Mon.–Fri. 🚇 Metro: Canillejas, then bus 101, 105, 151

PALACIO REAL DE EL PARDO
Originally a hunting lodge, this royal palace was embellished and extended by various monarchs over the centuries. The present structure is mostly 18th century with 19th-century decoration. Previously the official residence of General Franco, it is now used by visiting heads of state. There is a good selection of restaurants in the town of **El Pardo,** most of which specialize in local game. www.patrimonionacional.es 🅰 213 B4 ✉ Calle Manuel Alonso, 9 miles (14 km) northwest of Madrid ☎ 91 376 1500 ⏱ Closed Sun. p.m. 💲 $. Free Wed. for EU nationals 🚌 Bus: 601 from Moncloa

PALACIO REAL DE LA GRANJA DE SAN ILDEFONSO
This royal palace was built for Felipe V starting in the 1720s and reflects the French tastes of the first of the Bourbon monarchs. Designed by Teodoro Ardemans and several Italian architects, including Juvarra and Sacchetti, the palace comprises a series of elegantly decorated rooms. The excellent tapestry museum is closed for restoration until at least 2007. The high point is provided by the gardens, which were designed by René Carlier and contain spectacular fountains. Nearby in the village is the **Real Fábrica de Cristales** (*Paseo del Pocillo 1, tel 921 010 700, closed Mon. & Tues.*), a glass factory founded in 1770 where the glassware is on sale. www.patrimonionacional.es 🅰 213 B5 ✉ Plaza de España 17, La Granja de San Ildefonso, 56 miles (90 km) northwest of Madrid ☎ 921 470 019 ⏱ Palace closed Mon. 💲 $$. Free Wed. for EU nationals 🚌 Bus: La Sepulvedana from Paseo de la Florida 11 (tel 91 530 4800)

VALLE DE LOS CAÍDOS
General Franco chose the spectacular valley of the Guadarrama mountains as the site for his mausoleum. Marking the location is a granite cross that is 492 feet (150 m) high and can be seen for miles around. The sinister monument was built in the 1940s and 1950s by Republican prisoners, who were forced to dig into the rocky mountainside. The basilica was designed by Pedro Muguruza and contains an enormous crypt that houses the tombs of General Franco and José Antonio Primo de Rivera, the two most important figures of the Nationalist movement. The remains of 40,000 soldiers and civilians who died during the Civil War lie in ossuaries beside countless statues of Spanish saints and soldiers. The monument is slated to be remodeled in the near future as an exhibition center. www.patrimonio nacional.es 🅰 213 B5 ✉ Carretera de Guadarrama/El Escorial, Valle de Cuelgamoros, 7.5 miles (12 km) east of El Escorial ☎ 91 890 5344 ⏱ Closed Mon. 💲 $$ 🚌 Bus: 660 from El Escorial ∎

Travelwise

A postcard stand

TRAVELWISE INFORMATION.

PLANNING YOUR TRIP

WHEN TO GO

Madrid is welcoming all year round and, being small for a capital city (population about 3 million), it is compact and easy to explore, even on foot—the best way to get to know it. The most comfortable months as far as temperatures go are April–May and September–October, when Madrid's street life is at its most active.

August is traditionally family vacation month. Many head for the coast, and the smaller and most typical bars, restaurants, and shops tend to close. The museums and monuments do stay open, however, and the Veranos de la Villa (Summers in the City) festival, between June and September, fills the town with concerts, art exhibitions, and theatrical performances, many free of charge.

CLIMATE

Madrid is right in the middle of Spain. On the high *meseta* (plateau) at an altitude of 2,120 feet (646 m) above sea level, it is the highest capital in Europe. It is also the one with the most hours of sunshine. The city gets very hot in midsummer, not cooling down much even at night, and pretty cold and windy in midwinter. The rainiest months are October–December and April–May, so if you come then, bring rainwear. The atmosphere generally is very dry.

Average minimum/maximum temperatures
Jan. 36.7/49.5°F (2.6/9.7°C)
Apr. 45/63.5°F (7.2/17.5°C)
July 65.1/88.2°F (18.4/31.2°C)
Oct. 50.4/66.2°F (10.2°C/19°C)

MAIN EVENTS

Madrid has many festivals and fiestas, some national, some city wide, and others barrio based. The key Madrid festival is that of San Isidro, its patron saint, on May 15, a classic *romería* (pilgrimage) involving a religious procession, Mass, and offerings to the saint, a picnic, and then music and dancing. Centered around the church of San Isidro, it then shifts to the Pradera (meadow) of San Isidro, and concerts take place in Plaza Mayor and Las Vistillas park. The San Isidro bullfighting festival at Las Ventas offers prestigious bullfights every day for a month.

The Carnaval, in February or early March, celebrates the final days before Lent with a mixture of processions, fancy dress balls, and cultural events. The Baile de Máscaras at the Círculo de Bellas Artes is a 3,000-strong fancy-dress ball on Carnaval Saturday, and Sunday is a wonderful day out for children (disguised as pirates, princesses, or whatever they fancy), ending up with live music and theater.

Easter week (Semana Santa) can be in March or April; it fills the town with colorful medieval-style religious processions, and there's an enjoyable combination of ancient ritual and eating and dancing.

From August 6 to 15, Madrid celebrates three of its most thoroughly Madrileño festivals: San Cayetano, San Lorenzo, and the Virgen de la Paloma. The days are dominated by religious processions and the evenings by *verbenas* (outdoor dances). The locals dress in the classic Madrileño outfits: men in corduroy or finely checkered trousers, white shirt, neckerchief, black vest, and flat cap, and women resplendent in long dresses and scarves tied over their hair.

October sees the Festival de Otoño (Autumn Festival), offering music from the classical to the most modern, as well as dance and theater.

WHAT TO TAKE

You should be able to buy most necessities. Spaniards generally tend to dress more formally than North Americans and the British. While casual clothes and footwear are perfectly acceptable during the day, if you are going to a fancy restaurant or out for the evening, it is worth dressing up.

Most North American appliances (such as hair dryers) will require converters (see p. 238).

Bring any essential prescription medication. For other medicines, Spanish pharmacists are knowledgeable and helpful, and they will dispense many drugs that need prescriptions in other countries.

HEALTH

No vaccinations are required. Madrid tap water is safe to drink and remarkably soft and tasty. Plastic 1-liter or 1/3-liter bottles of mineral water are widely available. The primary health concerns are sunburn and dehydration. If you are out in the sun for a while, make sure you wear suitable clothing and put sunscreen on. During the hottest parts of the day in the summer, few local people will be out on the street if they can avoid it.

INSURANCE

Make sure that you have adequate travel and medical coverage for treatment and expenses, including repatriation, and baggage and money loss. Keep all receipts of your expenses. Report losses or thefts to the police and obtain a signed statement (*una denuncia*) from a police station to help you back up insurance claims.

HOW TO GET TO MADRID

ENTRY FORMALITIES

U.S. and Canadian citizens may enter Spain and remain there for up to 90 days without a visa.

The 90-day limit applies to the EU as a whole, so crossing an EU internal border does not extend it. U.S. and Canadian citizens planning a longer trip should submit visa application forms to their nearest Spanish consulate or embassy well ahead of time. British citizens can enter Spain without a visa for an indefinite period. It is advisable to keep your identity card or passport on you at all times.

BY AIR

The national carrier, Iberia, has regular direct flights to Madrid from New York, Chicago, and Miami. It also operates in collaboration with American Airlines in the U.S. from 20 other airports and with British Airways in Canada from Toronto, Montreal, and Vancouver. These flights often involve stopovers. Onward internal flights in Spain bought in conjunction with the international flight are often a very good value. U.S. airlines such as Delta also offer direct flights. Many European carriers, such as Air France, Lufthansa, and British Airways, have regular flights to Madrid.

USEFUL NUMBERS & INTERNET ADDRESSES
In Spain
   Air Europa, tel 902 401 501
   American Airlines, tel 902 115 570
   British Airways, tel 902 111 333
   Delta Airlines, tel 91 749 6630
   Iberia, tel 902 400 500

In the U.S. & Canada
   Air Europa, tel 212/921-2381, www.air-europa.com
   American Airlines, tel 800/433-7300 (English), 800/633-3711 (Spanish), www.aa.com
   British Airways, tel 800/247-9297 (U.S.) or 416/250-0880 (Toronto), www.britishairways.com
   Delta Airlines, tel 800/241-4141, www.delta.com

   Iberia, tel 800/772-4642 (U.S.) or 800/423-7241 (Canada), www.iberia.com

ARRIVING FROM THE AIRPORT
International flights to Madrid arrive at Barajas airport, which is 8 miles (13 km) from Madrid city center. A taxi ride to the center will cost roughly 25 to 30 euros ($30–$36) and take about 30 minutes, depending on the traffic and time of day. Buses run every 10 minutes to Avenida de América (not in central Madrid) from 5:36 a.m. to 11:30 p.m., costing 1 euro ($1.20) per passenger. To get into the center, you will still need to take a taxi, a subway train (metro), or a bus. The Barajas metro takes you as far as Nuevos Ministerios station (line 8). If you have heavy luggage, this is not advisable. Tickets cost 1 euro ($1.20), or 5.80 euros ($6.96) for a pack of ten (un bono de diez) and can also be used on Madrid buses. Punch them in the machine by the driver when you board.

Returning to the airport, Iberia, Air Europa, or Spanair ticket-holders can check in at Nuevos Ministerios metro station instead of Barajas. Some hotels have a direct shuttle to and from the airport.

BY TRAIN
Travelers can reach Madrid by train from London via the Eurostar from Waterloo Station, which goes through the Channel Tunnel before reaching Paris and the Gare du Nord. Changing stations, you catch the evening trenhotel (trainhotel) from Paris (Gare d'Austerlitz), on which you can eat, drink, and get a good night's sleep, to arrive at Chamartín station in Madrid the next morning.

GETTING AROUND

BY BUS
Madrid has an extensive bus

network, run by the Empresa Municipal de Transporte (EMT, Municipal Transport Company, tel 902 507 850 or 91 406 8810). All buses are air-conditioned and most have disabled-access facilities. Services operate every day from 6 a.m.–11 p.m., and there are night buses (búhos, or "owls"), with 25 different routes, starting from Plaza de la Cibeles, leaving every half-hour on the half-hour between midnight and 3 a.m., and hourly on the hour from 3–6 a.m. Drivers will stop only when hailed in good time from a bus stop or if a passenger inside presses the stop-request button. Dogs are admitted only if they are guide dogs for the blind or small dogs being carried.

BY CAR
In Madrid, finding a place to park a car can be very difficult (slightly easier in August) unless you have access to hotel or other private parking facilities. It is easy to see the city without a car, except perhaps for exploratory excursions outside town. Circling Madrid are three beltways, the innermost M-30, the M-40, and the M-50, which provide access to the highways leading out. Outside Madrid, the different road types are: autopistas (freeways) and autovías (state highways), which are almost all toll-free; carreteras nacionales (national roads), marked in red on the maps, old main roads that also carry local traffic; carreteras comarcales (local roads), smaller roads marked in yellow; and small country lanes, marked in white.

DRIVING INFORMATION
European Union driver's licenses are valid in Spain. U.S. and Canadian citizens should obtain International Driving Permits, available through the American and the Canadian Automobile Associations (www.aaa.com, www.caa.ca). You must carry ID. It is

compulsory to carry in the car two warning triangles, spare light bulbs for the headlamps, fuses, two reflective vests, and a spare tire. It is illegal for the driver to use a cell phone in the car, unless with a hands-free device, or to consume alcoholic drinks. Children under 12 are not allowed to ride in the front seats. The minimum legal age for driving is 18, and, for renting a vehicle, 21. If in your own vehicle, ensure that you have the appropriate insurance, including the green card, available from your insurers.

Breakdown assistance
Autopistas and autovías have emergency telephones, marked "S.O.S" at intervals along the roadside. A tow truck will be sent to help you. You are legally obliged to wear a reflective jacket if you leave the vehicle and to carry and use reflective triangles. If you belong to AAA, CAA, or AA, you can get help from RACE, their Spanish equivalent (tel 902 300 505).

Drinking & driving The alcohol limit for drivers is 0.25 milligram of alcohol per liter in a breath test or 0.5 gram of alcohol per liter in a blood test. The fine for exceeding this starts at 600 euros ($720). If you have had a driving permit for less than two years, the limits are 0.15 milligram and 0.3 gram.

Fines For exceeding the alcohol limit, fines start at 600 euros ($720); for speeding and seat-belt violations they begin at 300 euros ($360). Nonresidents of Spain are required to pay fines on the spot or to guarantee payment via a finance company that the traffic police (*Guardia Civil*) will put you in contact with. Nonpayment results in your vehicle being immobilized.

Fuel Fuel prices are controlled by the government and are typically slightly cheaper than U.K. prices, but nearly twice

those of the U.S. The types of fuel available are: *Super* (4-star), *Normal* (3-star), *Sin plomo* (Unleaded), and *Gasoleo* (Diesel).

Parking A continuous yellow line on the road or along the pavement means no parking or stopping. A broken yellow line means no parking, or time-limited parking where a sign indicates specified times. Blue lines indicate paid parking. Pay for your ticket at a dispensing machine (marked by a sign of a coin being pushed into a slot) and display it in your car. If your car has been towed away, look for an orange sticker on the pavement that gives details of your car, when it was removed, and the number to call.

Road signs If you are leaving Madrid on a car trip, finding the right road can sometimes be difficult. Signs sometimes appear at the last moment; often do not mention the destination, just the road number; and sometimes use old numbers (e.g. N-4, E-5) instead of the current one (e.g., A-IV). All distances in Spain are indicated in kilometers (1 km = 0.62 mile).

Seat belts Wearing seat belts is compulsory in the front seats, and in the back as well if the car is fitted with them.

Speed limits The speed limits are: autopistas and autovías 75 mph (120 kph); interurban roads either 62 mph (100 kph) or 56 mph (90 kph) as indicated; towns and built-up areas 31 mph (50 kph) or less, as indicated.

Traffic circles Vehicles already in a traffic circle have the right of way over those entering it, unless it is clearly marked otherwise.

What to do in a car accident See p. 240.

RENTING A CAR
Renting a car in Spain is straightforward and relatively cheap. There are many small companies as well as international ones, including Hertz and Avis.

Avis, tel 902 180 854
Europcar, tel 902 105 030
Hertz, tel 902 402 405

If you are planning a trip out of Madrid, it may make sense to go by public transportation and then rent a car for local travel. Check availability before leaving Madrid.

BY METRO
The subway system is the fastest mode of public transportation, running from 6 a.m. to 2 a.m., with rush hour (to be avoided) 7:30–9 a.m. Children under 4 travel for free. Each line has a distinct color code and two platforms, one in each direction, with the final station indicated. Keep your ticket for inspection until reaching the exit *(salida)*. It gets very hot underground in high summer. Customer service, tel 902 444 403.

BY PUBLIC TRANSPORT
Single tickets on the metro and on buses cost 1 euro ($1.20). The ten-journey Metrobús ticket is cheaper at 5.80 euros ($6.95) and works on the metro (except suburban line 12) and the bus network. It is on sale at metro stations, authorized newspaper stands, and tobacco shops (*estancos*, identified by a sign showing a yellow "T" and "tabacos" on a brown background), but not on buses. There is also a Tourist Travel Pass *(Abono Transportes Turístico)*, covering Madrid city (zona A) and valid for 1, 2, 3, 5, or 7 days. It costs from 3.50 to 18.40 euros ($4.20–$22.08), with children under 11 at half-price. These can also be bought in municipal tourist offices. There is also a monthly travel pass

(Abono Mensual de Transportes) for the metro and buses, which costs over-64s 9.55 euros ($11.46), and others between 25 and 130 euros ($30–$108). As in any major city, you should be sensibly security-conscious, especially during rush hours and nighttime.

BY TAXI

Downtown Madrid teems with taxis, which are white, with a diagonal red stripe on the front doors and the shield of Madrid on the side. If the roof light next to the "taxi" sign shows green, they are available for hire. Taxi stands are indicated by a white "T" on a blue sign. Taxis are not very expensive, and there are no charges for luggage or for dogs, but large dogs (except for guide dogs) will generally not be admitted. Trips to or from a bus or train station carry an extra charge of 2.20 euros ($2.64), and those to or from the airport cost an additional 4.20 euros ($5.04). Payment should be in cash. Private cab companies, charging the same rates, include Radio-Taxi Asociación Gremial: tel 91 447 5180 or 91 447 3232; Radio-Taxi Independiente: tel 91 405 1213 or 91 405 5500; Radio Teléfono Taxi/ Euro Taxi: tel 91 547 8200; and Teletaxi: tel 91 371 2131, 91 371 3711, or 630 907 990 (cell phone).

BY TRAIN

Renfe (Red Nacional de los Ferrocarriles Españoles) is Spain's main rail network, and a good way to explore sights beyond Madrid. The TALGO trains (Tren Articulado Ligero Goicoechea Oriol) and the high-speed AVEs (Alta Velocidad Española) are fast, comfortable, and include well-equipped bars with food. Madrid's main stations are Chamartín and Atocha. The fastest, most modern trains, the AVEs, leave from Atocha. Tickets can be bought from your home travel agent, from agents in Spain displaying a Renfe sticker, from

Renfe offices in central Madrid, in the Corte Inglés department stores, or at the railway stations. During rush hours and major holidays, trains are likely to be crowded. Arrive to catch your train with plenty of time to spare—trains have been known to depart early.

Return tickets are sold with a 20% discount if the round-trip is within a 60-day period. Children under 13 receive a 40% discount on all tickets. Under-4s travel for free if not occupying a seat. Inter Rail and Eurail passes are valid in Spain. For EU citizens, the Euro-Domino pass allows 3 to 8 days limitless travel within a one-month period for between 113 and 323 euros ($136–$388).

The Flexipass, available only to non-European residents, offers 3 to 10 days' unlimited travel within a two-month period for between 170 and 465 euros ($204–$558); under-26s and over-60s pay less. Additional supplements are charged for seat reservations and sleeping accommodation. First class is known as *Preferente* and second class as *Turista*. Check for new offers and discounts.

PRACTICAL ADVICE

COMMUNICATIONS

INTERNET

Most 3-star hotels and up offer their customers Internet access in some form. Madrid is full of cybercafés and Internet centers; here are a few of the more reliable ones.

BbiGG Internet & Games

www.bbigg.com
Calle Mayor 1, tel 91 531 2364. Metro: Sol. Open 9 a.m.–midnight; Fri. & Sat. until 2 a.m.
Calle Alcalá 21, tel 91 521 9207. Metro: Sevilla. Hours as above.
Calle Alcalá 399, tel 91 408 1812. Metro: Pueblo Nuevo. Open 10 a.m.–midnight.

Cost: 1.50 euros ($1.80)/hour.

Café Comercial

Glorieta de Bilbao 7, tel 91 521 5655. Metro: Bilbao. Open Mon.–Thurs. 8 a.m.–1 a.m., Fri. & Sat. 8 a.m.–2 a.m., Sun. 10 a.m.–1 a.m. Cost: 1 euro ($1.20)/50 minutes.

Cafetería Zahara

Gran Vía 31, tel 91 521 8424. Metro: Callao. Open 9 a.m.– 1 a.m. Coin-operated: about 2 euros ($2.40)/hour.

Casa de Internet

Calle Luchana 20, tel 91 594 4200. Metro: Bilbao. Open Mon.–Fri. 9 a.m.–12:30 a.m., Sat. & Sun. 10 a.m.–12:30 a.m. Cost 2.10 euros ($2.52)/hour.

POST OFFICES

A letter or postcard weighing less than 20 grams costs 0.28 euro ($0.34) to send within Spain, 0.53 euro ($0.64) within the EU, and 0.78 euro ($0.94) to North America. To send a registered letter *(carta certificada)* weighing less than 20 grams from a post office *(correos)* costs 2.2 euro ($2.65) within Spain, 2.73 euro ($3.28) within the EU, and 2.98 euro ($3.58) to North America. Stamps can also be bought in *estancos* (closed 2–5 p.m.).

Post offices are open 8:30 a.m.–8:30 p.m. Mon.–Fri., and 9:30 a.m.–1 p.m. Sat. A very few (e.g., Paseo Santa María de la Cabeza 42) are open on Sunday from noon until 10 p.m. American Express offices will hold letters (not packages) sent to cardholders. The Palacio de Comunicaciones post office in Plaza de la Cibeles will hold mail addressed to you at "Lista de Correos, Oficina Principal de Madrid, 28070, Spain" for 15 days only, after which it will be returned to sender.

TELEPHONES

All Spanish phone numbers have nine digits. The first two or three digits (91 in the case of Madrid) indicate the province but must always be dialed, even if you are calling from next door.

Numbers beginning with 6 are mobile phone numbers and suitably expensive. Toll-free numbers start with 900.

To call Spain from the U.S.
To call Spain from the United States, dial 011-34 (international and Spain country codes) and the nine-digit number.

To call from Spain
To call from Spain, dial 00 followed by the country code (1 for North America, 44 for the U.K.), then the area code and the telephone number. When ringing the U.K., the first 0 in the regional code is omitted.

Telephone cards
To make a call from telephone booths in Spain, you can use coins or (preferably) buy a tarjeta telefónica (phone card). Tarjetas telefónicas are sold at post offices and estancos, in denominations from 5 to 150 euros.

Operators & directory information
For calls within Spain, the operator's number is 1009; for Europe, North Africa, and Turkey, 1008, and for the rest of the world, 1005. For national directory information, dial 11818; for international, 11825.

CONVERSIONS
1 kilo = 2.2 pounds
1 liter = 0.2642 U.S. gallon
1 kilometer = 0.62 mile
1 meter = 1.094 yards

Women's clothing

U.S.	8	10	12	14	16	18
Spanish	36	38	40	42	44	46

Men's clothing

U.S.	36	38	40	42	44	46
Spanish	46	48	50	52	54	56

Women's shoes

U.S.	6-6.5	7-7.5	8-8.5	9-9.5
Spanish	38	39	40-41	42

Men's shoes

U.S.	8	8.5	9.5	10.5	11.5	12
Spanish	41	42	43	44	45	46

DISCOUNT CARD
The Madrid Card gives you free admission to 43 of Madrid's main museums, including the Prado, the Reina Sofía, and the Thyssen-Bornemisza; unlimited trips on the three Madrid Visión sightseeing bus routes; and free access to the Descubre Madrid (Discover Madrid) guided walking tours; free admission to the Madrid Parque de Atracciones (Amusement Park), the Zoo-Aquarium, the Teleférico (cable car), the Faunia nature park, and IMAX Madrid with its ultra-large and modern movie screens. It also entitles you to discounts in participating shops, restaurants, and shows.

The card costs 25 euros ($30) for 24 hours, 35 euros ($42) for 48 hours, and 40 euros ($54) for 72 hours, with discounts if bought online. It is available from municipal tourist offices, major railway stations, travel agencies, and selected hotels. Children's cards were introduced in 2006. Neoturismo, tel 902 877 996, www.madridcard.com.

ELECTRICITY
The standard electricity voltage in Spain is 220V, 50 Hz, not 110V as in North America. Most electrical equipment will need a transformer, except for some laptops which have automatic or manual voltage conversion features. Cheaper appliances, such as hair dryers or razors, may be worth buying in Spain. Most U.K. 240V appliances will work fine. Plugs have two round pins, so you will need adapters.

ETIQUETTE & LOCAL CUSTOMS
The Spanish siesta is not a myth, although it is often spent eating and talking rather than sleeping. Many shops shut from 1:30–4.30 p.m. or 2–5 p.m. It is unusual to start lunch, often the day's main meal, before 2 and it often it lasts until 5 p.m., or even longer on Sunday. The evening meal starts at any time between 9:30 and 11 p.m. If you eat earlier, it will be easier to get a table.

HOLIDAYS
Spain has national, regional, and local holidays, and Madrid has even more at barrio level. The Spanish national holidays are: January 1 (El Año Nuevo, New Year's Day), January 6 (El Día de los Reyes Magos, Epiphany), Maundy Thursday and Good Friday, May 1 (May Day or Labor Day), July 25 (Santiago Apostol, St. James the Apostle), August 15 (Asunción de la Virgen, Assumption of the Virgin), October 12 (Día de la Hispanidad, Spanish National Day), November 1 (Todos los Santos, All Saints), December 6 (Constitution Day), December 8 (Immaculate Conception), and December 25 (Día de Navidad, Christmas Day).

The Madrid-wide festivals are: May 2 (Madrid Day), May 15 (San Isidro, patron saint of Madrid), September 9 (Santa María de la Cabeza or La Melonera, the melon lady), and November 9 (La Almudena, Madrid's patroness). Madrid keeps functioning during these días festivos (holidays), their main effect (apart from the celebrations) being that national and local government buildings tend to close. If the holiday falls on Sunday, it is usually moved to Monday; if it falls on Tuesday or Thursday, it creates un puente (a bridge), resulting in the intervening Monday or Friday becoming a holiday too.

MEDIA

NEWSPAPERS
The three most popular daily newspapers are El País, El Mundo, and ABC. The left-leaning El País has the most in-depth international coverage. English-language newspapers are widely available in the more central parts of Madrid, particularly on the Gran Vía. The most common North American paper is the International Herald Tribune, and most of the British national newspapers are on same-day sale.

RADIO

The airwaves are full of national radio stations. The state-run Radio Nacional de España (RNE) has four stations covering classical and traditional music, pop music, news and current affairs, and sports. These are generally better than the local stations. The Voice of America is broadcast on shortwave, but moves around according to the time of day: Try 9700, 15205, and 15255 MHz. The same applies to the BBC World Service: Try 1323, 6195, 9410, 12095, 15565, and 17640. There is also Spectrum FM, an English-language pop and rock station, which broadcasts in Madrid on 107.0 FM.

TELEVISION

Spanish television has good news and sports coverage, but otherwise tends to be a mess of soap operas, celebrity gossip, and quiz and game shows. The TV will often be on in bars and even in restaurants. Madrileños generally take their soccer very seriously, and games involving either of the leading Madrid rivals, Real Madrid and Atlético Madrid, are shown in many bars.

There are two state-run national channels, TVE1 and TVE2, and two national independents, Antena 3 and Tele 5, plus a local channel, TeleMadrid. Hundreds of satellite channels are available in many bars and hotels, including English-language channels such as CNN, Fox News, BBC World Service, and Sky News. Films on satellite channels can often be returned to their original language via the remote control.

MONEY MATTERS

Spain's currency is the euro, which comes in coins of 1, 2, 5, 10, 20, and 50 cents (céntimos) and of 1 and 2 euros. Notes are available in 5, 10, 20, 50, 100, 200, and 500 euros. Many smaller businesses will not accept large bills, fearing counterfeits.

Try to arrive in Spain with some cash in euros; otherwise change some money at your arrival point. Take a combination of traveler's checks and credit or debit cards to get cash from the plentiful ATMs; most add a small charge for use. Major credit cards are widely accepted. Traveler's checks are a secure way to hold money and can be changed in banks (better exchange rates) and money-changing centers (longer opening hours).

OPENING TIMES

Banks are open from 8:30 a.m. to 2 or 2:30 p.m. (Mon.–Fri.) and from 8:30 a.m. to 1 p.m. on Saturdays. There are branches of Caja Madrid in Atocha and Chamartín stations, at the Puerta del Sol, and in Barajas airport (terminal 2) that are open from 8:15 a.m. to 7:45 p.m. (Mon.–Fri.) and from 10:15 a.m.–2:30 p.m. on Saturdays.

Most museums, apart from the Reina Sofía and a few others, are closed on Mondays.

Store opening times in Madrid vary: Large department stores, and shops in the Gran Vía and Sol areas, open at 9:30 or 10 a.m. and close at 10 p.m. Otherwise, shops and pharmacies open at 9:30 or 10 a.m., shut at 1:30 or 2 p.m., reopen at 4:30 or 5 p.m., and close for the night at 8 or 8:30 p.m. Almost all stores are closed on Sundays, but some open on the first Sunday of the month and on every Sunday during Christmas and the month of August.

Restaurants usually open about midday, close about 5 p.m., reopen at about 7 p.m., and often serve food until after midnight. Cafés open at 7 a.m., many bars at 8 a.m., and they tend to stay open all day, closing late. In the evening, bars often don't liven up until 11. Music bars usually close at 3 a.m. and discotheques at 7 a.m.

PLACES OF WORSHIP

When visiting churches, remember that most of them are still places of worship. You are not required to dress formally, but be aware of where you are and act accordingly.

RESTROOMS

Public toilets are rare outside the most tourist-oriented areas. But in Spain you are never very far from a bar or café and it would be unusual if you were not allowed to use the toilet. Carry toilet paper with you, as this is often in short supply.

TIME DIFFERENCES

Madrid is always six hours ahead of Eastern Standard Time in the U.S. (apart from one week a year), and one hour ahead of the U.K.

TIPPING

Service is already included in all restaurant bills, so you do not have to tip if you do not want to. However, Spanish service workers are generally poorly paid and a tip for good service would be a helpful thank-you gesture.

The Spanish often leave their small change when paying for drinks and tip about 5% in restaurants. Tip porters and cab drivers 1–2 euros.

TRAVELERS WITH DISABILITIES

Spain has only recently begun to cater seriously to the needs of people with disabilities. Newer buildings are more accessible than older ones, but there may still be problems. Check with hotels and restaurants before booking. Advice is available from:
Disabled Peoples' International (DPI)
748 Broadway, Winnipeg, MB R3G 0X3, Canada, tel, tel 204/287-8010, e-mail dpi@dpi.org, www.dpi.org
European Disability Forum
Rue du Commerce 39-41, B-1000 Brussels, Belgium, tel 32 2 282 4600, e-mail info@edf-feph.org, www.edf-feph.org

Mobility International U.S.A.
P.O. Box 10767, Eugene, Oregon, 97440, tel 541/343-1284, e-mail info@miusa.org, www.miusa.org
**RADAR
(Royal Association for Disability & Rehabilitation)**
12 City Forum, 250 City Rd., London EC1V 8AF, U.K., tel 020 7250 3222, e-mail radar@radar.org.uk, www.radar.org.uk

EMERGENCIES

EMBASSIES IN SPAIN
UNITED STATES
Calle Serrano 75, tel 91 587 2240, emergencies 91 587 2200. Metros: Rubén Dario, Núñez de Balboa. www.embusa.es
CANADA
Calle Núñez de Balboa 35, tel 91 423 3250. Metro: Velázquez. www.canada-es.org
UNITED KINGDOM
Calle Fernando El Santo 16, tel 91 700 8200. Metro: Alonso Martínez.
Consulate: Paseo de Recoletos 7-9, tel 91 524 970, emergencies 606 987 626. Metro: Colón. www.ukinspain.com.

SPANISH EMBASSIES
UNITED STATES
2375 Pennsylvania Ave., N.W., Washington, D.C. 20037, tel 202/452-0100, www.spainemb.org. Consulates in nine other cities.
CANADA
74 Stanley Ave., Ottawa, Ontario K1M 1P4, tel 613/747-2252, www.embaspain.ca. Consulates in eight other cities.
UNITED KINGDOM
39 Chesham Pl., London SW1X 8SB, tel 020 7235 5555.
Consulate: 20 Draycott Pl., London, SW3 2RZ, tel 020 7589 8989, www.conspalon.org. Consulates also in Manchester and Edinburgh.

EMERGENCY PHONE NUMBERS
The central emergency number for police, fire, and ambulance services is 112. If you have been the victim of a crime and want to report it to the police, at least to put it on the record, there is a 24-hour phone line, 902 102 112, where English speakers are available. You will be told which police station (comisaría de policía) to go to, to sign the official police report and to collect a copy of it.

POLICE
Spain has three distinct police forces. The Policía Municipal (or Local) is controlled by the local town hall and deals with minor matters like traffic infringements. The Policía Nacional is the main crime-fighting force in the cities. The Guardia Civil tends to operate in the countryside and on the highways, and it controls the borders and prisons.

LOSS OF CREDIT CARDS
American Express España, tel 902 375 637 (24 hours)
Diners Club Español, tel 901 101 011 (24 hours)
Mastercard, tel 900 971 231 (24 hours)
VISA International, tel 900 991 124 (24 hours)

WHAT TO DO IN A CAR ACCIDENT
The Guardia Civil operates special units to deal quickly with serious accidents. If your car has ended up where it might cause more accidents, mark its position as accurately as possible before moving it to the safest place nearby. Put on your reflective jacket(s). Set up reflective triangles, one in front of and one behind the car, at 165 feet (50 m) distance. If it is more than a minor accident, telephone 112 and wait for the police. If it is a minor accident with no injuries, but involving another vehicle, there is no need to call the police if both parties agree about what

occurred and who was responsible and reach a settlement. If you cannot agree, phone the police and get the name(s), address(es), car registration(s), and license number(s) of the other driver(s) involved and their insurance details. If there are witnesses, take their contact details. If you need repairs, call from an SOS emergency phone or call RACE on 902 300 505 (service available only to members of AAA, CAA, and AA). If the car is rented, phone the rental company.

HEALTH
Make sure that you have health insurance coverage for Spain. Most standard American policies do not include such coverage. Check whether your insurance covers an air-ambulance home should this prove necessary. EU citizens should carry a European Health Insurance Card (EHIC) issued in their home country, available in the U.K. from a post office or online from www.dh.gov.uk/travellers. This entitles the bearer only to state-provided medical care, so private health insurance may still be a sensible precaution. If it is an emergency, ring 112 and ask for an ambulance (ambulancia), or if near a hospital, head for urgencias, the emergency room. The U.S. Embassy maintains a list of English-speaking physicians in the Madrid area.
  The International Association for Medical Assistance to Travelers (IAMAT) is a nonprofit organization that anyone can join free of charge. Members receive a directory of English-speaking IAMAT doctors on call 24 hours a day, and they are entitled to services at a set rate. www.iamat.org
  United States: 162 Military Rd., Suite 279, Niagara Falls, NY 14304-1745, tel 716/754-4883
  Canada: 1287 St. Clair Ave. W., Suite 1, Toronto, Ontario M6E 1B8, tel 416/652-0137.

HOTELS & RESTAURANTS

From converted 17th-century palaces to cutting-edge modern hotels, from bullfighters' taverns to nouvelle-cuisine restaurants, Madrid is well prepared to welcome visitors. Although prices have gone up since the days when everything in Spain was unusually cheap, there has been a parallel improvement in quality and services provided.

HOTELS

Some hotels offer *media pensión* (breakfast and dinner included) or *pensión completa* (lunch as well) at good prices, so ask when reserving or on arrival. Madrid being justly famous for its late-running nightlife, it can be noisy in the town center, so if you are a light sleeper, it is worth asking for the quietest room available; but bear in mind that you may lose the good view.

Stars

Hotels in Madrid are graded with a star system of one to five, five being top of the range. The distinction is based on a mix of aesthetic and practical factors, such as the provision of heating and air-conditioning, the quality of bathroom facilities, and the size of the rooms. Any hotel with two or more stars should have an en suite bathroom; if three or more, with a bath and a shower. The cheaper *hostales* and *pensiones* have a separate system of one to three stars.

Note: 7% I.V.A. (Value Added Tax) is added to the quoted prices. Breakfast is usually not included in the quote. Most double rooms have twin beds; if you want a double bed, ask for a *cama de matrimonio*. The new smoking law requires smokers not to smoke in prohibited areas. In high season, reserve well in advance. You may be asked for a deposit or credit card and I.D./passport number.

Credit & debit cards

Many hotels accept all major cards—check whether they accept yours. Abbreviations used are: AE (American Express), DC (Diners Club), MC (Mastercard), and V (Visa).

RESTAURANTS

Madrid offers a wonderful array of food from all over Spain, as people from all over Spain have come to Madrid over time, bringing their dishes with them. Enormous quantities of fresh fish and seafood are also trucked into the capital every evening from the coast. If you want to see the menu, ask for *la carta*. If you ask for the *menú*, you will be told about the *menú del día*, usually offered only for lunch. This is a well-priced three-course set meal, where you can choose between limited options. In more expensive restaurants, the equivalent is the *menú degustación*, an avalanche of small portions. Many of the most authentic restaurants close in August.

Tapas bars, bars, & cafés

A regular Madrid bar is not a *bar de copas*, which is a drinking establishment, but a center of social life from early in the morning until whenever. According to legend, tapas started life as slices of ham or cheese placed on top of glasses of wine to stop the flies or dust getting in, *tapar* meaning "to cover." Once a free snack provided with every alcoholic drink ordered, now they have a price tag, but they are a wonderful way to try small portions of the food available. If you want a bigger portion, ask for a *ración* (plateful). The norm when *tape-ando* (eating tapas) is to have one or two, then change bars and start again. Typical Madrid tapas are *boquerones en vinagre* (fresh anchovies in salt and vinegar), *albóndigas* (meatballs), *callos* (tripe), *croquetas* (croquettes), and *tortilla de patatas* (Spanish potato omelette), but there are many more. The fact that the Spanish eat something every

time they have a drink makes public drunkenness rare. Many tapas bars also have restaurants —if the tapas convince you, have a full sit-down meal.

ORGANIZATION

Hotels, restaurants, and tapas bars have been listed by price, then in alphabetical order, within each neighborhood chapter division. For bars and cafés, see p. 261.

L = lunch   D = dinner

■ PLAZA MAYOR & OLD TOWN

HOTELS

⌂ HOTEL REYES CATÓLICOS
$$ *
CALLE ÁNGEL 18
TEL 91 365 8600
FAX 91 365 9867
www.hotelreyescatolicos.com
Near the Basílica de San Francisco el Grande, this hotel is one of the few in the Austrias barrio and is a good base for visiting the city. It has large, well-equipped, and well-maintained rooms.
🛏 38 🅿 🚇 Puerta de Toledo 🚭 🅰 🅰 All major cards

⌂ PETIT PALACE POSADA DEL PEINE
$$ **
CALLE POSTAS 17
TEL 91 523 8151
FAX 91 523 2993
www.hthoteles.com
The very central Posada del Peine started life as an inn near the edge of Madrid in 1610. It is now the oldest surviving hotel in Spain. Next to Plaza Mayor and the Puerta del Sol, it has been recently renovated and boasts highly modern facilities, making it one of the best hotels in Madrid.
ℹ 69 🚇 Sol 🚭 🅰 🅰 All major cards

🚭 Nonsmoking 🛗 Elevator 🅰 Air-conditioning 🌊 Indoor/🌊 Outdoor pool 🏋 Gym 🅰 Credit cards   **KEY**

HOTELS & RESTAURANTS

🏨 WESTERN CORTEZO
$$ ★★★
CALLE DOCTOR CORTEZO 3
TEL 91 369 0101
FAX 91 369 3774
www.hotelcortezo.com
Close to Plaza Mayor and the Puerta del Sol, this comfortable, simple hotel was last renovated in 1997 and is pleasantly modern. Many rooms have sitting areas with a desk and armchair. The public spaces match the guest rooms in freshness.
🛏85 🅿 🚇Tirso de Molina ⦿ ⦿ 🞬All major cards

RESTAURANTS

🍴 CASA LUCIO
$$$$
CALLE CAVA BAJA 35
TEL 91 365 3252
Simple dishes made with high-quality ingredients. Try the *huevos estrellados* (fried eggs mixed with potatoes), Madrid-style stewed tripe *(callos a la madrileña),* and the rice pudding *(arroz con leche).* Fine jabugo ham. Very *castellano* (Castilian).
🍽120 🕐Closed Sat. L & Aug. 🚇La Latina ⦿ 🞬All major cards

🍴 EL LANDÓ
$$$$
PLAZA DE GABRIEL MIRÓ 8
TEL 91 366 7681
Simplicity at its most sophisticated. Have some legendary *jamón ibérico* (Iberian ham) with *pan con tomate* (bread with crushed tomato) to prepare your taste buds. The restaurant uses excellent raw materials, deliciously prepared: *cocido madrileño, huevos estrellados,* lentils, stews, fish, meats, homemade cakes, and desserts, with very good wine. Reserve in advance.
🍽65 🕐Closed Sun. & Aug. 🚇La Latina 🅿 ⦿ 🞬All major cards

🍴 BOTÍN
$$$
CALLE CUCHILLEROS 17
TEL 91 366 4217
Reputed to be the world's oldest restaurant, and, according to Hemingway, the best, Botín was founded in 1725. Recommended are the traditional roast suckling pig *(cochinillo asado),* roast lamb *(cordero asado),* gazpacho, and *almejas marineras* (clams).
🍽260 🚇Sol ⦿ 🞬All major cards

🍴 CASA CIRÍACO
$$
CALLE MAYOR 24
TEL 91 548 0620
This very Madrileño restaurant first opened in 1917 and is still much frequented by high society. It has excellent home cooking: try *alubias* (kidney beans) *de La Granja, gambas al ajillo* (garlic shrimp), or their famed *pepitoria de gallina* (hen fricassée). *Cocido madrileño* (typical Madrid stew with meat, chickpeas, and sausage) is available only on Tuesdays. Advisable to reserve.
🍽65 🕐Closed Wed. & Aug. 🚇Sol ⦿ 🞬All major cards

🍴 CASA PACO
$$
PLAZA PUERTA CERRADA 11
TEL 91 366 3166
Typically Madrileño, child-friendly, and popular with bullfighters. Specializes in roast meat sold by weight, which turned the likes of Orson Welles into faithful customers. Also try their *cocido, callos, sopa de ajo* (garlic soup), and *pisto manchego* (La Mancha vegetable hash).
🍽100 🕐Closed Sun. & Aug. 🚇Sol ⦿ 🞬DC, MC, V

🍴 LA CAMARILLA
$$
CALLE CAVA BAJA 21
TEL 91 354 0207
A traditional old Madrileño

HOTELS
An indication of the maximum high-season cost of a double room with breakfast is given by $ signs.

$$$$$	Over $300
$$$$	$220–$300
$$$	$160–$220
$$	$80–$160
$	Under $80

RESTAURANTS
An indication of the cost of a three-course dinner, without drinks, is given by $ signs.

$$$$$	Over $80
$$$$	$50–$80
$$$	$35–$50
$$	$20–$35
$	Under $20

restaurant with a menu that changes with the seasons. Try *risotto de champiñón* (mushroom risotto), *cigalas* (crayfish), or *rollito de ternera con gratén de pato* (beef roll with duck au gratin), if available. Excellent *menú del día* at lunchtime for 11 euros.
🍽60 🕐Closed Mon. 🚇La Latina ⦿ 🞬All major cards

🍴 LA CHATA
$$
CALLE CAVA BAJA 24
TEL 91 366 1458
This restaurant, decorated in classical bullfighting style, offers good traditional Spanish cooking such as roast suckling pig, *rabo de toro* (bull's tail), *chopitos* (whole baby squid), *gambas al pulpo* (shrimp with octopus), and *bacalao a la Chata* (cod cooked to their secret recipe).
🍽250 🕐Closed Tues. & Wed. L 🚇La Latina ⦿ 🞬All major cards

🍴 TABERNA ARTE DIVINO
$$
PLAZA DE LA PROVINCIA 3
TEL 91 364 2706
A very good restaurant, in a 17th-century building, dedi-

---

cated to creative cooking and fine wine. Try their *bellota* ham, *foie* (liver pâté) with apple and wild mushrooms, *cecina a las cinco especies* (five-spiced cured meat), or *lasaña de verdura* (vegetable lasagna). Reserve in advance. 🛏 40 ⏱ Closed Tues.–Sat. L, Sun. D, Mon., & Aug. 🚇 Sol ♿ 🅰 All major cards

TAPAS BARS

CASA DANI
CALLE CALATRAVA 11
TEL 91 365 2621
Beautiful old-style bar, also known as Vinos 11, friendly, and chatty. Try the well-priced *longaniza picante* (spicy pork sausage), *chicharrones* (pork cracklings), *jamón*, the excellent *queso manchego*, and whatever other tapas are on offer.
⏱ Closed Mon. L & Sun,
🚇 La Latina

CASA LUCAS
CALLE CAVA BAJA 30
TEL 91 365 0804
Small bar with very good wine and inventive tapas. Try *revuelto de morcilla y tomate dulce* (scrambled eggs with blood pudding and sweet tomato), *solomillo de cerdo con cebolla confitada* (pork sirloin with onion confit), or *tataki de bonito con puré de manzana* (bonito tataki with apple purée).
⏱ Closed Wed. L
🚇 La Latina

CERVECERÍA MONJE
CALLE ARENAL 21
TEL 91 548 3598
The amiable Monje family serves a lovely seafood tapa with your drink, tempting you to order *raciones*—*ostras* (oysters), *gambas*, *percebes* (gooseneck barnacles), *berberechos* (cockles), or *mollejas de cordero* (lamb sweetbreads), to name a few. The freshest produce and good prices.
⏱ Closed Tues. 🚇 Ópera

EL ALMENDRO
CALLE EL ALMENDRO 13
TEL 91 365 4252
A bell rings out to call you to the kitchen hatch to pick up your freshly made food. This bar is almost always packed—let the bell ring for *pringá* (pork, sausage, and chickpea stew), *jamón*, *porra antequerana* (salmorejo Antequerastyle), or *roscas* (sweet pastries).
🚇 La Latina

EL BONANNO
PLAZA DEL HUMILLADERO 4
TEL 91 366 6886
Excellent, atmospheric bar, slighty pricy, and popular with the flamenco world. Good place to visit on Sunday morning on your way to the Rastro. Try their *paté de pato* (duck pâté), *cecina* (cured meat), and *boquerones en vinagre* (fresh anchovies in vinegar).
🚇 La Latina

LA ESCONDÍA
PLAZA DE PUERTA CERRADA 6
TEL 91 365 3419
Just by Plaza Mayor, this very Madrileño little bar is a good place to have a *caña* (draft beer) and a tapa in La Latina barrio. Try the *torta del Casar* (a strong, creamy sheep's cheese), some *morcón* (sausage made with chorizo and pork loin), *mojama* (salted tuna), or their *jamón*.
🚇 Tirso de Molina, La Latina

LAMIAK
CALLE CAVA BAJA 42
TEL 91 365 5212
This friendly Basque tapas bar, with a restaurant downstairs, offers inventive tapas such as *bocados de rabo de toro* (bull's tail snacks), *bacalao ajoarriero* (salt cod with peppers), *kokotxas* (cod or hake cheeks), *chipirones en su tinta* (squid cooked in their own ink), or *codorniz en salsa de chocolate* (quail in chocolate sauce).
⏱ Closed Mon. & Sun. D
🚇 La Latina

LA SALAMANDRA
CALLE ALFONSO VI 6
TEL 91 366 0515
Well-chosen wines by the glass or by the bottle. Their delicious seasonal dishes, on the pricey side, include *magret de pato* (duck breast), *torta de queso* (cheesecake), *solomillo de bellota* (pork loin), and inventive *revueltos* (scrambled egg dishes).
⏱ Closed Sun. D
🚇 La Latina

LA TABERNA DE LOS CIEN VINOS
CALLE NUNCIO 17
TEL 91 365 4704
A good place to taste Mediterranean tapas like *cecina con aceite de oliva* (cured meat with olive oil), *timbal de cous-cous con setas y paté* (meat pie with couscous, wild mushrooms, and pâté), or, in winter, *marmitako* (thick tuna and potato soup). Excellent selection of more than 150 wines.
⏱ Closed Mon. & Sun. D
🚇 La Latina

LA TORRE DEL ORO
PLAZA MAYOR 26
TEL 91 366 5016
A favorite bar of bullfighters since 1940 and full of memorabilia. It specializes in paella, fried fish, and excellent sausages.
🚇 Sol

SANLÚCAR
CALLE SAN ISIDRO LABRADOR 14
TEL 91 354 0052
Open since May 2002, this friendly Andalucían bar is already famed for its manzanilla sherry and for tapas such as *tortillitas de camarones* (baby shrimp pancakes), bellota ham, *langostinos* (king prawns), and *salmorejo* (cold vegetable soup).
⏱ Closed Sun. D & Mon.
🚇 La Latina

🚭 Nonsmoking 🛗 Elevator ❄ Air-conditioning 🏊 Indoor/ 🏊 Outdoor pool 💪 Gym 🅰 Credit cards   **KEY**

HOTELS & RESTAURANTS

PALACIO ROYAL & AROUND

HOTELS

SOMETHING SPECIAL

⊞ CASA DE MADRID

This discreet and luxurious seven-room hotel is one of Madrid's best-kept secrets. In a beautiful 18th-century building in the old city, facing the Teatro Real opera house, it feels like the noble family home that it was until 2003. Spacious rooms and excellent service.

$$$$ ★★★★★
CALLE ARRIETA 2
TEL 91 559 5791
FAX 91 540 1100
www.casademadrid.com
🛈 8 🅿 🚇 Ópera 🔁
📇 All major cards

⊞ TRYP AMBASSADOR

$$$$ ★★★★
CUESTA DE SANTO
DOMINGO 5 & 7
TEL 91 541 6700
FAX 91 559 1040
www.solmelia.com
This 19th-century ducal palace in the heart of historic Madrid became a hotel in 1990 and retains many original features, such as the sweeping staircase and the attractive greenhouse. The elegant rooms are large, with mahogany furniture.
🛈 182 🚇 Santo Domingo, Ópera 🔁 🔁 📇 All major cards

⊞ CARLOS V

$$ ★★★
CALLE MAESTRO VICTORIA 5
TEL 91 531 4100
FAX 91 531 3761
www.hotelcarlosv.com
On a pedestrian-friendly street by the Puerta del Sol, this amiable family-run hotel has an unusual art nouveau entrance. Rooms are large and elegantly decorated—ask for one with a balcony. The top-floor rooms have ter-

races. Shuttle service to airport. Breakfast included. Cafeteria.
🛈 67 🅿 🚇 Sol 🔁
📇 All major cards

⊞ HOTEL ÓPERA

🍴 $$ ★★★
CUESTA DE SANTO DOMINGO 2
TEL 91 541 2800
FAX 91 541 6923
www.hotelopera.com
Near the opera house, this hotel has comfortable rooms with large windows, some with balconies. Customer service is friendly. Non-smoking rooms available. The hotel restaurant, **El Café de la Ópera** (*$$$$, Calle Arrueta 6, tel 91 542 6382*), is well-regarded, serving Spanish and international food while regaling you with opera and *zarzuela* (Spanish light opera) music. Sometimes waiters—opera singers between jobs—join in.
🍴 79 🚇 Ópera 🔁 🔁
📇 All major cards

⊞ MARIO

$$ ★★
CALLE CAMPOMANES 4
TEL 91 548 8548
FAX 91 559 1288
www.room-matehoteles.com
Often known by its previous name (Campomanes), the Hotel Mario has a clean, modern design and helpful, friendly service. Good breakfast included. Close to the opera house.
🛈 54 🚇 Ópera 🔁 🔁
📇 All major cards

⊞ PETIT PALACE ARENAL

$$ ★★★
CALLE ARENAL 16
TEL 91 564 4355
FAX 91 564 0854
www.petitpalacearenalhotel-madrid.com
In a restored 19th-century palace near the Puerta del Sol, this hotel has large rooms, friendly customer service, beautiful decor, and good

bed-and-breakfast deals. One floor is kept for non-smokers. Technologically well equipped.
🛈 64 🚇 Ópera 🔁 🔁
📇 All major cards

RESTAURANTS

🍴 ENTRE SUSPIRO Y SUSPIRO

$$$
CALLE CAÑOS DEL PERAL 3
TEL 91 542 0644
Good Mexican food in a lovely old palace. Excellent *cebiche* (raw fish or seafood in lemon juice). The corn quesadillas filled with *cuitlacoche* (corn mushrooms) and jalapeño chilis are very tasty, as is the *ensalada mandinga* (shrimp, mango, onion, and coriander salad). Good margaritas and tequilas.
🪑 65 🅿 🕐 Closed Sat. L & Sun. 🚇 Santo Domingo, Ópera 🔁 📇 All major cards

🍴 EL PATO MUDO

$$
CALLE COSTANILLA DE LOS ÁNGELES 8
TEL 91 559 4840
In the middle of the *casco viejo* (old quarter), good traditional Mediterranean cooking, especially paellas and rice dishes with duck, fish, or vegetables. Cozy, bohemian atmosphere. Call ahead on weekends.
🪑 55 🕐 Closed Sun. 🚇 Santo Domingo, Ópera 🔁 📇 All major cards

🍴 CASA MINGO

$
PASEO DE LA FLORIDA 34
TEL 91 547 7918
A large tavern-style restaurant with long tables where everyone sits together—noisy, but a good opportunity to get to know the locals. On the menu: roast chicken, chorizo sausages, empanadas, salad, and plenty of Asturias cider. No reservations. Summer terraces.
🪑 300 🚇 Príncipe Pío 🔁
📇 All major cards

⑪ LA BOLA
$
CALLE BOLA 5
TEL 91 547 6930
Founded in 1870, this excellent corner restaurant serves typical Madrid food and is something of a shrine to *cocido madrileño*. The *caldo* (stock) is served as a soup and, as a stew, you get the delicious *garbanzos* (chickpeas), *chorizo*, *morcilla* (blood pudding), chicken, pork and ham, cabbage, leeks and potatoes, all cooked up over oak embers. Other specialties include *callos a la madrileña* (tripe Madrid-style) and roast lamb, and for dessert *buñuelos de manzana* (apple fritters).
🔲 100 🅿 ⏰ Closed Sun. D
🚇 Santo Domingo ⛔

TAPAS BARS

ANCIANO REY DE LOS VINOS
CALLE BAILÉN 19
TEL 91 559 5332
A delightful century-old bar, with beautiful tiles, serving very good wines and sherries. With each drink they offer a savory biscuit or a tapa of *cabrales* (strong Asturian cheese) or *anchoa con tomate* (anchovy with tomato). Try *escabeche* (soused fish), *pavías de bacalao* (fried salt cod in saffron batter), or *albóndigas*. A specialty is *torrijas*, milky bread fried in batter with honey or sugar and wine.
⏰ Closed Wed. 🚇 Ópera

CAFÉ DE ORIENTE
PLAZA DE ORIENTE
TEL 91 541 3974 OR 91 547 1564
On top of the ruins of the 17th-century San Gil convent (whose vaulted ceilings still survive), the café offers imaginative cooking and good draft beer. Its excellent tapas include *mero confitado en aceite de almendras con brandada de arenque ahumado* (slow-cooked sea bass in almond oil with strips of smoked herring). If you want a full sit-down meal, book in advance.
🚇 Ópera

SOMETHING SPECIAL

TABERNA DEL ALABARDERO
With a French Basque flavor and offering a modern take on traditional dishes, this restaurant serves tapas in its bar. Try the *bacalao con tomate* (cod with tomato) or *con pisto* (vegetable hash), the *chipirones en su tinta* (baby squid in their own ink), or the house specialty, *chistorra*, a tasty Basque sausage.
CALLE FELIPE V 4 & 6
TEL 91 547 2577
🚇 Ópera

⬛ DOWNTOWN MADRID

HOTELS

🏨 QUO PUERTA DEL SOL
$$$ ★★★★
CALLE SEVILLA 4
TEL 91 532 9049
FAX 91 531 2834
www.hotelesquo.com
This hotel opened in a very central early 20th-century building in 2003. The interior is very cleanly designed, sharp, and modern. Good views from the rooms on the main street and little noise through the double-glazed windows. Friendly and helpful staff.
ⓘ 62 🚇 Sevilla 🅢 ⬌ 🅢
🅢 All major cards

🏨 SUECIA
⑪ $$$ ★★★★
CALLE MARQUÈS DE CASA RIERA 4
TEL 91 531 6900
FAX 91 521 7141
www.hotelsuecia.com
Next door to the Círculo de Bellas Artes (Fine Arts Club) and close to Cibeles, this hotel is in a 1951 building renovated in 2000, with airy rooms and modern art on the walls. It has two restaurants. On the top floor is a balcony, reportedly frequented by Hemingway, with lovely views.
ⓘ 128 🚇 Banco de España
🅢 ⬌ 🅢 🅢 All major cards

SOMETHING SPECIAL

🏨 DE LAS LETRAS
⑪
The 1917 neoclassic exterior encloses an avant-garde interior with a literary theme. It has a library, and the corridors are lined with interesting quotations. The bar on its summer roof terrace has excellent views of Madrid. Very modern, well equipped, and with good service. It has a successful new restaurant, **DL's** *(Calle Caballero de Gracia 11, tel 91 523 7850, $$)*, whose chef, Ernesto Hinojal, offers an original cosmopolitan take on traditional dishes like *cocido madrileño*. Standouts include *brocheta de chipirón* (baby squid kebab), the carpaccios, the sushi, and *taco de atún a la plancha* (grilled tuna bites).
$$ ★★★★
GRAN VÍA 11
TEL 91 523 7980
FAX 91 523 7981
www.hoteldelasletras.com
ⓘ 107 🚇 Gran Vía, Sevilla
⬌ 🅢 🎽 🅢 All major cards

🏨 LIABENY
$$ ★★★★
CALLE SALUD 3
TEL 91 531 9000
FAX 91 532 7421
www.liabeny.es
Large and modern, the hotel is two minutes from the Puerta del Sol and Gran Vía. It has marble bathrooms and all the facilities expected of a four-star hotel. Helpful and courteous staff. Easy parking.
ⓘ 220 🅿 🚇 Sol, Gran Vía
⬌ 🅢 🎽 🅢 All major cards

🏨 PARIS
$$ ★★
CALLE ALCALÁ 2
TEL 91 521 6496
FAX 91 531 0188
Built in the 1870s, an old-style Madrid hotel and very central—right on the corner of the Puerta del Sol. It is a charmingly old-fashioned establishment, with a dark wood-paneled reception area. Clean and comfortable. Some of the rooms and bathrooms are on the small side. Good value.
🛏 120 🚇 Sol 🔌 🛗 🚫 All major cards

🏨 PETIT PALACE DUCAL
$$ ★★★
CALLE HORTALEZA 3
TEL 91 521 1043
FAX 91 521 5064
www.hthoteles.com
In a recently refurbished 19th-century palace just off the Gran Vía, this hotel is now modern, high-tech, and a good base for exploring the city.
🛏 58 🚇 Gran Vía 🛗 🔌 🚫 All major cards

🏨 REGINA
$$ ★★★
CALLE ALCALÁ 19
TEL 91 521 4725
FAX 91 522 4088
www.hotelreginamadrid.com
This centrally located hotel is comfortable, clean, and recently renovated. Spacious rooms for the tired sightseer. No restaurant. Breakfast included in the rate.
🛏 180 🅿 🚇 Sevilla 🔌 🛗 🚫 All major cards

🏨 VINCCI CENTRUM
$$ ★★★★
CALLE CEDACEROS 4
TEL 91 360 4720
FAX 91 522 4515
www.vinccihoteles.com
Opened in March 2004, this centrally located hotel (very close to the three main art museums) is stylish, modern, and well equipped, and the staff multilingual and friendly.

Some of the more expensive (superior) rooms have balconies with lovely views of the Madrid skyline.
🛏 87 🚇 Sevilla 🔌 🛗 🚫
🚫 All major cards

RESTAURANTS

🍴 LA TERRAZA DEL CASINO
$$$$$
CALLE ALCALÁ 15
TEL 91 532 1275
This Casino de Madrid restaurant has grand dining rooms and a beautiful summer terrace. Its chef, Paco Roncero, a creative disciple of the Catalan genius Ferrán Adriá, has already achieved his first Michelin star. Imaginative modern Mediterranean cuisine—try anything, as the textures, aromas, and flavors are wonderful. Famous dishes include *tortilla en tres pisos* (three-story omelette), served in a glass.
🪑 65 🅿 🚇 Closed Sat. L, Sun., Aug., & Easter week
🚇 Sevilla 🔌 🚫 All major cards

🍴 LA CASTAFIORE
$$$$
CALLE MARQUÉS DE MONASTERIO 5
TEL 91 310 6651 OR 91 319 4221
Named after the co-star of several Tintin adventures, this restaurant has waiters who are opera singers between jobs. They will sing for your supper (not at lunchtime) and end the evening with an ensemble performance, so don't go for a quiet conversational dinner. The food is Mediterranean with a Basque touch. Try *merluza rellena de langostinos* (hake filled with king prawns), *lubina a la espalda con patatas panaderas tosca* (grilled sea bass with roast breaded potatoes), or *solomillo de buey con salsa de boletus* (ox sirloin with boletus sauce). Reserve in advance.

🪑 125 🚇 Closed Sat. L & Sun. 🚇 Recoletos, Colón 🔌 🅿 🚫 All major cards

SOMETHING SPECIAL

🍴 LHARDY
Established in 1839, this place is legendary. Upstairs is the restaurant, ornate in its original Isabelline style and famed for its *cocido madrileño*, its seasonal game, and its excellent fish—try the *lubina al horno* (baked sea bass). Reserve in advance. Downstairs is a very fancy stand-up snack bar, serving delicious croquettes, *hojaldres* (light, flaky pastries), tapas, and, famously, a stupendous consommé poured into porcelain cups from silver samovars. If you fancy a dash of *jerez* (sherry) in it, don't hesitate to ask.
$$$$
CARRERA DE SAN JERÓNIMO 8
TEL 91 521 3385
🪑 130 🚇 Closed Sun. D & Aug. 🚇 Sol, Sevilla 🔌 🚫 All major cards

🍴 EL MENTIDERO DE LA VILLA
$$$
CALLE SANTO TOMÉ 6
TEL 91 308 1285
In this modern Spanish

restaurant, decorated with wooden fairground horses and a trompe l'oeil ceiling, chef José Ynglada is nothing if not imaginative. Try his *crujiente de morcilla sobre salsa de miel y gengibre* (crunchy blood pudding in honey and ginger sauce) or the *pularda rellena de foie con salsa de boletus y trufas* (hen stuffed with pâté in boletus and truffle sauce). Disabled access. Reserve in advance.
🔲 50 🅿 🕐 Closed Sat. L, Sun., & Aug. 🚇 Chueca, Colón 🚇 🏧 All major cards

🍴 ERROTA-ZAR
$$$
CALLE JOVELLANOS 3
1ST FLOOR
TEL 91 531 2564
This restaurant offers excellent traditional Basque cooking, an impressive wine list, and a large selection of cigars (*puros*). Try *boletus al horno* (roast boletus mushrooms), *kokotxas de merluza en aceite* (hake cheeks in olive oil), and the delicious homemade sheep's-milk yogurt (*cuajada*). Reserve in advance.
🔲 142 🕐 Closed Sun. & Aug. 🚇 Banco de España, Sevilla 🚇 🏧 All major cards

🍴 BOCAÍTO
$$
CALLE LIBERTAD 4
TEL 91 532 1219
This friendly restaurant offers Andalucían cooking with an occasional Madrileño touch. The fish menu varies with today's catch. Delicious on toast: *berberechos* (cockles), *gambas* (shrimp), and *trigueros* (wild asparagus). Regular stewed dishes: on Wednesday, *judiones de la granja con almejas* (huge fresh beans with clams); on Thursday *cocido madrileño;* and on Fridays *potaje castellano* (vegetable and pulse stew from Castilla). Good tapas.
🔲 80 🕐 Closed Sat. L, Sun.,

& Aug. 🚇 Chueca 🚇
🏧 All major cards

🍴 CARMENCITA
$$
CALLE LIBERTAD 16
TEL 91 531 6612
Open since 1850, a favorite of García Lorca, Dalí, Neruda, and Buñuel. Beautiful decor. Good, reasonably priced cooking, mainly Basque, using quality produce. Try *habitas* (baby broad beans) and clams, *cordero troceado al chilindrón* (chopped-up lamb with tomatoes and peppers), *pez espada en roquefort* (swordfish in Roquefort), or *tortilla de bacalao* (cod omelette). *Cocido madrileño* only on Thursdays. Good *menú del día* at lunchtime.
🔲 45 🕐 Closed Sat. L, Sun., & Aug. 🚇 Chueca 🚇
🏧 All major cards

🍴 LA PAELLA DE LA REINA
$$
CALLE LA REINA 39
TEL 91 531 1885 OR 91 531 6014
This Valencian restaurant specializes in paellas and rice dishes, as its name suggests— *paella de bogavante* or de *marisco* or *de la casa* or *valenciana* (lobster or seafood or house or Valencian paella); *arroz a'banda* or *negro* or *caldoso con bogavante* (rice in fish broth, or with shrimp and cuttlefish and its ink, or soupy with lobster). Fine desserts and good wines. Reserve in advance.
🔲 70 🚇 Banco de España 🚇 🏧 All major cards

🍴 ZARA
$
CALLE INFANTAS 5
TEL 91 532 2074
The friendliest Cuban restaurant in Madrid, serving delicious *ropa vieja* (literally, "old clothes," but here a meat stew). Delicious *tortilla de plátano* (banana omelette), *yuca frita* (fried cassava), and *picadillo de ternera con arroz y plá-*

tano (minced beef with rice and banana). Famous daiquiris. Small, with no reservations, so go early.
🔲 45 🕐 Closed Sat., Sun., & Aug. 🚇 Chueca, Gran Vía

TAPAS BARS

BODEGAS LA ARDOSA
CALLE COLÓN 13
TEL 91 521 4979
This friendly bar has been selling drinks (including Irish beers and vermouth on tap) and tapas since 1892. Their *salmorejo* (a thick, cold soup, similar to gazpacho, but with ham and egg and without peppers and cucumber) is historic. Try *cecina de León* (cured beef), *fabes con calamares* (Asturian beans with squid), or their varied croquetas.
🚇 Tribunal

CASA LABRA
CALLE TETÚAN 12
TEL 91 531 0081
Here since 1860, this bar is famous as the birthplace of the Spanish Socialist Workers' Party in 1879. It specializes in croquetas and in *bacalao* (cod), of which the freshly fried *tajadas* (slices) are particularly tasty.
🚇 Callao

LA COSA NOSTRA
CALLE DE LA CRUZ 3
TEL 91 521 2153
This bar's name refers to its decorative theme, not to its regular customers. Very central, it offers straightforward and rapidly served food, based on *crepes dulces* or *saladas* (sweet or savory pancakes) and empanadas.
🚇 Sevilla

LA CRUZ BLANCA
CALLE DE LA CRUZ 11
TEL 91 521 0770
Owned by the brewery, this establishment sells very good Cruzcampo draft beer and good *raciones* of *pulpo a la gallega* (octopus Galician-

HOTELS & RESTAURANTS

style), *chopitos* (baby squid), and *sepia* (cuttlefish), as well as other seafood and good cheese and ham.

🕐 Closed Mon. 🚇 Sevilla

TABERNA DE ÁNGEL SIERRA

CALLE GRAVINA 11
TEL 91 531 0126

A very typical 1917-vintage Madrid bar with a beautiful facade. Excellent draft beer and very good vermouth on tap, with fine tapas including *anchoas* (anchovies) and wonderful escabeches.

🚇 Chueca

■ AROUND PLAZA DE SANTA ANA

HOTELS

🏨 HOTEL HARD ROCK REINA VICTORIA
$$$$

PLAZA DE SANTA ANA 14
TEL 91 531 4500
FAX 91 522 0307
www.hardrockhotelmadrid
.com

Open since March 2006, right in Plaza de Santa Ana, the first Hard Rock hotel in Europe has transformed the old Grand Hotel Reina Victoria into a calm and discreetly high-tech temple of contemporary cool, while retaining its traditional beauty. The rooftop bar has beautiful views over the city, and it turns into something of a hotspot come the evening. Inside, there are plenty of good places to hang out. Friendly and efficient 24-hour service.

🛏 192 🅿 🚇 Sol 🔄 🔄
📺 🏧 All major cards

🏨 INGLÈS
$$ ★★★

CALLE ECHEGARAY 8
TEL 91 429 6551
FAX 91 420 2423
www.ingleshotel.com

Opened in 1886, this hotel—where Virginia Woolf and other writers and artists used

to stay—has few frills, but it is well situated near Plaza de Santa Ana and very close to iconic bars like Viva Madrid and Los Gabrieles. Clean, friendly and well-priced. No restaurant.

🛏 58 🅿 🔄 🏧 All major cards

🏨 MIAU
$ ★★★

CALLE DEL PRÍNCIPE 26
TEL 91 369 7120
FAX 91 429 3068
www.hotelmiau.com

Welcoming family-run hotel, behind a beautiful 18th-century facade, on Plaza de Santa Ana. Some of the rooms have small balconies overlooking the square. Reasonably priced and close to public parking facilities.

🛏 20 🚇 Antón Martín, Sevilla 🔄 🔄 🏧 All major cards

RESTAURANTS

🍴 EL RINCÓN DE ESTEBAN
$$$

CALLE SANTA CATALINA 3
TEL 91 429 9289

Cozy and elegant, much frequented by politicians, this restaurant's specialties include *manda huevos* (fried eggs, thin-cut potato fries, shavings of *jamón ibérico*, and baby eels), *merluza con almejas* (hake with clams), and *perdiz estofada a la toledana* (Toledo-style partridge stew). In May and December, it opens on Sundays for lunch.

🪑 60 🅿 🕐 Closed Sun. & Aug. 🚇 Sevilla 🔄 🏧 All major cards

🍴 PRADA A TOPE
$$

CALLE PRÍNCIPE 11
TEL 91 429 5921

Delicious reasonably priced food from the León village of El Bierzo. Good tapas at the bar. Try their local specialty, *botillo* (chickpeas, cabbage, potatoes, and pork ribs),

chorizo cooked in wine, or their famous *codillos* (pig's trotters), served with chorizo, potatoes cooked in their skins, cabbage, and refried vegetables.

🪑 45 🕐 Closed Sun. D & Mon. 🚇 Sevilla, Sol 🔄 🏧 DC, MC, V

🍴 ZERAIN
$$

CALLE QUEVEDO 3
TEL 91 429 7909

This friendly country-style Basque restaurant specializes in cider (hence the large barrels). Their grilled fresh fish and meat is delicious. Also try their *tortilla de bacalao* (cod omelette), *alubias de Tolosa* (Tolosa kidney beans), or their more elaborate fish dishes.

🪑 140 🕐 Closed Sun. & Aug. 🔄 🏧 All major cards

🍴 ¡CUANDO SALÍ DE CUBA!
$

CALLE TERNERA 4
TEL 91 522 9318

This friendly Cuban joint was one of Hemingway's favorite *tabernas* in Madrid. It offers unpretentious Cuban food and a well-priced lunch menu as well as good daiquiris and mojitos. Live Cuban music, 10:30 p.m.–2 a.m., Wed.–Sat.

🪑 40 🕐 Closed Sun. 🚇 Callao, Santo Domingo 🔄 🏧 DC, MC, V

🍴 LA BIOTIKA
$

CALLE AMOR DE DIOS 3
TEL 91 429 0780

A warm and cozy macrobiotic vegetarian hangout that makes delicious salads and homemade soups as well as tofu-based dishes. Near Plaza de Santa Ana.

🪑 25 🚇 Antón Martín 🏧 Not accepted

🍴 LA VACA VERÓNICA
$

CALLE MORATÍN 38
TEL 91 429 7827

A small, informal, romantic

Argentine restaurant, quiet and beautifully decorated. Delicious beef, as you would expect, cooked over hot stones, but also other meats and fresh fish, as well as a wide selection of salads. Try the homemade pastas, the one with *carabinero* (large grilled red shrimp) being legendary. Some impressive chocolate desserts. Reserve in advance.
🛏 60 🕐 Closed Sat. L
🚇 Antón Martín 🔾
🅰 All major cards

TAPAS BARS

CASA ALBERTO
CALLE HUERTAS 18
TEL 91 429 9356
This bar and restaurant, dating from 1827, is much loved by bullfighters and aficionados. It is famous for its *rabo de toro estofado* (stewed bull's tail). Vermouth on tap, delicious with a good tapa. Try the *callos*, *jamón ibérico*, *albóndigas* (meatballs), or *croquetas*.
🕐 Closed Mon., Sun. D, & Aug. 🚇 Antón Martín

CERVECERÍA ALEMANA
PLAZA DE SANTA ANA 6
TEL 91 429 7033
A lovely bar, open since 1904 and right in Plaza de Santa Ana, it is little changed since the days when Hemingway used to drink there, by the window. Tapas include good salads, *surtido de ahumados* (selection of smoked fish), *esparragos y palmitos* (asparagus and palm hearts), and *ensalada de tomate con queso de cabra* (tomato salad with goat's cheese).
🕐 Closed Tues. 🚇 Sevilla

LA AGUJA
CALLE AVE MARÍA 25
If you fancy listening to rock, blues, and jazz while you eat tapas and you're up for a bit of a party, then this is your place. Try the *tortilla de patatas al curry* (curried potato omelette), *croquetas de espinaca* (spinach cro-

quettes), or *tostas de lacón con albhaca* (pork shoulder with fresh basil on toast) as you swallow your draft beer.
🚇 Lavapiés

LA TABERNA DE ANTONIO SÁNCHEZ
CALLE MESÓN DE PAREDES 13
TEL 91 539 7826
Named In the early 19th century after the original owner's son, who died in the bullring, the *taberna* still retains its connections with the bullfighting world. The food is suitably Madrileño: *caracoles guisados* (stewed snails), *acelgas con almejas* (Swiss chard with clams), *tortilla San Isidro* (cod omelette), and *huevos estrellados*. Try the *torrijas*—milk-soaked bread fried in batter and sweetened with honey or sugar and wine.
🕐 Closed Sun. D
🚇 Tirso de Molina

LA TRUCHA
CALLE MANUEL FERNÁNDEZ Y GONZÁLEZ 3
TEL 91 429 5833
Very Andalucían bar, both in decor and in tapas, and hence the accent on frying. Try the *pescaíto frito* (small whole fried fish), the *berenjenas fritas* (fried sliced eggplant), the *alcachofas fritas* (fried artichoke), and the *verbena de ahumados* (smoked fish selection). Summer terrace.
🚇 Sevilla, Sol

LA VENENCIA
CALLE ECHEGARAY 7
TEL 91 429 7313
Famous for its wines and sherries, along with excellent tapas such as *mojama* (salted tuna), *lomo embuchado* (pork loin sausage), *encurtidos* (pickles), and very good *anchoas* (anchovies). A hang-out for wine experts, so avoid asking for a glass of soda—or risk being surrounded by raised eyebrows.
🚇 Sevilla

TABERNA LA DOLORES
PLAZA DE JESÚS 4
TEL 91 429 2243
Founded in 1908, this is one of the best known old-style bars in Madrid, with its lovely tile facade. Delicious *boquerones* (fresh anchovies), empanadas, and good draft beer.
🚇 Sevilla, Antón Martín

◼ PASEO DEL PRADO

HOTELS

🏨 PALACE
🍴 $$$$$ ★★★★★
PLAZA DE LAS CORTES 7
TEL 91 360 8000 OR 888/625-5144 (U.S. OR CANADA)
FAX 91 360 8100
www.palacemadrid.com
Inaugurated by King Alfonso XIII in 1912, the Palace has sumptuous public spaces with period furniture, chandeliers, and tapestries. The enormous stained-glass cupola in one of the salons is impressively beautiful. Rooms are small, but interior furnishings and bathrooms are first-class. A new Chinese-accented restaurant, **Asia Gallery,** has recently opened to acclaim.
ℹ 465 🅿 🛗 🔾 🎮
🅰 All major cards

🏨 RITZ
🍴 $$$$$ ★★★★★
PLAZA DE LA LEALTAD 5
TEL 91 701 6767
FAX 91 701 6776
www.ritz.es
Built in 1910 for King Alfonso XIII, who realized that there was no hotel in Madrid grand enough for the guests invited to his wedding to Queen Victoria's granddaughter. The hotel is full of beautiful antiques and chandeliers, and it is surrounded by gardens.
ℹ 167 🅿 🛗 🔾 🎮
🅰 All major cards

SOMETHING SPECIAL

🏨 VILLA REAL
🍴

A modern hotel in an ideal location, built to blend in with older surroundings. The reception area, salons, and rooms are decorated in the French style. It boasts wonderful modern and antique sculptures, paintings, tapestries, and other art, including a collection of third-century Roman mosaics. Guest rooms have sitting areas with mahogany furniture and bathrooms with Carrara marble. Suites have balconies and saunas.

$$$$ ★★★★★
PLAZA DE LAS CORTES 10
TEL 91 420 3767
FAX 91 420 2547
www.derbyhotels.es
🛏 120 🅿 🚇 🚭
💳 All major cards

🏨 HOTEL MORA
$ ★★
PASEO DEL PRADO 32
TEL 91 420 1569
FAX 91 420 0564
www.hotelmora.com
Close to Atocha railway station, the major museums, and parks, this friendly five-story hotel is well priced and recently refurbished. Rooms on the upper stories are quieter. Good bar.
🛏 62 🚇 Atocha 🚭 🚭
💳 All major cards

RESTAURANTS

🍴 BALZAC
$$$$
CALLE MORETO 7
TEL 91 420 0177
Balzac's chef, Andrés Madrigal, is inventive, original, and a master of aromas. His dishes are constantly evolving, so trying the *menú degustación* may be a sensible decision on the first visit. Madrigal is famous for his seafood dishes. Reserve in advance.
🪑 70 🚇 Closed Sat L, Sun., & second half Aug. 🚭
💳 All major cards

🍴 PARADÍS RF CASA DE AMÉRICA
$$$
PALACIO DE LINARES
PASEO DE RECOLETOS 2
TEL 91 575 4540
Cutting-edge Catalan and Mediterranean cuisine under the guidance of famed chef Ramón Freixa, in a modern minimalist setting inside the Palacio de Linares. The restaurant is noted for its rice and codfish dishes and inventive use of the freshest seasonal raw materials. Good wine selection. You could also try the sister restaurant inside the Thyssen-Bornemisza museum.
🪑 60 🅿 🚇 Closed Sat. L & Sun. 🚇 Banco de España 🚭
💳 All major cards

🍴 AROLA MADRID
$$
REINA SOFÍA MUSEUM
ALLE ARGUMOSA 43
TEL 91 467 0202
Inside the brand-new Nouvel-designed wing of the Reina Sofía museum and looking onto the beautiful enclosed plaza, this very modern restaurant is the younger (and cheaper) sibling of the two-Michelin-starred La Broche (see p. 253). Try the *pastel de bacalao con naranja y cebolleta* (codfish pie with orange and spring onion) before moving on to the *espuma de chocolate blanco* (white chocolate foam).
🪑 104 🅿 🚇 Closed Mon. (from 9 p.m.) & Tues. 🚇 Atocha 🚭 💳 All major cards

🍴 PARADÍS MUSEO THYSSEN
$$
PASEO DEL PRADO 8
TEL 91 429 2732
Excellent restaurant inside the Thyssen-Bornemisza museum, its cooking overseen by Catalan super-chef Ramón Freixa. It specializes in rice and fish dishes and salads. Try the *merluza sobre crema de patatas* (hake on a creamed

potato bed), *buey con setas* (ox with wild mushrooms), or *arroz negro con sepia* (cuttlefish rice in its ink).
🪑 60 🚇 Closed Mon. 🚇 Banco de España 🚭
💳 All major cards

🍴 IBOO CIBELES
$
CALLE ALCALÁ 55
TEL 91 781 1555
This is one branch of a very original chain invented by the successful young chef Mario Sandoval; it has high-class Mediterranean food, fast-food-style, at popular prices. Delicious salads, fish and meat dishes, and desserts in a modern and sophisticated setting. Open all day. Other branches at Calle Sor Ángela de la Cruz 17 (*metro: Cuzco*) and at Calle Génova 4 (*metro: Alonso Martínez*).
🪑 120 🚇 Banco de España 🚭 💳 All major cards

■ PARQUE DEL RETIRO & AROUND

HOTELS

🏨 AC PALACIO DEL RETIRO
$$$$$ ★★★★★

(see p. 253)

HOTELS
An indication of the maximum high-season cost of a double room with breakfast is given by $ signs.

$$$$$ Over $300
$$$$ $220–$300
$$$ $160–$220
$$ $80–$160
$ Under $80

RESTAURANTS
An indication of the cost of a three-course dinner, without drinks, is given by $ signs.

$$$$$ Over $80
$$$$ $50–$80
$$$ $35–$50
$$ $20–$35
$ Under $20

CALLE ALFONSO XII 14
TEL 91 523 7460
FAX 34 91 523 7461
www.ac-hotels.com
In an early 20th-century palace, restored and converted into a hotel in late 2004, this impressive but cozy hotel has excellent facilities and a good combination of traditional and modern design. With lovely views of the Parque del Retiro, it is perfectly situated for visiting the major museums.

[1] 50 P 🚇 Retiro 🟢 🔼
🔼 🎦 🗎 All major cards

🏨 HOTEL WELLINGTON
🍴 $$$$$ ★★★★★
CALLE VELÁZQUEZ 8
TEL 91 575 4400
FAX 91 576 4164
www.hotel-wellington.com
A lovely, traditional hotel, with beautiful views of the Parque del Retiro. Popular with bullfighters, who dress here before leaving for the bullfight. Well furnished and decorated, it has a lovely garden with a swimming pool. Its associated modern Basque restaurant, **Goizeko Wellington** (*Calle Villanueva 34, tel 91 577 0138, $$$$, closed Sat. D, July, & Aug, all major cards*) is very good, with a mix of traditional dishes like *kokotxa de merluza* (hake cheeks) and original ones like *ensalada de ostras con granizado de gin tonic* (oyster salad topped by gin tonic slush).

[1] 300 P 🚇 Retiro 🟢
🔼 🟢 🏊 🗎 All major cards

🏨 NH NACIONAL
$$$ ★★★★
PASEO DEL PRADO 48
TEL 91 429 6629
FAX 91 369 1564
www.hotelnhnacional.com
Located in the "Art Triangle," close to Atocha railway station and overlooking the Botanic Garden, this grand and spacious hotel was completely rehabilitated in 1997 and now has a modern,

understated decor. It is also equipped with up-to-the-minute technology. The lobby, with its tall columns underneath a glazed dome, is particularly impressive. Two bars and a restaurant.

[1] 214 🚇 Atocha P 🔼
🔼 🎦 🗎 All major cards

RESTAURANTS

🍴 HORCHER
$$$$$
CALLE ALFONSO XII 6
TEL 91 522 0731
Set up in 1943 by a Berlin restaurateur escaping the war, this elegant establishment now also serves more international cooking, specializing in seasonal wild game dishes, such as wild boar *(jabalí)*, venison *(venado, ciervo)* and duck *(pato)*. It also has good fish and desserts. Dress formally. Reserve in advance.

🔳 70 P 🕐 Closed Sat. L, Sun., & Aug. 🚇 Retiro 🟢
🗎 All major cards

🍴 CASA RAFA
$$$$
CALLE NARVÁEZ 68
TEL 91 573 1087
Said by many to serve the best seafood in Madrid—but the meat dishes are also good. The chef is extremely rigorous in selecting his raw materials, mainly from the Cantabrian coast. Delicious *gambas a la plancha* (grilled shrimp), *percebes* (gooseneck barnacles), *rodaballo* (turbot), *centolla* (spider crab), *salpicón de marisco* (seafood salad), and delicious stews like *langostinos con verduras en fideuá* (king prawns and vegetables in noodles). Mouth-watering. Reserve in advance.

🔳 80 P 🕐 Cosed Mon. D
🚇 Ibiza 🟢 🗎 All major cards

🍴 VIRIDIANA
$$$$
CALLE JUAN DE MENA 14
TEL 91 523 4478
Named after Buñuel's 1961

film masterpiece, this is one of the very best restaurants in Madrid. It is led by the creative chef Abraham García, who is also a writer, a film buff, and a lover of bullfighting and horse racing, as the decor reflects. He serves the freshest seasonal foods, free-range or wild meat and fish, with glorious taste and aroma. Try absolutely anything. Highly rated wine list. Reserve in advance.

🔳 60 P 🕐 Closed Sun.
🚇 Banco de España, Retiro
🟢 🗎 All major cards

🍴 LA GAMELLA
$$$
CALLE ALFONSO XII 4
TEL 91 532 4509
Established here in 1988 by an American owner and looking onto the Parque del Retiro, La Gamella serves excellent, delicate, and imaginative Spanish and American dishes. Try the *steak tártar al Jack Daniel's, magret de pato en salsa agridulce de frutas rojas* (duck breast in sweet-and-sour red-fruit sauce), or just go for a top-quality hamburger. Welcoming and relaxing. Reserve in advance.

🔳 48 🕐 Closed Sat. L, Sun., & first half Aug. 🚇 Retiro
🟢 🗎 All major cards

🍴 CASA DOMINGO 1920
$$
CALLE ALCALÁ 99
TEL 91 431 1895
This friendly family restaurant, serving typical Madrileño food since 1920 in an art nouveau setting, is a historical monument. Try the *gallina en pepitoria* (hen fricassée), *pastel de cabracho* (scorpionfish pie), *estofado de rabo de toro* (bull's tail stew), or their famous *callos* (tripe). On the dessert front, their crêpes suzettes are, appropriately, legendary. Reserve in advance.

🔳 150 P 🚇 Retiro 🟢
🗎 All major cards

🍴 CASA PELLO
$
CALLE DOCTOR CASTELO 2
TEL 91 574 0103
A small and friendly family restaurant offering fine local fare, well priced. Don't miss their *cocido madrileño, pimientos rellenos de bacalao con gambas* (peppers stuffed with cod and shrimp), and *croquetas de espinacas y roquefort* (spinach and Roquefort croquettes). Reserve in advance.
🔩 35 🕐 Closed Sun.
🚇 Ibiza 🖘 All major cards

TAPAS BARS

LA ANTIGUA
CALLE O'DONNELL 12
TEL 91 576 4198
Have a *caña* (glass of draft beer) and a good traditional tapa or *ración* at the bar. This regular joint fills up at lunchtime because of the tasty food and very good prices.
🚇 Príncipe de Vergara, Retiro

LA TABERNA DE BUENDI
CALLE DOCTOR CASTELO 15
TEL 91 578 2737
This fine, friendly, and typically Madrileño bar is like an extension of your own home but with more people and less work. Good Spanish wine selection. Try their *jamón iberico, boquerones en vinagre* or canapés on toast—like *cabeza de jabalí con brie fundido* (boar's head with melted Brie) and *bacalao ahumado* (smoked cod).
🚇 Ibiza

LUCHARNA
CALLE MENORCA 9
TEL 91 573 2243
Friendly family atmosphere with a good selection of wine and tapas. Choose one of the many clear soups on offer or try their *gallega* (Galician) specialties such as *empanada de zamburiñas* (scallop pastries) or, from elsewhere, their *bacalao ajoarriero* (salt cod

with peppers) or *ensalada de ventresca con pimientos del piquillo* (tuna belly meat with red peppers).
🕐 Closed Sun. 🚇 Ibiza

TABERNA DEL PUERTO
CALLE FERNÁN GONZÁLEZ 50
TEL 91 504 6699
Excellent Andalucían cooking: Concentrate on fish and seafood, often in batter, fast-fried, crunchy on the outside and mouth-watering on the inside. The sister restaurant is at Calle Diego de León 58 *(tel 91 309 2887, metro: Diego de León)*. Try the *salmonetes frescos* (fresh red mullet), *acedía* (plaice), *calamares en fritura* (frittered squid), *boquerones fritos* (fried fresh anchovies), or *chirlas guisadas* (stewed clams).
🅿 🕐 Closed Sun. D
🚇 Ibiza

⬛ LA CASTELLANA & SALAMANCA

HOTELS

🏨 ADLER
$$$$$ ★★★★★
CALLE VELÁZQUEZ 33
TEL 91 426 3220
FAX 91 426 3221
www.lesein.es/adler
Opened in 2001 in a completely rehabilitated 1884 palace in the Salamanca barrio, this hotel is well equipped and well furnished, welcoming and cozy. The service is friendly and attentive. It has a haute-cuisine restaurant, with a very good wine list.
🛏 45 🔩 55 🅿
🚇 Velázquez 🖘 🖘
🖘 All major cards

🏨 VILLA MAGNA
🍴 **$$$$$ ★★★★★**
PASEO CASTELLANA 22
TEL 91 587 1234
FAX 91 431 2286
www.madrid.park.hyatt.com
This hotel's modern facade contrasts with the Carlos IV-

style interiors. Rooms are decorated with plants in the bathrooms. The hotel also has two fine restaurants: The walnut-paneled **Berceo** specializes in fish, and **Tse-Yang** serves the highest quality Chinese cuisine in the capital. The hotel is surrounded by wonderful gardens and has a terrace to dine on in summer.
🛏 182 🅿 🚇 Rubén Darío
🖘 🖘 🖘 🖘 All major cards

SOMETHING SPECIAL

🏨 PUERTA DE AMÉRICA
🍴

A brand-new hotel, opened in 2005, with each of its 12 floors designed by a different cutting-edge architect (including Jean Nouvel, Zaha Hadid, Norman Foster, and Arata Isozaki). Impressively well designed and well equipped. Outside the center, but quieter for it. Its restaurant, **Lagrimas Negras** *($$$$, tel 91 744 5400)*, is led by the up-and-coming chef José Luis Estevan. It offers such imaginative food as *cangrejo de caparazón blando* (soft-shelled crab), fried to be both crunchy and juicy, and *tórtolas asadas* (roast turtle doves).
$$$$ ★★★★★
AVENIDA DE AMÉRICA 41
TEL 91 744 5400
FAX 91 744 5401
www.hotelpuertamerica.com
🛏 342 🅿 🚇 Cartagena 🖘
🖘 🖘 🖘 All major cards

SOMETHING SPECIAL

🏨 SANTO MAURO
🍴

Built in neoclassic style by the Duke of Santo Mauro in 1894, this palace has interiors by Josep Joanpere, combining the original cornices and Italian marble fireplaces with contemporary furniture and textiles. No two rooms are the same. In the basement is an amazing pool with columns and vaulted ceilings. Its restaurant, **Santo**

Mauro *(closed Aug.)*, occupies the old library, still lined with books. Try the *ensalada templada de vieiras* (warm scallop salad), *rodaballo salvaje asado con crujiente de verduras y salsa de lima y gengibre* (roast wild turbot with crunchy vegetables and lime and ginger sauce), or *lomo de cordero presalé asado con ensalada crujiente especiada de verduras* (roast lamb loin with crunchy spicy vegetable salad). There is a beautiful garden where you can eat in summer months.

$$$$ *****
CALLE ZURBANO 36
TEL 91 319 6900
FAX 91 308 5477
www.ac-hotels.com
🛏51 🔁56 🅿 🚇 Gregorio
Marañón 🔁 🅢 🖥 🖦
🅢 All major cards

🏨 BAUZÁ
🍴 $$ ****
CALLE GOYA 79
TEL 91 435 7545
FAX 91 431 0943
www.hotelbauza.com
Opened in 1999, this fashionable boutique-style hotel is in the heart of the Salamanca barrio. Away from Madrid's nightlife, it is peaceful and comfortable, with attentive service. The restaurant offers fresh Mediterranean food with a hint of Japanese influence and a creative, often changing menu.
🛏167 🅿 🚇 Goya,
Velázquez 🔁 🅢 🖦
🅢 All major cards

🏨 GALIANO
🍴 $$ ***
CALLE ALCALÁ GALIANO 6
TEL 91 319 2000
FAX 91 319 9914
www.hotelgaliano.com
Originally a convent, this beautiful little palace now houses a noble family's private home as well as the hotel. It is nicely quiet for somewhere so central. With Chueca on one side and Salamanca on the other, it is well placed

for exploring.
🛏29 🅿 🚇 Colón 🔁 🅢
🅢 AE, MC, V

RESTAURANTS

🍴 JOCKEY
$$$$$
CALLE AMADOR DE LOS RÍOS 6
TEL 91 319 2435
Ranked among the top restaurants in Spain, Jockey has an elegant, old-fashioned, British-influenced decor of wood paneling and racing prints. Start with the house aperitif, Gin Jockey. Specialties include *langostinos crudos al caviar con crema fresca* (thinly sliced raw king prawns with caviar and fresh cream), *tuétano con patatas, foie gras y salsa de champagne* (squash with potatoes, foie gras, and champagne sauce), *mollejas* (sweetbreads), and *faisán a las uvas con vino de Oporto* (pheasant with grapes in port). Excellent wines and ports. Dress up and reserve well in advance.
🔁100 🅿 🕐 Closed Aug.
🚇 Colón 🅢 🅢 All major cards

SOMETHING SPECIAL

🍴 LA BROCHE SERGI AROLA
This restaurant's elegant and minimalist decoration is the setting for the artistry of its hugely successful young Catalan chef and ex-rock guitarist, Sergi Arola. A disciple of Ferrán Adriá, he has already won himself two Michelin stars. The food is original, creative, imaginative—new dishes often appear on the menu—and delicious. Try the *sardinas ahumadas con crujiente de huevo frito* (smoked sardines with crunchy fried egg), *lubina asada con chutney de mango y yogurt* (roast sea bass with mango and yogurt chutney), *medallón de langosta con cuscús de arroz y especias africanas* (lobster medallion with rice couscous and African

spices), or follow your nose or the waiter's advice. With only 40 seats, the restaurant is full every night, so don't fail to reserve in advance.
$$$$$
CALLE MIGUEL ANGEL 29
TEL 91 399 3437
🔁40 🅿 🕐 Closed Sat., Sun., Aug., & Easter week
🚇 Gregorio Marañón 🅢
🅢 All major cards

SOMETHING SPECIAL

🍴 SANTCELONI
In the Hotel Hesperia, the Madrid wing of the celebrated chef Santi Santamaría's Barcelona base has already earned two Michelin stars. The cooking is supervised by his disciple Óscar Velazco. Fresh, seasonal, and innovative, without ever losing touch with tradition. Try the *mero marinado con puré de manzana ahumado* (marinated sea bass with smoked apple purée), *terrina de pularda y foie gras con trufas* (terrine of fattened hen and foie gras with truffles), *jarrete de ternera blanca con puré de patata* (white beef hock with potato purée), or *esparedeñas con mollejas de cordero* (sea cucumber with lamb sweetbread). Legendary. Reserve well in advance.
$$$$$
HOTEL HESPERIA
PASEO DE LA CASTELLANA 57
TEL 91 210 8840
🔁45 🕐 Closed Sat. L, Sun., & Aug. 🅿 🚇 Gregorio Marañón 🅢 🅢 All major cards

🍴 ZALACAÍN
$$$$$
CALLE ÁLVAREZ DE BAENA 4
TEL 91 561 4840
The restaurant that introduced nouvelle cuisine to Spain is still one of its top kitchens. The much-admired Basque chef Benjamín Urdaín, recently awarded his second Michelin star, offers a mixture of Zalacaín classics along with

new fruits of his creativity. Always fresh and seasonal. Try the *manitas de cerdo rellenas de cordero* (pig's trotters stuffed with lamb), *ostras en salsa verde* (oysters in green sauce), the potato soufflé with anything, or the *tartar de bonito con beluga y pimienta verde* (bonito tartar with Beluga caviar and fresh pepper). Dress up and reserve well in advance.

🛏 120 🅿 🕐 Closed Sat. L, Sun., Aug., & Easter week 🚇 Gregorio Marañón 🈂 🈹 All major cards

🍴 EL AMPARO
$$$$
CALLE PUIGCERDÁ 8
TEL 91 431 6456

This charming Basque restaurant led by Carlos Posadas offers a creative take on that culture's traditional cuisine. Stand out dishes include *foie caliente a la sartén con crujiente de calabaza dulce y salsa perigord* (goose liver heated in the skillet with crunchy sweet squash and Périgord sauce), *cigalas salteadas con ravioli de queso y romero* (sautéed Dublin Bay shrimp with cheese and rosemary ravioli), and *lechona confitada con puré de manzana y membrilla* (honeyed suckling pig with apple purée and quince jelly). The hot chocolate soufflé is exquisite. Excellent wine cellar. Reserve in advance.

🛏 65 🅿 🕐 Closed Sat. L. & Sun. 🚇 Serrano 🈂 🈹 All major cards

🍴 EL BODEGÓN
$$$$
CALLE PINAR 15
TEL 91 562 8844

Traditional Basque cooking with a Catalan element and original touches, headed by chef José Machado. Formal, but friendly. Try the *menú degustación* to explore, or start with *potaje de lentejas y perdiz* (lentils and partridge soup), vichyssoise, or any of the fish soups, and then

move on to *lomo de salmonete en caldo gelatinoso de hinojo* (red mullet in jellied fennel stock), *pichón con ciruelas* (pigeon with plums), or the classic filet mignon à la béarnaise. Dress up and reserve in advance.

🛏 60 🅿 🕐 Closed Sat. L, Sun., & Aug. 🚇 Gregorio Marañón 🈂 🈹 All major cards

🍴 LOS CLARINES
$$$
CALLE BOCÁNGEL 2
TEL 91 356 9859

Very Madrid, very close to Las Ventas bullring, and very bullfight-aficionado. Its menu stays on track, from *rabo de toro* (bull's tail) to *estofado de toro* (bull stew). Also good fish, such as *merluza a la cosquera* (hake in shellfish sauce). During the Feria de San Isidro, from mid–May to early June, it stays open all day, every day, except during the bullfights (roughly 7–9 p.m.).

🛏 70 🕐 Closed Mon. except during San Isidro 🚇 Ventas 🈹 All major cards

🍴 PRÍNCIPE DE VIANA
$$$
CALLE MANUEL DE FALLA 5
TEL 91 457 1549

One of the best loved restaurants in the city, with Basque-Navarrese cuisine. Try these specialties: *menestra de verduras de Tudela* (asparagus stewed with other vegetables), *bacalao ajoarriero con langosta* (cod with peppers and lobster), or *merluza en salsa verde* (hake in parsley, garlic, and olive oil sauce). The ham croquettes are famous. Reservations essential.

🛏 80 🅿 🕐 Closed Sat. L & Sun. 🚇 Santiago Bernabéu 🈂 🈹 All major cards

🍴 DONDE LEO
$$
CALLE PEDRO HEREDIA 22
TEL 91 356 6561

One of the favorite restaurants of the bullfighting fraternity, this very Madrileño restaurant is presided over by the Virgen de la Paloma and portraits of bullfighters. Stand-out dishes: *rabo de toro con caracoles* (bull's tail with snails) and the croquetas.

🛏 75 🕐 Closed Mon. except during San Isidro 🚇 Ventas 🈹 All major cards

🍴 LA CASUCA
$$
CALLE AGUSTÍN DE FOXÁ 16–18
TEL 91 314 5696

A great opportunity to try classic Cantabrian cooking and more, in the hands of Antonio Hoyas. The stews and roasts are excellent. Try typical northern dishes like *cocido montañés* (stew of kidney beans, blood sausage, cabbage, pork, chorizo, cabbage, and pig's ears), *rabas* (fried squid), *marmitako de bonito* (bonito stew), or *brandada de bacalao con vinagreta de pulpo* (cod strips with octopus vinaigrette). Reserve in advance.

🛏 90 🅿 🕐 Closed Sun. D 🚇 Plaza de Castilla, Chamartín 🈂 🈹 All major cards

🍴 LA TABERNA DE BUE-NAVENTURA

$$

CALLE HERMOSILLA 69

TEL 91 575 8365

Popular old-style Madrid restaurant offering high-quality local dishes, including a famed *cocido madrileño, callos a la madrileña* (Madrid-style tripe), and fresh fish dishes. A *cupletista* (cabaret singer) livens up Saturday nights. Reserve in advance.

🔢 96 🕐 Closed Mon., Sun. D, & Aug. Ⓜ Goya 🅢
🅢 DC, MC, V

TAPAS BARS

EL RINCÓN DE JAÉN

CALLE DR. GÓMEZ ULLA 6

TEL 91 355 4011

DON RAMÓN DE LA CRUZ 88

TEL 91 401 6334

These friendly and generous bar/restaurants are said by some to have the best Andalucían food in Madrid. Delicious fried fish, seafood, sausages, and salads.

Ⓜ Manuel Becerra

FINOS Y FINAS

CALLE ESPARTINAS 6

TEL 91 575 9069

A popular bar (and small restaurant) with inventive, high-quality tapas. Try the *pimientos de piquillo rellenos de níscalos y jamón ibérico* (red peppers filled with wild mushroom and ham), *tartaletas de calamares,* or *de pollo en pepitoria* (squid or fricasséed chicken pies), or croquetas.

🕐 Closed Sun. D, Aug.
Ⓜ Velázquez, Príncipe de Vergara

LA TABERNA DEL BUEY

CALLE GENERAL PARDIÑAS 7

TEL 91 578 1154

Popular tapas bar, offering delicious Swiss cheese, *ahumados* (smoked fish), *gulas* (baby eels), *pimientos de piquillo rellenos de bacalao* (red peppers stuffed with cod), with perfect *patatas*

paja (fine-cut crunchy fried potatoes) and fine canapés.
Ⓜ Velázquez

O'CRUCEIRO

CALLE NUÑEZ DE BALBOA 29

TEL 91 577 8447 OR 91 577 7302

This *gallego* restaurant offers first-rate seafood in its bar: *vieiras* (scallops), *percebes* (gooseneck barnacles), *ostras* (oysters), *navajas* (razor shells), and *langostinos*. Excellent empanadas of *vieira* and of *bacalao con pasas* (cod with raisins), as well as *pulpo a la gallega* (Galician-style octopus).

🅿 🕐 Closed Sun. D
Ⓜ Goya

■ PLAZA DE ESPAÑA & WESTERN MADRID

HOTELS

🏨 HUSA PRINCESA

$$$ ★★★★★

CALLE PRINCESA 40

TEL 91 542 3500 OR 2100

FAX 91 542 7328

www.hotelhusaprincesa.com

Spacious, modern hotel, completely redone in 2001, on the edge of the historic center and not far from the parks. The outdoor terrace is open from May to October. Facilities for the disabled.

🛏 275 🅿 Ⓜ Argüelles 🅢
🔁 🅢 🎽 🎦 🅢 All major cards

🏨 EL COLOSO

$$ ★★★★

CALLE LEGANITOS 13

TEL 91 548 7640

FAX 91 547 4968

www.hotelelcoloso.com

Comfortable hotel, close to the center, and well equipped. Attentive service. Good deals in the low season.

🛏 132 🅿 Ⓜ Plaza de España, Santo Domingo 🔁
🅢 🅢 All major cards

🏨 T3 TIROL

$$ ★★★

CALLE MARQUÉS DE URQUIJO 4

TEL 91 548 1900

FAX 91 541 3958

www.hotel-tirol.com

Recently renovated, a comfortable, modern hotel with good facilities. It is outside the center, but very close to the metro station. Up-to-half-price offers available at times.

🛏 98 Ⓜ Argüelles 🔁 🅢
🅢 All major cards

RESTAURANTS

SOMETHING SPECIAL

🍴 CLUB ALLARD

In a beautiful art deco building, this used to be a private politicians' and bankers' club, but it is now a wonderful restaurant led by chef Diego Guerrero, who has worked with some of the finest Basque and Catalan chefs. Try starters such as terrine of goose liver with a honey vinaigrette or *huevos con pan y panceta sobre crema ligera de patata* (eggs with bread and belly pork over lightly creamed potato). Good meat courses include *coquelet de Bresse confitado en grasa de pato con jugo de uvas* (young Bresse chicken confit in duck fat with grape juice) and *cochinillo confitado con canela y comino* (suckling pig confit with cinnamon and cumin). The menu keeps developing, but the fish section changes every day according to which wild fish are brought in. Excellent wine list. Dress up and reserve in advance.

$$$$

CALLE FERRAZ 2

TEL 91 559 0939

🔢 70 🅿 🕐 Closed Sun., Sat L, & Mon. D Ⓜ Plaza de España 🅢 🅢 All major cards

🍴 LAS CUATRO ESTACIONES

$$$$

CALLE GENERAL IBÁÑEZ ÍBERO 5

TEL 91 553 6305
Classic yet modern French-influenced Mediterranean food in a quiet setting. The fresh, seasonal menu includes *gazpacho con bogavante* (cold tomato-based soup with lobster), *foie caliente a las uvas* (goose liver cooked with grapes), and *verduras a la plancha* (grilled vegetables). Their *callos a la madrileña* are famed, as are their steak tartare and their potato soufflé. Excellent wine list.

130 🕓 Closed Sat. L, Sun., Aug., & Easter week 🚇 Gúzman el Bueno 🅿 💳 🚫 All major cards

🍴 BOKADO
$$$
AVENIDA JUAN DE HERRERA 2
TEL 91 549 0041
This fine restaurant in the Museo del Traje (Clothing and Costume Museum) also has a lovely terrace by the Moncloa gardens. Take your choice of two *menus degustación*, or try the terrine of foie gras with crème fraîche and canteloupe, *rape negro en salsa de almejas* (black monkfish in clam sauce), or *ravioli de changurro con jugo de carabinero con verduritas fritas* (crab ravioli with shrimp juice and fried vegetables). Children's menu available.

90 🅿 🕓 Closed Mon. & Sun. D 🚇 Ciudad Universitaria 💳 🚫 DC, MC, V

🍴 LAS BATUECAS
$$
AVENIDA REINA VICTORIA 17
TEL 91 554 04 52
Good, traditional food in this restaurant, unchanged in 50 years. Try their famed *tortilla con callos* (omelette with tripe sauce), *puerros gratinados* (leeks au gratin), croquetas, *berenjenas rebosadas* (sliced and battered eggplant), or *cordero asado* (roast lamb). Reserve in advance.

60 🕓 Closed Mon.–Wed.

D, Thurs.–Fri. L, Sat. D, Sun., & Aug. 🚇 Cuatro Caminos 💳 🚫 Not accepted

🍴 SAL GORDA
$$
CALLE BEATRIZ DE BOBADILLA 9
TEL 91 553 9506
A cozy, traditional, and reasonably priced restaurant. Recommended dishes include *bacalao ajoarriero* (cod in garlic, pepper, and tomato sauce), *lomo de buey* (ox fillet), or *pencas de acelgas rellenas de jamón* (ham-filled Swiss chard). Reserve in advance.

65 🕓 Closed Sun. & Aug. 🚇 Guzmán el Bueno 💳 🚫 All major cards

🍴 CON DOS FOGONES
$
CALLE SAN BERNARDINO 9
TEL 91 559 6326
Fusion cuisine in this small, country-style, but modern restaurant, designed for both vegetarians and carnivores. Try the *hamburguesa de merluza* (hake burger) with tomato sauce, squash tempura, soy sauce, and honey, or the *bacalao confitado con pisto de hongos y crema de ajos* (cod confit with wild mushroom hash and garlic cream). Very reasonable prices. Reserve for dinner.

45 🚇 Plaza de España 💳 🚫 All major cards

TAPAS BARS

CUENLLAS WINE BAR
CALLE FERRAZ 5
TEL 91 542 5621
A gem in a tapas-rich street, this bar offers excellent tapas and canapés and has a restaurant as well. Try *soldaditos de Pavía en fritura ligera a la madrileña* (cod fritters Madrid-style), Beluga caviar, or *cecina con aceite de oliva* (cured meat with olive oil). A treat.

🕓 Closed Sun. 🚇 Ventura Rodríguez

ENTREVINOS
CALLE FERRAZ 36
TEL 91 548 3114
Wonderful wines, tapas, and *raciones* in this good-looking bar/restaurant. Try their meat or fish carpaccios, *cecina artesana* (cured meat prepared here), the excellent *jamón ibérico de bellota* (ham from acorn-fed pigs), or the cheese board.

🕓 Closed Sun. & Aug. 🚇 Ventura Rodríguez, Plaza de España

PRADA A TOPE
CUESTA DE SAN VICENTE 32
TEL 91 547 8020
Like its twin in the Santa Ana barrio, this bar and restaurant offers food from the village of El Bierzo in León. Try the *botillo* (chickpeas, cabbage, potatoes, and pork ribs), *codillos* (pig's trotters), or the *morcilla* (blood pudding).

🚇 Plaza de España

TABERNA LOS PORCHES
PASEO PINTOR ROSALES 2
TEL 91 542 4900
With lovely views of the park and the ancient Templo de Debod, this *taberna* has a friendly family atmosphere. Good *ahumados* (smoked fish), *morcilla de Burgos* (Burgos blood pudding), and *tostas* (servings on toast). Crowded on weekends.

🕓 Closed Mon. 🚇 Ventura Rodríguez

SHOPPING

Shopping in Madrid can transport you across centuries within a few steps. Old, established, family-run shops selling shawls and mantillas and convents selling sweets and pastries made by unseen nuns reflect Madrid's old traditions. On the other hand, boutiques offering clothes by some of Europe's most imaginative, ground-breaking designers represent the extraordinary creative explosion that followed Franco's death in 1975—a burst of artistic development that continues to this day.

Central Madrid has three main shopping areas. The first centers around the Puerta del Sol, including the pedestrian-only street Preciados that connects Plaza de Callao to the Gran Vía. At Sol's southern end, it stretches from Plaza Mayor to Plaza de Canalejas. This area includes department stores, fashion chains, and modern stores selling everything from clothes to shoes to jewelry to crafts to books and music. It includes many tourist outlets, but you will also come across typically Madrileño shops, unusual and generations old.

The second area is in the exclusive Salamanca barrio, a chic and glamorous district with the not inaccurate nickname La Milla de Oro (the Golden Mile). It is concentrated around these streets: Serrano, Castelló, Claudio Coello, Goya, Velázquez, Jorge Juan, Núñez de Balboa, and Ortega y Gasset. The area houses the international haute couture establishments and classy Spanish design houses, which—while not cheap—are better-priced here than abroad.

Close by is the third area, centered around Madrid's gay barrio Chueca, as well as on Fuencarral, where the fashion tends to be less formal, younger, and hipper; here you will find the newest designers to hit the street. In Chueca, wander down Hortaleza, Almirante, Argensola, Augusto Figueroa, and their side streets. On Fuencarral, which also has a good mix of other stores, dive into the Mercado Fuencarral, with its 60 up-to-the-minute shops.

OPENING TIMES
See p. 239.

PAYMENT
Supermarkets, chain stores, and many (but not all) smaller stores accept credit cards backed by I.D., which you should carry. Check the signs on the door as you go in, and, if in doubt, check with an assistant (*¿Aceptan tarjetas de crédito?* "Do you accept credit cards?").

RETURNS
If you have any complaints about a purchase, return it as soon as possible with the receipt (*el recibo*) as proof of purchase. Items bought on sale are usually nonrefundable.

EXPORTS
A 16% purchase tax, known as IVA, is included in the price of most retail goods; for books it is 4%. Non-EU citizens are entitled to claim back the IVA element if they have spent 90.16 euros ($108.19) or more in one store and will be removing the goods from the EU within three months. Ask the shop for an invoice (*una factura*) showing the price, the IVA paid for each item and identifying the vendor and the purchaser (you must show your passport/I.D.). When leaving Spain, you must have the invoice stamped by customs (*aduana*). Either mail it back to the vendor, who will mail you the refund, or take the invoice to the nearest Banco Exterior branch (there's one at Barajas airport), where you will get your refund, if the relevant shop has an arrangement with them.

TYPICAL MADRILEÑO STORES
Belloso
Calle Mayor 23
tel 91 366 4258
Metro: Sol
Making and selling religious artifacts—vestments, images, chalices, figures—since 1893.
Capas Seseña
Calle Cruz 23
tel 91 531 6840
Metro: Sol
Beautiful capes sold to high society—from the Spanish royal family to Hillary Clinton—for over a century.
Casa de Diego
Puerta del Sol 12
tel 91 522 6643
Metro: Sol
Calle Mesoneros Romanos 4
Metro: Callao
Classic silver-handled walking sticks, umbrellas, sunshades, castanets, ornamental combs, shawls, and fans since 1858.
Casa Hernanz
Calle Toledo 18
tel 91 366 5450
Metro: Sol, Ópera
Selling hats and shoes, including espadrilles, since the 1840s.
Casa Jiménez
Calle Preciados 42
tel 91 548 0526
Metro: Sol
Gorgeous embroidered shawls and lace mantillas, as well as fans and combs; the store also rents formal clothes.
Casa Yustas
Plaza Mayor 30
tel 91 366 5084
Metro: Sol, Ópera
Founded in 1894, Casa Yustas sells hats ranging from *boinas* (berets), through patent-leather Guardia Civil tricorne headgear, to elegant men's and women's styles.
El Caballo Cojo
Calle Segovia
tel 91 366 4390
Metro: Sol, Ópera
An old-fashioned store with beautiful ceramics, particularly from the 17th and 18th centuries, and handicrafts and furniture.

El Convento de las Carboneras
Plaza Conde de Miranda 3
tel 91 548 3701
Metro: Sol
The convent shop sells delicious sweets and pastries made by a closed order of Hieronymite nuns.

El Flamenco Vive
Calle Conde de Lemos 7
tel 91 547 3917
Metro: Ópera
For flamenco aficionados, everything from guitars, *castañuelas,* and drum chests to dresses or waistcoats and trousers.

Filatelia Arias
Plaza Mayor 28
tel 91 366 4499
Metro: Sol
A beautiful store for collectors of stamps and old or ancient coins—including Greek and Roman examples.

La Favorita
Plaza Mayor 25
tel 91 366 5877
Metro: Sol
Selling hats since 1894.

La Pajarita
Calle Villanueva 14
tel 91 435 7454
Metro: Recoletos
Quality candies and chocolates. The specialty: *pajaritas* (little birds) of chocolate.

La Violeta
Plaza de Canalejas 6
tel 91 522 5522
Metro: Sevilla
A Madrileña candy store since 1915, named after its famous violet-shaped and -colored delights.

Maravillas Trajes Regionales
Calle Sal 3
tel 91 366 5248
Metro: Sol
Spanish men's and women's regional costumes, flamenco outfits, capes and shawls, and fancy dress clothes.

BOOKS
Booksellers
Calle José Abascal 48
tel 91 442 8104
A large selection of books in English.

Casa del Libro
Gran Vía 29
tel 91 524 1900
Metro: Gran Vía
Calle Maestro Victoria 3
tel 91 521 4898
Metro: Callao, Sol
Large, comprehensive stores, with limited English section.

J&J
Calle Espíritu Santo 47
tel 91 521 8576
Metro: Noviciado
Bookstore (and café/bar) with plenty of secondhand books in English, run by an American woman and her Spanish husband. They don't close for lunch.

Libros Madrid
Calle Campomanes 5
tel 91 547 8736
Metro: Ópera
The largest seller of antique and secondhand books in Madrid.

CLOTHING
High-fashion Spanish designers

Adolfo Domínguez
Calle Serrano 18
tel 91 577 8280
Calle Serrano 96
tel 91 576 7053
Metro: Serrano
Classic but relaxed, well-made clothes for men and women, at very reasonable prices.

Ágatha Ruiz de la Prada
Calle Serrano 27
tel 91 319 0501
Metro: Serrano
Madrid-born designer who came to fame in the 1980s *movida;* colorful and imaginative men's and women's fashions.

Amaya Arzuaga
Calle Lagasca 50
tel 91 426 2815
Metro: Velázquez
Bold, sensual design for men and women. She also sells wine from her father's bodega.

Ángel Schlesser
Calle Claudio Coello 46
tel 91 435 4869
Calle Don Ramón de la Cruz 2
tel 91 575 5574
Metro: Serrano
Restrained, timeless, chic urban daywear and spectacular evening wear for women.

Antonio Miró
Calle Lagasca 65
tel 91 426 0225
Metro: Velázquez
Often inspired by painters, his style is colorful, bold, and innovative. For men and women.

The Deli Room
Calle Santa Bárbara 4
tel 91 521 1983
Metro: Tribunal
All Spanish designers and all young. An excellent and funky place to eyeball the future of Spanish fashion. Mainly for women.

Elena Benarroch
Calle Lagasca 88
tel 91 435 5144
Metro: Núñez de Balboa
Best known for her coats and leather clothes, she also stocks designer labels. For men and women.

El Jardín de Serrano
Calle Goya 6–8
tel 91 577 0012
Metro: Serrano
A luxurious 23-store shopping center packed with pricy designer labels.

Hoss Homeless
Calle Serrano 16
tel 91 781 0612
(also at Tetuán 19 and Fuencarral 16)
Young, hip, and Spanish—original young women designing for women.

Javier Larraínzar
Calle Castelló 16
tel 91 577 8835
Metro: Príncipe de Vergara, Velázquez
A reinvented classicism and elegance for women, with the focus on evening wear and suits made to order.

Jesús del Pozo
Calle Almirante 9
tel 91 531 3646
Metro: Chueca, Colón
Classic and beautiful Spanish style for women from a leading young designer, much frequented by young actresses.

Kina Fernández
Calle Claudio Coello 75
tel 91 426 2420
Metro: Serrano, Núñez de

Balboa
Ultra-feminine urban style, beautifully cut and structured.
La Compañía Multihispana
Calle Hortaleza 30
tel 91 532 3833
Metro: Gran Vía
Women's clothes from their
own collection and from designers like Sybilla and Hoss
Homeless. Well priced.
Loreak Mendian
Calle Argensola 5
tel 91 319 4716
Metro: Alonso Martínez
Cutting-edge men's fashion from
a Basque designer.
Mercado Fuencarral
Calle Fuencarral 45
tel 91 521 4152
Metro: Tribunal
A 60-store shopping center in
an old market building, with
young designers focused on the
hip crowd with clothes, shoes,
jewelry, and accessories.
Paco Casado
Calle Castelló 6
tel 91 431 0150
Metro: Avenida de América
Well-established and popular,
noted for his showy and glamorous women's wear.
Pedro del Hierro
Calle Serrano 24 and 63
tel 91 575 6906
Metro: Serrano
Sophisticated and simple clean
lines for men and women from
this creative Madrileño.
Pedro Morago
Calle Almirante 20
tel 91 521 6628
Metro: Colón
Hip designer for men and women:
colorful, daring, and classic.
Purificación García
Calle Serrano 28
tel 91 577 8370
Metro: Serrano, Colón
Elegant, well made, and discreet
clothes for women by this well-
known designer.
Roberto Verino
Calle Claudio Coello 27
tel 91 577 7381
Calle Serrano 33
Metro: Serrano
Famous for his elegant but simple and comfortable clothes for
men and women.

Supreme
Calle Martín de los Heros 24
tel 91 541 0042
Metro: Ventura Rodríguez
Young, feisty, with up-and-
coming labels for men and
women.
Sybilla
Callejón Jorge Juan 12
tel 91 578 1322
Metro: Serrano
Flowing, elegant, and original
women's clothes, with a more
affordable younger line.
Victorio y Lucchino
Calle Lagasca 75
tel 91 431 8786
Metro: Núñez de Balboa
These famous designers from
Seville make theatrical, well-
made flamenco-inspired clothes
for women and have now
moved into menswear.

Other clothing

Algarabía
Calle Ayala 74
tel 91 575 6291
Metro: Goya
Women's fashion from well-
known designers at low prices.
Ararat
Calle Almirante 10/11
tel 91 531 8156
Metro: Recoletos
Sophisticated suits and cosmopolitan party clothes for
women.
Cristina Guisado
Calle Doctor Fourquet 1
tel 91 528 8788
Metro: Lavapiés
New and secondhand 1960s and
'70s clothes plus accessories.
Imaginative and well priced.
Escuela de Divinos
Calle Zurbarán 16
tel 91 308 2816
Metro: Rubén Dario
Spanish designer clothes at
reduced prices.
Lefties
Calle Carretas 10
tel 91 531 2188
Metro: Sol
End-of-line fashions, many from
Zara, at very low prices.
Mango
Calle Fuencarral 70
tel 91 523 0412

Metro: Tribunal
In most shopping areas,
you'll find a branch of this
good-quality and inventive
women's fashion chain.
Restaurante Cambalache
Calle San Lorenzo 5
tel 91 310 0701
Despite the name, secondhand
clothes with high quality and
low prices, plus accessories.
Zara
Gran Vía 34
tel 91 521 1283
Metro: Gran Vía
Excellent chain store for good
well-priced women's and children's clothes, and menswear.
There are Zara stores in most
shopping barrios.

CRAFTS
Adamá
Avenida Felipe II 24
tel 91 435 9988
Metro: Goya
Top contemporary Spanish
ceramics.
Antigua Casa Talavera
Calle Isabel la Católica
tel 91 547 3417
Metro: Santo Domingo
Excellent ceramics shop, selling
yellow and blue Talavera pottery
and fine work from Manises in
Valencia.
Cántaro
Calle Flor Baja 8
tel 91 547 9514
Metro: Santo Domingo
Beautiful handmade pottery.
Casa Julia
Calle Almirante 1
tel 91 522 0270
Metro: Recoletos, Chueca
Experimental furniture and
modern paintings, plus antiques
and unusual souvenirs.
El Arco
Plaza Mayor 9
tel 91 365 2680
Metro: Sol
Contemporary Spanish handicrafts, pottery, jewelry, glass, and
leatherware.
La Tierra
Calle Almirante 28
tel 91 521 2134
Metro: Chueca
Beautiful arts and crafts shop,
from terra-cotta ceramics and

sevillano tiles to traditional kitchenware.

Mercado Puerta de Toledo
Ronda de Toledo 1
tel 91 366 7200
Metro: Puerta de Toledo
Once a 19th-century fish market, now a modern shopping center. Good for antique, craft, and design stores.

DEPARTMENT STORE
El Corte Inglés
Calle Serrano 47
tel 91 432 5490
Metro: Serrano
(Also at Preciados 1, 2, 3, & 9, Princesa 41, 47, & 56, Goya 76 & 85, Plaza de Callao, and elsewhere) The top department store chain in Spain, covering what seems to be everything and doing it well. Good toy section, bargains, and food.

FOOD, WINE, & SPIRITS
La Oleoteca
Calle Juan Ramón Jiménez 37
tel 91 359 1803
Wonderful olive oil from all over Spain. More easily transportable are the wooden cooking and salad utensils.
Lavinia
Calle José Ortega y Gasset 16
tel 91 426 0604
Metro: Núñez de Balboa
Huge wine (and spirits) store, stocking 4,500 wines and staffed by multilingual experts.
Mariano Aguado
Calle Echegaray 19
tel 91 429 6088
Over 150 years of selling wine and spirits, underneath an eye-catching painted ceiling.
Mercado de la Paz
Calle Ayala 28
tel 91 435 0743
Metro: Velázquez
In this beautiful market, the stars are the cheeses and prepared meats, but all the food is good quality. Built by Gustave Eiffel in the 19th century, it became a market only in 1943.
Mercado de Maravillas
Calle Bravo Murillo 122
tel 91 534 8429
Metro: Alvarado, Cuatro Caminos

The biggest traditional market in Madrid, with the largest offering of fresh fish in town and all the bustle and spectacle of a good market—plus a famous sculpture by Luis Muguruza.

LEATHER & SHOES
Acosta
Calle Hermosilla 36
tel 91 710 3026
Metro: Velázquez
A long-established shoemaker, producing high-quality, comfortable, and expensive shoes.
Camper
Calle Preciados 2
tel 902 364 598
Metro: Callao
(Also at Ayala 13, Princesa 75, Gran Vía 54, and Serrano 24) A very stylish chain with original and well-made footwear, cheaper in Spain than abroad.
Guantes Luque
Calle Espoz y Mina 3
tel 91 522 3287
Metro: Sol
This glove shop, over 100 years old, has even more gloves than years, but persevere and you will find some fitting beauties.
Loewe
Calle Serrano 26 for women
tel 91 577 6056
Calle Serrano 34 for men
tel 91 426 3584
Metro: Serrano, Gran Vía 8 for both
Top-class leather purses, belts, and clothes.
Nere Denda
Calle Castelló 38
tel 91 435 9723
Metro: Velázquez
Purses, shoes, and other leather goods by young, imaginative designers.
Piamonte
Calle Marqués de Monasterio 5
tel 91 522 4580
Metro: Chueca, Recoletos
Calle Villanueva 16
tel 91 435 3747
Metro: Serrano
Very modern and colorful Spanish designer shoes, bags, and belts; the Villanueva shop is cheaper, as it sells remainders.

STREET MARKETS
El Rastro
Calle Ribera de Curtidores/Plaza de Carrasco
tel 91 588 2900 (Madrid Tourist Office)
Open every Sun. 7 a.m.–2 p.m.
Metro: La Latina
Dive into one of the finest flea markets in the world, selling everything from antiques to leather goods to absolute rubbish. Very lively and noisy, with plenty of cafés if you need a break. Payments in cash. Watch out for pickpockets, and don't forget to bargain.
Feria del Libro
Cuesta de Claudio Moyano
Metro: Atocha
By the Jardín Botánico and the Parque de Retiro. Rare and unusual books, all year round.
Mercado de Monedas y Sellos
Plaza Mayor
Metro: Sol
Every Sunday morning, the beautiful old square is lined with stalls selling antique coins and stamps.

TOYS
Bazar Mila
Gran Vía 33
tel 91 531 8728
Metro: Gran Vía
An old-style toy store for the younger (pre-computer games) child.
Gepetto
Calle Diego de León 47
tel 91 563 4507
Metro: Diego de León
Puppets and handmade wooden toys of every kind. Expensive, but unique and exquisite.
Sanatorio de muñecos
Calle Preciados 21
tel 91 521 0447
Metro: Sol, Callao
The oldest toy shop in Madrid, dating from the 1910s. Specializes in dolls, from old-style to modern, and dolls' houses, but also has other toys, such as cars and tin soldiers.

ENTERTAINMENT

Madrid is packed with bars, cafés, and things to do in the evenings. Madrileños tend to stay up very late, often until sunrise, and really know how to enjoy themselves. The weekly *Guía del Ocio* is an excellent guide to what is going on. You can also pick up information on entertainment and events from tourist information centers, often in English.

For tickets for the theater, cinema, concerts, bullfights, and football all over Spain, phone or reserve online (commission added) at:

Caixa Catalunya tel 902 101 212, www.telentrada.com
El Corte Inglés tel 902 400 222, www.elcorteingles.es /entradas
Entradas.com tel 902 488 488, www.entradas.com
Localidades Galicia Plaza del Carmen 1, tel 91 531 9131 & 91 531 2732, www.eol.es/lgalicia
ServiCaixa tel 902 332 211, www.serviticket.es

BARS
Biombo
Plaza del Biombo
Metro: Ópera
Lovely small bar much favored by the film and TV world. Great terrace in summer. Closed Mon.
Casa del Pueblo
Calle León 3
tel 91 429 0515
Metro: Sevilla
Designer meets bohemian with a jazz background. Closed Mon.
Los Gabrieles
Calle Echegaray 17
tel 91 429 6261
Metro: Sevilla
Beautiful old tiled Madrileño bar with a flamenco tradition (live concerts on Tues.).
Museo Chicote
Gran Vía 12
tel 91 532 6737
Metro: Gran Vía
An award-winning classic cocktail bar, associated with writers and stars such as Hemingway and Elizabeth Taylor, but always up-to-date. Closed Sun.
Viva Madrid
Calle Manuel Fernández González 7
tel 91 429 3640
Metro: Sevilla

A beautifully tiled bar, with bullfighting connections. Tapas during the day, drinking and talking at night.

BULLFIGHTING
Plaza de Toros Monumental de las Ventas
Calle de Alcalá 237
tel 91 356 2200
Metro: Ventas
Spain's biggest bullring, open mid-March to Oct. The most important *corridas*, in the Feria de San Isidro, are daily from mid-May to early June. Buy in advance; the best seats are in the shade (*sombra*). Tickets from the bullring or authorized ticket agencies.

CAFÉS & CHOCOLATERÍAS
Madrid is full of cafés—these are a few of the best. There are fewer chocolaterías, which are dedicated to hot chocolate and *churros* (sweet fritters).
Café Central
Plaza del Ángel 10
tel 91 369 4143
Metro: Antón Martín
Unusual café, often with live music, mainly jazz. A haunt of the intelligentsia.
Café Comercial
Glorieta de Bilbao 7
tel 91 521 5655
Metro: Bilbao
Traditional old-style café, as charming and talkative as a century ago.
Café de Barbieri
Calle Ave María 45
tel 91 527 3658
Metro: Lavapiés
Quiet but lively, this very traditional café looks onto Plaza de Lavapiés. Films show in the evening (small fee), usually in the original language.
Café del Espejo
Paseo de Recoletos 33

tel 91 308 2347
Metro: Colón
Beautiful and elegant, with a magnificent shaded summer terrace and lovely coffee.
Café del Círculo de Bellas Artes (La Pecera)
Calle Marqués de Casa Riera 2
tel 91 521 6942
Metro: Banco de España
Beautiful and quiet; good for chatting or reading.
Café de Oriente
Plaza de Oriente 2
tel 91 547 1564
Metro: Ópera
On the ruins of an old convent, with lovely views of the royal palace. Elegant and old-fashioned. Serves breakfast, snacks, and tapas and has a restaurant.
Café Español
Calle del Príncipe 25
tel 91 420 1755
Metro: Sevilla
The café of the Teatro Español. Daily classical music concerts on the upper level and magic shows every Thurs. Closed Mon.
Café Gijón
Paseo de Recoletos 21
tel 91 521 5425
Metro: Banco de España, Colón
Traditional meeting point for poets and writers, also serving a good lunch.
Café Libertad 8
Calle Libertad 8
tel 91 532 1150
Metro: Chueca, Banco de España
A traditional haunt of the anti-Franco opposition, now hosting theatrical shows, storytelling, and live music (usually acoustic). Open late.
Chocolatería San Ginés
Pasadizo San Ginés 5
tel 91 365 6546
Metro: Sol
Open Mon.–Tues. 6 p.m.–7 a.m., Wed.–Sun. 10 a.m.–7 a.m.
Open all night, every night: a chocolate paradise for the sleepless, with excellent churros.
Maestro Churrero
Plaza de Jacinto Benavente 2
tel 91 369 2406
Metro: Sol
Open until 11 p.m. or, on weekends, 2 a.m. Part of a chain, but with good churros.

ENTERTAINMENT

CHILDREN'S ACTIVITIES
Faunia
www.faunia.es
Avenida de las Comunidades 28
tel 91 301 6210
$$$$
Metro: Valdebernardo
A cross between a zoo and a
theme park, re-creating the
world´s different ecosystems.
Enjoyable and educational.
Museo de Cera (Wax
Museum)
www.museoceramadrid.com
Paseo de Recoletos 41
tel 91 319 2649
Closed 2:30–4:30 p.m. Mon.–Fri.
$$$
Metro: Colón
From Frankenstein to Bart
Simpson, including a multimedia
history of Spain.
Parque de Atracciones
www.parquedeatracciones.es
Casa de Campo
tel 91 463 2900
Open daily May–mid-September,
& otherwise mainly on week-
ends.
$$$$
Metro: Batán
Huge amusement park, with
roller coasters, train rides, boat
trips, puppet theaters. Plenty of
cafés and restaurants.
Parque del Retiro
Plaza de la Independencia
Metro: Retiro, Ibiza, Menéndez
Pelayo
A lovely park to visit with
children for a walk, the swings,
or a boat trip on the lake.
Especially nice on weekends,
when there are puppet shows,
mimes, and jugglers.
Planetario (Planetarium)
www.planetmad.es
Avenida del Planetario 16
Parque Tierno Galván
tel 91 467 3461
Closed Mon., open Tues.–Fri.
5–7:45 p.m., Sat.–Sun. 11
a.m.–1:45 p.m., 5–8:45 p.m.
$
Metro: Méndez Álvaro
Magical eclipses and journeys
through outer space.
Safari Madrid
Finca El Rincón
Aldea del Fresno
tel 91 862 2376

Open daily 10:30 a.m.–6:30 p.m.
(winter) & 9:30 p.m. (summer)
$$$
Take highway A-5 or N-5 to
Navalcarnero, exit at km 32, and
head for Aldea del Fresno. Best
to visit this beautiful nature
reserve by car to see the wild
animals in a natural setting. The
reserve also has birds of prey
and insect and reptile houses.

CINEMA
These central cinemas show
films in their original language
(versión original).
Alphaville Calle Martín de los
Heros 14, tel 91 559 383, metro:
Plaza de España.
Cine Doré (Filmoteca
Nacional) Calle Santa Isabel 3,
tel 91 369 1125, metro: Antón
Martín.
Pequeño Cinestudio Calle
Magallanes 1, tel 91 447 2920,
metro: Quevedo.
Princesa Calle Princesa 3, tel
91 559 9774, metro: Plaza de
España.
Renoir Cuatro Caminos
Calle Raimundo Fernández
Villaverde 10, tel 91 541 4100,
metro: Cuatro Caminos.
Renoir Plaza de España Calle
Martín de los Heros, tel 91 541
4100, metro: Plaza de España.
Renoir Retiro Calle Narváez
42, tel 91 541 4100, metro: Ibiza.
Verdi Calle Bravo Murillo 28,
tel 91 447 3930, metro:
Quevedo.
Yelmo Cineplex Ideal Calle
Doctor Cortezo 6, tel 902 220
922, metro: Tirso de Molina.

DISCOTHEQUES
El Sol
Calle Jardines 3
tel 91 532 6490
Metro: Sol
A classic disco since the 1980s
movida, but now with the
hippest DJs: everything from
acid jazz, hip-hop, Brit and funk
to whatever's happening. Closed
Sun. & Mon.
Joy Eslava
Calle Arenal 11
tel 91 366 3733
Metro: Sol
Very successful and stylish, with

the accent on techno and
house, packed with people from
the movie, fashion, sports, and
TV worlds. Open 11:30 p.m.–
6 a.m. every day.
Kapital
Calle Atocha 125
tel 91 420 2006
Metro: Atocha
Huge disco with seven floors
and a roof terrace, each floor
offering different vibes: house
music or funk or R&B or
Spanish and Latin or live shows
or karaoke. Closed Mon.–Wed.

FLAMENCO
Café de Chinitas
Calle Torija 7
tel 91 559 5135
Metro: Santo Domingo
Good, traditional, and authentic
flamenco from 9:30 p.m.; all the
greats have played here. Food
(not cheap) and drink served.
Closed Sun.
Candela
Calle del Olmo 2
tel 91 467 3382
Metro: Antón Martín
A cult bar where flamenco pro-
fessionals and enthusiasts meet.
Sessions are held almost daily;
one or more unannounced
artists may start singing, dancing,
or playing. Authentic.
Cardamomo
Calle Echegaray 15
tel 91 369 0757
Metro: Sevilla
New, young flamenco in a bar-
like setting, with interesting programming. At the Cardamomo
sessions every Wednesday
evening, recognized flamenco
artists mix their art with jazz
and pop.
Corral de la Morería
Calle Morería 17
tel 91 365 8446
Metro: Ópera
Open since 1956 and once frequented by Frank Sinatra and
Ava Gardner. From 9:30 p.m.
La Soleá
Calle Cava Baja 34
tel 91 365 5264
Metro: La Latina
A classic Madrileño Gypsy joint,
sometimes enlivened by the
unforeseen intervention of

artists moved to join in.
Entrance fee includes a drink.
Taberna Casa Patas
Calle Cañizares 10
tel 91 369 0496
Metro: Antón Martín
Top flamenco singers, dancers,
and guitarists. Reservations
needed. Try the bull meat.
Closed Sun.

OPERA & CLASSICAL MUSIC
Auditorio Nacional de Música
Calle Príncipe de Vergara 146
tel 91 337 0140
Metro: Cruz de Rayo
Classical music.
Teatro Monumental
Calle Atocha 65
tel 91 429 8119
Metro: Antón Martín
Classical music and sometimes
one-off concerts such as
flamenco.
Teatro Real
Plaza de Oriente
tel 91 516 0606
Metro: Ópera
The grandest theater in Madrid
for opera and ballet.
Teatro de la Zarzuela
Calle Jovellanos 4
tel 91 524 5400
Metro: Banco de España, Sevilla
Devoted to zarzuela, the Spanish
light opera genre.

POP, ROCK, & JAZZ
Berlín Cabaret
Calle Costanilla de San
Pedro 11
tel 91 366 2034
Metro: La Latina
Lovely old 1930s-style cabaret
joint, recently renovated. Shows
during the week as late as 1:30
a.m. On weekends, it becomes a
regular bar. No cover. Closed
Sun.
Calle 54
Paseo de la Habana 3
tel 91 561 2832 OR 902 141 412
Metro: Nuevos Ministerios
A jazz club—Latin, Afro-Cuban,
international—along with two
restaurants and a cinema.
Closed Sun.
Clamores
Calle Alburquerque 14

tel 91 445 7938
Metro: Bilbao
Originally a jazz club, now also
fusion, flamenco, Latin, and eth-
nic music. Concerts generally
start at 10 p.m. Post-concert
jam sessions until 3 a.m. on Fri.
& Sat.
Galileo Galilei
Calle Galileo 100
tel 91 534 7557
Metro: Islas Filipinas
A stage mainly for stand-ups and
singer-songwriters, but also for
poetry readings and other cul-
tural events.
Honky Tonk
Calle Covarrubias 24
tel 91 445 6886
Metro: Alonso Martínez
A classical rock and pop venue,
going since the 1980s, all week.
Also has a restaurant.
La Boca del Lobo
Calle Echegaray 11
tel 91 429 7013
Metro: Sevilla
Music, film shows, and theater.
Music is varied: rock, Spanish,
ethnic, reggae. Gigs start at
10:30 or 11 p.m. Closed Sun.–
Tues.
La Sala
Avenida Nuestra Señora de
Fátima 42
tel 91 525 5444
Metro: Carabanche
Big two-story place offering
modern Spanish and interna-
tional music.
Oba Oba
Calle Jacometrezo 4
Metro: Callao
Brazilian joint with live
weekend concerts, often with
Brazilian artists, and lively
all week.
Populart
Calle Huertas 2
tel 91 429 8407
Metro: Antón Martín
Live jazz from 11 p.m. Free
entry.
Siroco
Calle San Dimas 3
tel 91 593 3070
Metro: San Bernardo
Small, with two floors, one with
concerts, and one with quiet
music. Closed Sun.–Wed.

THEATER
A good place to catch Madrid-
style theater is at Madrid's
Theater Festival, from late
October to the end of
November, featuring all forms of
theater, including dance.
Cuarta Pared
Calle Ercilla 17
tel 91 517 2317
Metro: Embajadores
Contemporary theater.
Children's programming on
Sundays.
El Canto de la Cabra
Calle San Gregorio 8
tel 91 310 4222
Metro: Chueca
Popular, modern, and experi-
mental theater.
Teatro Abadía
Calle Fernández de los Ríos 42
tel 91 448 1627
Metro: Quevedo
A mix of classical and modern
theater, dance, and musicals.
Teatro Alfil
Calle del Pez 10
tel 91 521 4541
Metro: Noviciado
A popular venue for stand-up
comics, mainly Spanish.
Teatro Calderón
Calle Atocha 18
tel 91 429 5890
Metro: Tirso de Molina
The biggest theater in Madrid,
with more than 2,000 seats. Big
musical productions.
Teatro de Bellas Artes
Calle Marqués de Casa Riera 2
tel 91 532 4437
Metro: Banco de España
Classical theater.
Teatro Pavón
Calle Embajadores 9 (Plaza de
Cascorro)
tel 91 528 2819
Metro: La Latina
A beautifully restored mod-
ernista theater, currently housing
the Compañía Nacional de
Teatro Clásico, while that com-
pany waits for restoration work
to be finished on the Teatro de
la Comedia in 2007–2008.

LANGUAGE GUIDE & MENU READER

USEFUL WORDS & PHRASES

excuse me *perdón*
hello *hola*
good-bye *adios*
please *por favor*
thank you *gracias*
you're welcome *de nada*
good morning *buenos días*
good afternoon/evening *buenas tardes*
good night *buenas noches*
today *hoy*
yesterday *ayer*
tomorrow *mañana*
now *ahora*
later *más tarde*
this morning *esta mañana*
this afternoon/this evening *esta tarde*
Do you speak English? *¿Habla inglés?*
I am American *Yo soy norteamericano/a*
I don't understand *No entiendo*
where is...? *dónde está ...?*
I don't know *No sé*
at what time? *¿A qué hora?*
when? *¿Cuándo?*
Do you have...? *¿Tiene...?*
    a single room *una habitación individual*
    a double room (double bed) *una habitación con dos camas (con cama de matrimonio)*
    for one night *para una noche*
I need a doctor/dentist *Necesito un médico/dentista*
Can you help me? *¿Me puede ayudar?*
hospital *hospital*
police station *comisarìa de policía*
I'd like *Me gustaría*
How much is it? *¿Cuánto es?*
Do you accept credit cards? *¿Aceptan tarjetas de crédito?*
cheap *barato*
expensive *caro*
post office *correos*
visitor information center *oficina de turismo*
open *abierto*
closed *cerrado*
every day *todos los días*

MENU READER

desayuno breakfast
almuerzo/la comida lunch
cena dinner
me gustaría pedir I'd like to order
¿Está incluido el servicio? Is service included?
carta menu
menú del día fixed-priced three-course meal including a drink
a la carta Ordering anything other than menú del día
lista de vinos wine list
la cuenta the check
cubiertos knives and forks

a la parrilla grilled
a la plancha grilled on a hotplate
ahumado smoked
crudo raw
estofado stew
el pan bread
frito fried
horno oven
empanada savory pastry
ración portion, helping
tapa small snack taken with a drink
tortilla Spanish omelette made with potatoes

BEVERAGES & CONDIMENTS

un agua mineral mineral water
    sin gas still
    con gas sparkling
el azúcar sugar
un café americano large black coffee
un café con leche large white coffee
un café descafeinado decaffeinated coffee
un café solo short black coffee/espresso
una cerveza beer
la leche milk
la sal salt
un té tea
un vino blanco white wine
un vino tinto red wine
un zumo de naranja orange juice

MEAT & POULTRY

callos tripe
cerdo pork
chorizo spicy sausage
conejo rabbit
cordero lamb
jamón ham
lomo loin (usually of pork)
pato duck
pavo turkey
perdiz partridge
pollo chicken
salchicha sausage
ternera beef

SEAFOOD

almejas clams
atún tuna
calamares squid
camarones shrimp
cangrejo crab
chipirones small squid
gambas shrimp
langosta lobster
lenguado sole
lubina sea bass
mejillones mussels
merluza hake
ostra oyster
pescadilla whiting
rape monkfish
vieira scallop

VEGETABLES

alcachofa artichoke
arroz rice
berenjena eggplant
calabacín zucchini
cebolla onion
champiñones mushrooms
col cabbage
espárragos asparagus
espinacas spinach
guisantes peas
habas broad beans
judías beans
lechuga lettuce
patatas fritas fried potatoes
pepino cucumber
puerro leek
seta wild mushroom
zanahoria carrot

FRUIT

albaricoque apricot
cereza cherry
ciruela plum
frambuesa raspberry
fresa strawberry
limón lemon
mandarina tangerine
manzana apple
melocotón peach
naranja orange
sandía watermelon
uva grape

ILLUSTRATIONS CREDITS

One of the world's largest nonprofit scientific and educational organizations, the National Geographic Society was founded in 1888 "for the increase and diffusion of geographic knowledge." Fulfilling this mission, the Society educates and inspires millions every day through its magazines, books, television programs, videos, maps and atlases, research grants, the National Geographic Bee, teacher workshops, and innovative class-room materials. The Society is supported through membership dues, charitable gifts, and income from the sale of its educational products. This support is vital to National Geographic's mission to increase global understanding and promote conservation of our planet through exploration, research, and education.

For more information, please call 1-800-NGS LINE (647-5463) or write to the following address:

National Geographic Society
1145 17th Street N.W.
Washington, D.C. 20036-4688
U.S.A.

Visit the Society's Web site at www.nationalgeographic.com.

Special Offer! Order today and get one year of National Geographic Traveler, the magazine travelers trust, for only $14.95. Call 1-800-NGS-LINE and mention code TRAC3A6.

Travel the world with National Geographic Experts:
www.nationalgeographic.com /ngexpeditions

Published by the National Geographic Society
John M. Fahey, Jr., *President and Chief Executive Officer*
Gilbert M. Grosvenor, *Chairman of the Board*
Nina D. Hoffman, *Executive Vice President,*
    President, Books and School Publishing
Kevin Mulroy, *Senior Vice President and Publisher*
Marianne Koszorus, *Design Director*
Kristin Hanneman, *Illustrations Director*
Elizabeth L. Newhouse, *Director of Travel Publishing*
Cinda Rose, *Art Director*
Carl Mehler, *Director of Maps*

Staff for this book:
Barbara A. Noe, *Series Editor & Project Editor*
Kay Kobor Hankins, *Designer*
Jane Menyawi, *Illustrations Editor*
Patricia Daniels, *Text Editor*
Xander Fraser, *Researcher*
Judith Klein, *Editorial Consultant*
XNR Productions, *Map Research and Production*
Chapel Design & Marketing Ltd., *Map Art*
R. Gary Colbert, *Production Director*
Mike Horenstein, *Production Manager*
Rebecca Hinds, *Managing Editor*
Meredith Wilcox, *Illustrations Assistant*
Robert Swanson, *Indexer*
Jack Brostrom, Dana Chivvis, Steven D. Gardner, Lawrence Porges, Jane
    Sunderland *Contributors*

Artwork by Maltings Partnership, Derby, England (pp. 74–74,128–129, & 230–231)

ISBN-10: 0-7922-5372-8
ISBN-13: 978-0-7922-5372-3

Printed and bound by Mondadori Printing, Verona, Italy.
Color separations by Quad Graphics, Alexandria, VA.

Visit the society's Web site at http://www.nationalgeographic.com.

The information in this book has been carefully checked and to the best of our knowledge is accurate. However, details are subject to change, and the National Geographic Society cannot be responsible for such changes, or for errors or omissions. Assessments of sites, hotels, and restaurants are based on the author's subjective opinions, which do not necessarily reflect the publisher's opinion. The publisher cannot be responsible for any consequences arising from the use of this book.

For information about special discounts for bulk purchases, please contact National Geographic Books Special Sales: ngspecsales@ngs.org

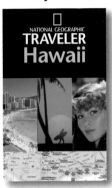